Design and Planning of Retail Systems

Design and Planning of Retail Systems

David Gosling BA (ARCH) DIP TP M ARCH (MIT) MCP (YALE) RIBA ARIAS MRTPI

Barry Maitland BA DIP ARCH MA RIBA

Whitney Library of Design: New York

First published in the United States in 1976
by The Whitney Library of Design,
an imprint of Watson-Guptill Publications,
a division of Billboard Publications, Inc.,
One Astor Plaza, New York, New York   10036

Designed by Graham Mitchener
Copyright © David Gosling and Barry Maitland 1976
First published in 1976 in Great Britain

Reprinted 1977

Manufactured in Great Britain

A note about scales

Unless otherwise indicated, all plans are shown at 1 : 4000
scale, so that 25 mm or 1 in represents 100 m or 328 ft. This
scale has been chosen to suit the whole range of sizes of
buildings discussed, and although some clarity may be
lost at the smaller end of the scale it was felt that the
benefits of showing all plans on a comparative basis
outweigh this disadvantage. Similarly all sections, unless
otherwise stated, are at 1 : 2000 scale.

Library of Congress Cataloging in Publication Data

Gosling, David.
   Design and planning of retail systems.

   Bibliography: p.
   1. Shopping centers.   2. Shopping centers—
Design and construction.   3. Retail trade.
I. Maitland, Barry, joint author.   II. Title.
HF5430.G67   711'.552   75-38806
ISBN 0-8230-7138-3

Contents

Acknowledgements

The authors particularly want to acknowledge the advice of many individuals and organisations, without whose assistance this book would not have been possible:

Great Britain
Godfrey Golzen, Keith Kneebone, Alexandra Artley, Miss W. G. Constable and the late John Bailey of The Architectural Press Ltd.; Susan Balfour, Doreen Spurr, Jack Bricklebank and Hella Davies of the University of Sheffield; Mary Stonelake, Tony Scott of Irvine Development Corporation; David Dean (Librarian), J. F. van der Wateren (deputy librarian) of the Royal Institute of British Architects; K. Alsop and A. J. M. Heselden of the Building Research establishment; R. K. Turner of the Freight Transport Association Ltd.; Jim Howrie: Head, Birmingham Polytechnic School of Architecture

Great Britain: Commercial Organisations
Tom Baron (Managing Director), Dan Donohue (Director) of Christian Salvesen Properties Ltd.; Kenneth Eyles (Managing Director), Dick de Broekert (Project Manager) of Grosvenor Estates Ltd.; Fred Maynard (Managing Director), W. Mathieson (Director), Donald Finlayson (Project Manager) of Ravenseft Properties Ltd.; Sam Chippendale (Deputy Chairman) Town and City Properties Ltd.; Percy Gray (Consultant Architect) Town and City Properties Ltd.; R. I. Northern (Director) Capital and Counties Property Co. Ltd.; Terence Conran (Chairman) and Ginny Pepper, Habitat Ltd. and Conran Associates; David Hall (Director) Melville Dundas and Whitson; D. G. West (General Manager), C. A. Thoday (Estates Manager) Woolco Ltd.; Aylett Moore (Managing Director) Wheatsheaf Trading Ltd.; M. T. Middleton Evans (Director) and Avril Cliff, James Galt & Co. Ltd.; I. B. Wakefield (Property Manager) Mac Fisheries Ltd.; Stephen Beaven: National Cash Register Co. Ltd

Great Britain: Officials
F. J. E. Robotham (Real Estate Officer) Multiple Shops Federation; Ron Turton (Chief Executive) Halton District Council

Great Britain: Architects
Gordon Cullen; Keith Smith (Deputy Chief Architect), Brian Williams (Librarian) Runcorn Development Corporation; Derek Walker (Chief Architect) Milton Keynes Development Corporation; Ken Davie (Chief Architect) Cumbernauld Development Corporation; Pat Garnett of Garnett Cloughley, Blakemore Associates; Michael Wilford of James Stirling and Partner; Professor George Grenfell-Baines and Mary Smallbone of Building Design Partnership; Lewis Womersley of Sir Hugh Wilson and Lewis Womersley; Norman Foster and Ian Ritchie of Foster Associates; Peter Cook of Archigram; Richard Burton of Ahrends, Burton and Koralek; Terrence Farrell of Farrell/Grimshaw partnership; Eric Lyons of Eric Lyons, Cunningham and Partners; Michael Bayer of Sir Robert Matthew, Johnson-Marshall and Partners; Robert Chapman and Nigel Woolner of Chapman, Taylor and Partners; T. J. Hoggett of Peter Black and Partners; F. Cleveland of Arthur Swift and Partners; John A. Graham of Sir Frederick Gibberd and Partners; Frederick Jennet of Sir Percy Thomas Partnership; K. E. Gilham of Scott Brownrigg and Turner

United States of America: Commercial Organisations
International Council of Shopping Centres (New York); Joan M. Walker (President) Property Consultants Inc.; Erica Kipp, Ezra Stoller and Associates

United States of America: Architects
Terry Rankine (Partner), Cambridge Seven Associates, Cambridge, Mass.; Benjamin Thompson and Jane McC. Thompson of Benjamin Thompson Associates, Cambridge, Mass.; William Remington of Hellmuth, Obata and Kassabaum, St. Louis, Missouri; Kathleen Kershaw of Esterick Hornsey, Dodge & Davis, San Francisco; Avner Naggar, California; Welton Becket and Associates, Los Angeles; Callister, Payne and Bischoff, California; Ulrich Franzen, New York; Jim Burns of Lawrence Halprin and Associates, San Francisco; Barbara Solomon, San Francisco; Charles Luckman, Los Angeles; Kenzo Tange and Urtec of Tokyo and McCue, Boone and Toomsick, San Francisco; Cesar Pelli, Gruen Associates California; Wurster, Bernadi and Emmons, San Francisco; Charles Moore, Connecticut; Louis Skidmore of Skidmore, Owings & Merrill, Chicago

Canada: Architects
Ray Affleck and James Cummings (Arcop Associates) Montreal; Johan de Villiers of Diamond and Myers, Toronto; Barrie Briscoe, Toronto; Henry Fleiss of Fleiss and Murray, Ontario

Denmark: Commercial Organisations
Paul Hock of A.B. Hasle Klinker, Copenhagen; Ole Kerndal: Institut for Center Planlaegning, Copenhagen; Alan Jessen (Faellesforeningen for Danmarks Brugsforeninger); Albertslund, Denmark

Denmark: Architects
Gunnar Krohn of Krohn and Hartvig Rasmussen, Copenhagen

Sweden: Commercial Organisation
Hans Ax (Managing Director) Haken Thylen (Assistant Manager) Brigitta Crone (Administrative Assistant) of IKEA, Almhult, Sweden; Roland Davidsson (Manager) IKEA, Malmo, Sweden

Sweden: Architects
Leif Reinius of Sven Backstrom and Leif Reinius AB, Stockholm; Hjalmar Klemming, Stockholm; Ralph Erskine, Drottingholm, Sweden

Finland: Architects
Erkki Karvinen, Helsinki

Switzerland: Architects
Professor Alfred Roth, Lucerne; Suter and Suter, Basel

Germany: Architects
Hans Bandel, Berlin; Prof. Helmut Striffler, Mannheim

France: Commercial Organisations
James Jeffreys: International Association of Department Stores, Paris; Michel Berroeta (Director) Christian Salvesen, France S.A.; L. Poujade and Co., Paris

France: Architects
Claude Balick, Paris

Japan: Architects
Minoru Takeyama, Tokyo; Michele Chiuini, Calabria, Italy

Belgium: Architects
Marcel Blomme, Brussels

Italy
Gae Aulenti, Milan; Ignazia Favata, Studio Joe Colombo, Milan; Studio Bellini, Milan; Caterina Zaina, *Domus*

David Gosling would also like to thank the University of Sheffield for its generous grant from the University Research Fund to enable him to collect research material in Scandinavia and France

Finally we both would like to thank our wives, Miriam and Sarah, for their encouragement and amazing patience

Photographic Acknowledgements

Tim Street-Porter/The Architectural Review: 1·01; *Courtesy of The Architectural Review*: 1·02–03; *David Gosling*: 1·04, 1·09–10, 3·24, 3·28, 3·30, 4·10, 4·35, 4·60, 4·89, 4·92–9·7, 5·06, 6·39, 7·17–18; *J. R. Johnson*: 1·05; *H. de Burgh-Galway/The Architects' Journal*: 1·06; Penelope Reed: 1·07; *Fox Photos Ltd/courtesy of Harrods Ltd*: 1·08; *Gadek, Juchnowicz & Skòczek*: 2·01; *Whitmore Thomas Design Associates*: 2·02; *Joshua Freiwald*: 3·01, 3·16; *Welton Becket & Associates*: 3·07–09; *Jowett*: 3·20; *FDB*: 3·32–36; *Park Studios*: 3·40; *Jacoby*: 3·45–46, 3·48, 7·01, 7·12; *Jacoby/Milton Keynes Development Corporation*: 4·18–20; *John Donat/Milton Keynes Development Corporation*: 4·01, 4·15; *John Donat*: 5·03–05; *G. E. Kidder Smith*: 4·02; *Hugo Priivits*: 4·03; *Strüwing*: 4·08–09, 4·11; *Bryan & Shear Ltd*: 4·25–26; *Bill Toomey/The Architects' Journal*: 4·27; *Ateljé Sundahl*: 4·28; *John Mills Photography Ltd/Runcorn Development Corporation*: 4·30–31, 4·53, 4·91, 6·01, 6·08–09, 6·12, 6·14–18, 6·30–31; *Foto Vrijhof*: 4·32; *Building Design Partnership*: 4·37–38; *Sydney W. Newbery*: 4·44; *André Muelhaupt*: 4·46–47; *Ralph Erskine*: 4·28; *Robert Häusser/ Helmut Striffler*: 4·51–52; *Sam Lambert*: 4·54, 5·15; *Sam Lambert/The Architects' Journal*: 4·56; *Jack Bricklebank/ Gordon Cullen*: 4·61; *Gordon Cullen*: 4·62–64, 5·20–21; *Jack Bricklebank*: 4·65; *Gordon Bishop*: 4·66; *Simo Rista*: 4·67–68; *Hedrich-Blessing*: 4·72–73; *Michael Drummond*: 4·78–80; *Jeremiah O. Bragstad*: 4·82; *Peter Heman*: 4·86; *Keith Gibson*: 4·90, 7·20; *John McCann/Frederick Gibberd & Partners*: 4·98; *Roger Sturtevant/Wurster, Bernadi & Emmons Inc.*: 4·100; *Peter Dodge/Esherick, Homsey, Dodge & Davis*: 4·101 (left); *Kathleen Kershaw*: 4·101 (right); *Mario Mulas*: 5·01; *Stig Holm/Stenbergs Bilder*: 5·07; *Courtesy of Ikea*: 5·08; *Ralph Marshall/courtesy of James Galt & Co Ltd*: 5·11; *Ezra Stoller*: 5·12; *Dorchester Photographers*: 5·14; *Press Promotions Ltd*: 5·16–17; *Keystone Press Agency Ltd*: 5·18; *Robert Hill/Garnett, Cloughley Blakemore & Associates*: 5·19; *Robert Perron: Osamu Murai*: 5·27; *Entwistle, Thorpe & Co Ltd*: 6·04; *Product Support (Graphics) Ltd*: 6·22–23; *Vernon Monaghan*: 6·32–34; *Tony Scott*: 6·35, 6·37–38; *Saul Steinberg*: 7·02; *JBW Photography*: 7·09; *C. Mascaro*: 7·21; *Terry Cryer*: B·6

Preface

The idea of this book arose from the experience of the authors in working on integrated shopping development projects without the benefit of a source of comprehensive background information. It appeared that, while much knowledge had been accumulated in the various aspects of the design and implementation of these building types, it was generally incomplete or inaccessible. With each new project therefore it was necessary to go over ground which had already been well covered elsewhere, without gaining from the previous experience. This applied in varying degree to each of the parties involved in the development process, and indicated the need for a technical source book relating to the more complex shopping centre buildings which had been developed by the early 1970s.

Since that time, a number of books have appeared in the UK and USA which examine in greater depth than was previously available both particular shopping building types and also specialised aspects of their development or management. The ways in which these types have evolved and are continuing to evolve, and the relationships between what has become an amazing proliferation of shopping building types, has not, however, been adequately discussed, and it is with these topics that this book is primarily concerned. In attempting to cover the whole range of shopping buildings in this way, discussion of a number of aspects is necessarily much shorter and more superficial than the authors would wish, and to compensate for this, two case studies are included of particular projects in which the circumstances of their development are more thoroughly discussed. Similarly it has not been possible to discuss anything like a majority of important shopping developments, and the selection of appropriate examples has to some extent been arbitrary.

Since this book was first mooted the circumstances surrounding shopping centre development have altered considerably. Forecasts of future economic growth, patterns of investment, costs of high energy systems and attitudes to widespread urban reconstruction have all changed. The period of development covered by this book thus appears now to have a completeness which was not apparent at the beginning. It is hoped that this book will contribute something to the assessment of that period and to the creation of the new generation of shopping buildings which will follow it.

Throughout the book metric measures have been used, and while accurate conversions may be made, the majority of dimensions relating to gross areas and overall lengths can be adequately translated by the approximate conversions: 1 ha to 2·4 acres, 1 m² to 10 ft², and 1 m to 1 yd. For accurate conversion tables North American readers are referred to the *VNR Metric Handbook*, and British readers to the *AJ Metric Handbook*.

1·1 Introduction

The efficient distribution of goods is of such fundamental importance to a modern industrial society that it must appear strange that so little attention was paid to this process until comparatively recently. Canon Paley's opinion in 1814, that 'distribution becomes of equal consequence to the population with the production',[1] does not seem to have been generally shared by economists until the depression and the publication of Keynes' 'General Theory'[2] created a new interest in the distributive function.

With regard to the buildings which the process of distribution demands, neglect has been ever more prolonged. The great department stores of Chicago in the 1880s and 1890s must have seemed as vital an expression of that city's proto-modern architecture as the skyscraper office blocks which were their neighbours. Yet there is hardly a reference in the history of modern architecture to retailing or any other structures of distribution beyond this point. With few exceptions, modern architecture in its pioneering phase between the World Wars had nothing to say on the subject of an industry employing one worker in ten, accounting for 12% of the Gross Domestic Product and whose structures stood in relation to the community both as a vital service to it and as a focus of its communality.

Part of the reason for this silence must lie with the nature of the industry itself, for the Modern Movement most clearly expressed itself in areas where a demand for innovation, whether organisational or structural, could be felt or interpolated. But at this time, the business of distribution, fixed still in the Utopian patterns of the 19th century, demanded no new solutions. This apparent chauvinism and stability of the industry was not, however, altogether real.

It is of the nature of the distributive industry that, sooner or later, it must respond to pressures for change deriving from three sources. In the first place, there are those changes which occur in the manufacturing industry by which it is supplied. The introduction of new inventions or processes in manufacturing industry, such as the development of transparent polymeric packaging films, or improved refrigeration techniques, may not require changes in the distribution sector, although its most enterprising members may see the opportunity for parallel new forms of marketing. But other developments on the manufacturers' side may force changes in retailing or in the structure of the distributive organisations. Such a development was the massive increase in the use of advertising by large manufacturers to appeal directly to the consumer and create markets for brand products without the traditional intermediary of the retailer.

The second source of change comes from the consuming public which the distributor serves. Again the distributor's reaction may be positive or negative. He may recognise some new development, such as a rapid increase in car ownership, and devise new retailing structures to exploit this fact. Alternatively, he may be forced to change by the decline of traditional markets.

The distributive industry itself forms a third origin of change. These arise in fact from that industry's position in the economy as a whole by which it shares in the general tendencies of all industries. Thus the increasing cost of labour and the structural tendency towards units of greater size are aspects of change in the retail trade which it has shared with the other industries of Western Europe and North America in this century.

The element of competition in these countries has acted as a major factor in encouraging distributive industry, with its traditionally ambivalent attitude towards change, to recognise the pressures for change from all these sources, and to adopt radical new solutions; as indeed the department stores and Co-operative movements of the 19th century had been. By 1946, after the shocks of the Depression and the physical destruction of the Second World War, the industry was again in a position to require strange new building types. These, the out-of-town centres, hypermarkets, supermarkets, superettes, launderettes, et al, have proliferated now into a whole family of shop and shopping centre types which have sprung up in our cities and suburbs without benefit of architectural precedent from the twenties. It seems highly unlikely, moreover, that the development of these new types is now complete, for their more fine response to the nuances of specific markets makes them all the more susceptible to technical and social change.

These new shopping buildings are the subject of this book, as is the planned groupings of such buildings into the shopping centres which have been a special feature of post-war retailing construction. Although rarely the product of individual retailers, these display the characteristics of the industry as a whole and represent, as do the new shop types, the options and responses of the industry in its social and economic milieu. As planned buildings in their own right, these concentrations of shopping are also the point at which the relationship between the retail industry and the public becomes crucial. They are also of special interest in that they introduce a new party into this relationship, the property development company or public authority, concerned, not with the process of distribution itself, but with the provision of the buildings it requires. Acting neither as retailers, nor simply as bankers, these bodies have developed specialist skills which have been important in the evolution of the modern pattern of shopping.

Current shopping patterns are the result of long growth. From the time of the first exchange of goods between producing areas, the process of distribution and marketing has developed, layer upon layer, with each new development in the society around it. From the point of view of this study, the patterns begin to look recognisable in the early part of the 19th century, when the growth of urban populations and the manufactured production of standardised goods together brought about a retailing industry to match. Yet even before 1800 the marketing processes, though increasingly alien to modern eyes, give some interesting insights into the patterns of today.

1·2 Pre-1800

'The two classic forms of the market, the open place or covered bazaar, and the booth or shop-lined street, had possibly found their urban form by 2000 BC at latest.'[3] Certainly, by the Roman period the retail function had been identified and articulated as an element of the urban structure. This is perhaps most clearly seen in those Roman 'New Towns' established around the periphery of the empire, and since a major function of those settlements was to service the empire's system of distribution, it is appropriate that this should be so.

Unlike the early European immigrants to America, whom Vincent Scully describes as having 'never felt

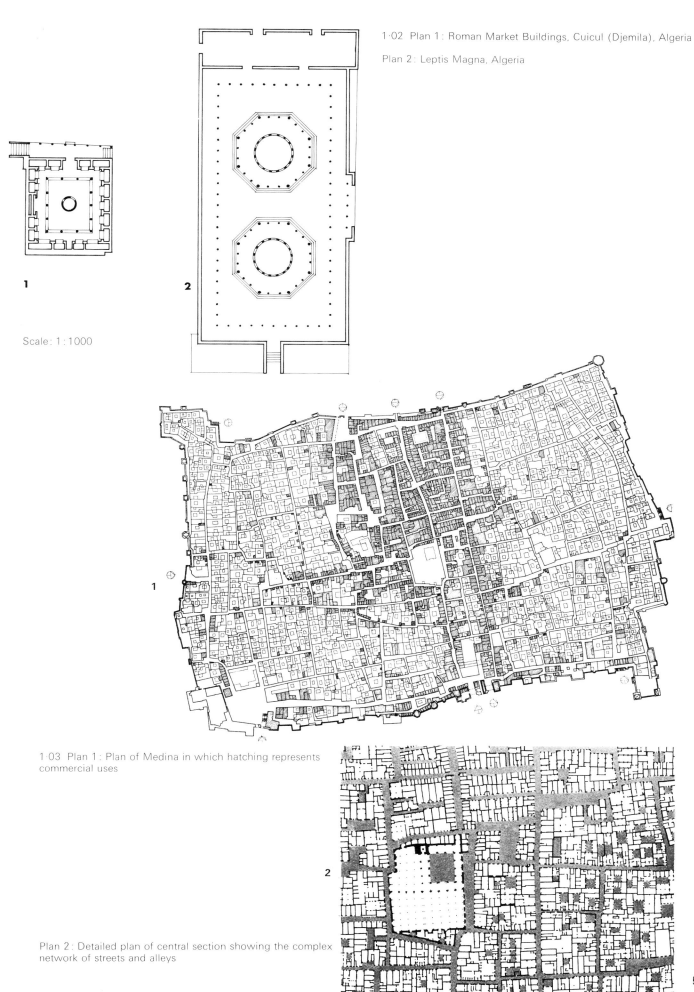

1·02 Plan 1: Roman Market Buildings, Cuicul (Djemila), Algeria

Plan 2: Leptis Magna, Algeria

1

2

Scale: 1:1000

1·03 Plan 1: Plan of Medina in which hatching represents
commercial uses

1

2

Plan 2: Detailed plan of central section showing the complex
network of streets and alleys

5

entirely fixed in place upon the continent',[4] the Romans established their new towns with an almost machine-like precision, with the result that they display an uncanny resemblance to modern shopping centres, with their orderly disposition of elements of varying 'draw' along simply arranged routes. The retailing unit was a similarly standardised solution of peristyle court surrounded by small shop units. The permanence and stability of these establishments may be seen at Leptis Magna where the stone tables are worn by the use of certain trades, as in the case of the butcher's bench, and marked with official measures.

In the Middle Ages, one might argue that the job of providing an ordered framework for retailing passed from the builder to the lawyer. Retailing emerged at this time as a separate business function out of the fairs, bazaars and guild-controlled shops of the period and grew as the concept of competition grew. In spite of this, a system was evolved which effectively eliminated competition. Prices of consumer goods were determined by the guilds, who issued detail specifications to master workmen who produced the articles: the number of these master workmen was restricted so that competition between them was limited; and finally, the fairs were restricted in duration and sold goods which did not compete with the products of the guild craftsmen. A remnant of this system still survives in England, where street markets are limited in number by law, so that the market towns are geographically separated by 6⅔ miles, being a third of a day's walk.

Mediaeval retailing was controlled by a body of commercial law, the three major crimes of which illustrate the nature of the system. These were: forestalling, meaning to buy before the market was open or from vendors before the product reached the market; regrating, which involved reselling at a price higher than originally paid; engrossing, implying an intention to resell by buying in larger than retail lots. Since these precautions are aimed at a potential wholesaler it is perhaps the emergence of this figure which indicates most clearly the collapse of the mediaeval system under the pressures of the industrial revolution.

1·04 The Rows, Chester, England. Two-level shopping with an upper-level covered walkway dating back to the Middle Ages

1·3 The Nineteenth Century

Le Corbusier located the start of modern architecture in 1790. With the demonstration in France that a decisive point had been reached in the transformation of rural agricultural economy into an urban one, based on manufacture and trade, we may say that that year, symbolically at least, marks also the beginning of modern retailing. Another symbolic event occurred five years later, when the French government offered a prize of 12,000 francs for the invention of a practical method of food preservation as a means of provisioning its wartime armies. This application, which led to the canning process, summarised the problem which led to the emergence of the modern distributive industry, namely the application of technology to service large masses of people separated from their agricultural base.

Consumers

The first prerequisite for the growth of modern retailing was the movement of population from the land to the manufacturing centres, coupled with overall growth in the population as a whole. This created mass markets and a dependence of those markets upon retail outlets for all goods and services. The decline in rural populations, the increase in agricultural productivity through mechanisation and the gradual increase in living standards through the 19th century, as evidenced by increased per capita consumption of meat and high protein foods as against bread and cereals, all required a more elaborate distribution system to serve cities no longer able to rely upon the immediate rural hinterland.

Technology

The second requirement for the development of modern retailing was the application of technology to the problem of serving mass markets. Primarily this involved the mechanized production of goods in vast numbers and to a consistent pattern, a process which was well established by the beginning of the 19th century. With regard to the manufacture of cloth, for example, the inventions of the 18th century, from Kay's shuttle, to Hargreaves spinning jenny and Arkwright's water-frame, made possible the production in Britain in 1812 of yarn on Crompton's mules equivalent to that of 4 million women at hand spinning wheels. One important consequence of this standardised mass production was that selling, which in the Middle Ages had been a skilled job involving the detailed inspection and costing of individually made goods, could now in many areas be handled by relatively unskilled staff.

As well as such direct applications of technology to manufacturing, a growing number of inventions profoundly affected the forms of distribution and the markets they served, and it is worth considering a few of the most significant.

Transportation

The opening of the Liverpool and Manchester Railway line in 1830 began the development of the railway systems which were to have two great effects on retailing. In the first place, it led to great increases in the speed and efficiency of the system of distribution. And secondly, it encouraged the process of urbanization and, with the development of the suburban networks, increased the potential size and mobility of the urban populations.

In the case of Britain, whose agricultural hinterland was limited, the railway and canal systems were complemented by the shipping lines. The development of the screw propeller during the 1830s hastened the mechanization of that part of the distribution system also, with the result that the English cities had, by the end of the century, effectively extended their sources of supply from the immediate sub-region outward to cover the world. The old specialisation of small country areas in the production of raw materials and basic foodstuffs was now effected on a global scale, requiring not merely an inflation, but a complete restructuring of the distributive function. Cities grew around the key points of distribution, the ports and railway nodes, and developed new building types to serve their function, as in the grain silos and meat packing plants of Chicago and the sugar and tobacco warehouses of Liverpool.

The second effect of improved communications, within the cities themselves, was reinforced by new urban transportation systems to supplement the suburban railways. The earliest passenger tram system opened in New York in 1832, and by the 1860s horse-drawn trams were operating in London and Liverpool. The first four miles of underground railway were built in London in 1863 and the first electric tramway in 1883. These systems, which made the city centres immediately accessible to large numbers of people, created the conditions for new forms of retail outlets and organisations, and in particular for the department store.

Food Processing

The French government's 12,000 francs was claimed with a process of food preservation using glass jars. This method was soon superseded by the use of tin cans which reached English shops in 1830 and were in widespread use in the USA by 1839. The technique was improved by the use of closed steam pressure retorts for canning in 1874, and by the introduction of the sanitary or open top can in 1905.

These developments meant that food could not only be preserved, but also arrive at the retail outlet in standard, packaged units of predictable weight, quality and cost, with the result that food retailing could become simplified and the customer's choice shifted from a selection of the raw material to a selection of manufacturers' brands. Throughout the century, mechanization extended into the preparation of non-tinned foods, such as bread, with similar results.

One final limitation on the world-wide distribution of food, made possible by steamship lines and rail-roads, was overcome in 1880 with the first shipment of refrigerated fresh meat from Australia to London, and although the full exploitation of this technique really belongs to the 20th century, its use confirmed the 19th century development of the separation of producer and consumer.

One final point should be made regarding 19th-century food technology and that concerns the development of a scientific basis for its achievements. It was not until Pasteur's work in the 1860s that the reasons for successful canning and bottling were understood. Gradually, however, the theoretical base was expanded, leading to the equal participation of the chemist and biologist with the engineer in the developments of the next century.

Consumer Durables

1830 was a significant year, not only for transportation,

with the opening of the first steam railway line, but also for the development of an expanding range of non-food products, the consumer durables. For in that year were invented the sewing machine and the lawn mower, soon to be joined by such essential commodities as the Bissell carpet sweeper (1876) the Edison phonograph (1877) and the Waterman fountain pen (1884). The proliferation of labour-saving, instructive or simply amusing gadgets thus widened the scope of retailing at the same time as industry was standardising the objects of sale.

Building Technology

Perhaps the most dramatic public demonstration of the application of technology to building in the 19th century was the Crystal Palace at the Great Exhibition in London in 1851. Its use of light cast-iron frame structure had been already applied in new market halls for the distributive industry, such as the Market Hall of the Madeleine, Paris 1824, and Hungerford Fish Market in London, 1835, and its appropriate use in the new intensive forms of retailing buildings on expensive urban sites was soon proved.

Perhaps of even more significance for these buildings was the application of technology to building services. The department store at its full development relied upon a great number of these services. The first steam-driven safety lift was installed in a New York department store, E. G. Haughwont and Co., by Elisha Otis in 1857, and the first electric lifts in Macy's and Wanamaker's in New York in 1889. The general use of steam or hot water heating systems in the 1860s, and the introduction of the escalator, the telephone, the electric light and the pneumatic tube, all contributed to the department store's development.

Wholesalers

The outcome of the social and technical developments described above was so radically different from what had gone before that the old prescripts against wholesaling had to be abandoned. The process of distribution had become so enlarged, both in distance and time, that some stockholding and ordering function, standing between the manufacturer and retailer, was required. With regard to the great number of small retailers who served the urban populations, the wholesaler provided a buying service which compensated for their limited knowledge of the widely varying sources of supply. With transport networks formed, but still relatively slow, the wholesaler had the resources, which each small retailer had not, to carry stock for considerable periods to meet peak demands, and he could aggregate demand from dispersed markets. Equally the wholesaler acted as salesman for a large number of manufacturers, often small and specialised in their production, and could place bulk orders in advance of demand. The buildings which the wholesaling function made were among the earliest to use the new materials of iron and glass. The market halls noted earlier show the application of the materials to the problem of wide-span roofs over large areas, while a parallel development in city blocks of high land value was the use of the multi-storey iron frame. The Jamaica Street Warehouse in Glasgow, 1855–56, Waterhouse's Fryer and Bunyon Warehouse in Manchester, 1856, and the Wellington Williams Warehouse in London, 1858, are examples of this development.

Retailers

Although 19th-century developments in retailing can be seen now as logical responses to new situations, it can have been by no means obvious at the time what structure of industry would emerge. Certainly, each new form which was tried—department stores, chain stores, mail order houses— was regarded by retailers generally with hostility and as a threat to the small independent retailers who formed the bulk of the trade.

19th century Britain saw the consolidation of the corner shop as the main community service shop. In the 18th century the general merchants were established in small shops with a relatively limited range of services including grocery and provision merchants, linen drapers and haberdasheries. In the 19th century there was a great expansion in the range of shops and existing examples in Greater London include cornchandlers, hairdressers, cheese shops, secondhand clothiers, drysalter and colour stores, chemists, hardware stores, pie shops, umbrella shops, violin shops as well as the more common grocery, draper and general stores. Andrew Lawson notes in an article on these shops (*The Sunday Times* 30th March 1975) that Charles Dickens in 'Sketches by Boz' bewailed the disappearance of the musty old shops and their replacement by more brash and grandiose shops. He quotes Dickens: 'Six or eight years ago, the epidemic began to display itself among the linen drapers and haberdashers. The primary symptoms were an inordinate love of plate glass and a passion for gas lights and gilding . . .' As Lawson points out, the expansion and amalgamation of small shops eventually led to the first department stores.

Department Stores

The outstandingly successful development of the 19th century was the department store. In Britain, the Board of Trade defines a department store for the purposes of retail sales analysis as any large shop actively engaged in the sale of a wide range of commodities, one of which must be clothing. In 1948, the definition of size was established in the USA as 25 or more employees, and in 1957, after an earlier attempt at a definition in terms of turnover, the American definition was adopted in Britain also. Whatever definition is taken now, the essential characteristic of selling a variety of goods through a series of 'departments' within a shop does not seem to have been present at the birth of the idea. Aristide Bouçicaut is credited with this in the early part of the century, when he adopted new methods in his then small shop, the Bon Marché in Paris. These were different in four main respects from contemporary trading habits:

1 The aim was high stock-turn rather than high mark-up
2 The retailer accepted a degree of responsibility for goods which could be returned by a customer
3 Prices were marked, in place of haggling
4 Entrance was free with no obligation on the customer to buy

These revolutionary methods succeeded and the business expanded, increasing the number of lines which then became organised by departments. The new trading methods, coupled with Giedion's description of the department store's origins as 'more a storage place' and 'a place where goods were kept in quantity for cheap retail sales'[5] point to a location of the early department stores in the same tradition as the discount houses of the early 20th century and the hypermarkets of today, as low cost operations located in cheap warehouse-type structures at highly

1·05 Cast-iron framed department store, Broadway, New York City
Architect: J. P. Gaynor

8

accessible points in relation to transportation networks. The John Wanamaker 'Grand Depot' in Philadelphia, 1876, was firmly of this type, being a huge, 2-acre, single-storey dry-goods store housed in a converted freight depot of the Pennsylvania Railroad. The department stores, however, developed into quite another animal. Housed in increasingly sophisticated multi-storey buildings, making use of the latest innovations of building services and structure to provide flexibility of operation and customer comfort, and providing a high degree of personal service together with a wide range of commodities in separate sections of the store, they established an alternative tradition, examples of which will be found in modern urban shopping centre complexes.

From its beginnings in Paris, the development of the department store moved to the USA, where general merchandise stores and ready-made clothing concerns converted by broadening stocks and setting up departments. Lord and Taylor in New York originated in 1826, as did A. T. Stewarts. In 1863, the A. T. Stewart store, later sold to John Wanamaker, occupied a building using James Bogardus' system of cast-iron construction enabling the pre-fabrication of parts for multi-storey warehouse-type structures. This building had seven storeys and six lifts. Macy's of New York began in 1858, Strawbridge and Clothier in Philadelphia in 1868 and Emery-Bird-Thayer in Kansas City in 1863. The movement reached its peak in Chicago, where Marshall Field became the largest department store in the world.

The department store idea spread throughout Europe and, by the end of the century, to Canada and Australia. In Paris, in 1876, Gustave Eiffel and L. A. Boileau built a new store for Bon Marché, which had begun the idea, and, with its numerous light wells, slim iron columns and bridges and large glass sky lights, it is, fittingly, perhaps the most elegant of them all.

Mail Order Houses

Another development in retailing, which required no retailing buildings at all, was mail-order selling. In this respect, it belongs to a third trading tradition, that of the pedlar, the costermonger, and, today, the slot-machine. Like the last of these, mail-order trading depended upon the arrival of an appropriate technology, the parcel post, which the US Mail introduced after the Civil War. It also depended in the USA upon large un-urbanized areas of country with a population ready to enjoy the fruits of industrial society, but poorly served by the high cost retailing methods of small town and village general shops. Like the department store, the new idea was regarded at first with suspicion and then hostility by small traders who predicted the end of the village shop and, in some states, managed to have laws passed which prohibited mail-order trading. In spite of this resistance, the mail-order houses flourished, with Montgomery Ward, which began in 1872, and Sears Roebuck in 1893, emerging as the leaders in the field.

In Britain, where the conditions of large populations distant from cities did not exist, the mail-order method of trading awaited another innovation, that of the mass circulation popular press.

Co-operative Societies

One of the few forces in 19th-century retailing whose development was predominantly European, rather than American, was the consumer co-operative movement. It began with a number of experiments based on Owenite ideals

1·06 Barton Arcade, Manchester

1·07 (Right) The Galleria, Milan

before the successful pattern was established. In 1821, the London Co-operative and Economical Society attempted to sell at cost and in 1827 the Brighton Society to capitalize profit. Both failed, but in 1844 the Rochdale Pioneers opened a store which charged current market prices and credited each member with a share of the surplus in proportion to his purchases. By 1863 Co-operative Society membership in Britain had passed the 100,000 mark, and in the last decades of the century, the membership trebled. Societies also developed in Europe, most successfully in the Scandinavian countries, while in France and Italy, Producers Co-operative Societies were formed on the basis of co-partnership among employees.

The case of Chicago forms an effective summary of the story of 19th-century retailing. Between 1837 and 1850, Chicago's population grew from 4,000 to 30,000, over half of whom were immigrants from outside the USA. The development of the railway system between 1848 and 1869 linked Chicago to its region and beyond and rapidly established its predominance over trade in the north-west and other sectors. Its population now grew more rapidly, reaching 1,100,000 in 1890, and double this figure in 1910. In 1851 it became the largest corn market in the USA, in 1854 the largest wheat trade centre and in 1856 the largest timber centre. By 1862 it had surpassed Cincinnati as a pork-packing centre and went on to achieve primacy in livestock and the meat-packing industry.

Chicago thus became a prime example of a city of distribution, built around the railroads, and when the great fire of 1870 destroyed most of its buildings, it went on to demonstrate a commercial architecture appropriate to this function. 'In Chicago the tall buildings would seem to have arisen spontaneously in response to favourable physical conditions. . . . The future looked bright. The flag was in the breeze. . . .'[6] Sullivan's optimism was matched in a succession of office buildings and the de-

partment stores of the '80s and '90s which used the 'Chicago frame' to make a new architecture of efficiency. William le Baron Jenney's Leiter building of 1889–90, and Sullivan's Carson, Pirie and Scott Department Store of 1889–91 and 1903–04 show this clearly enough.

1·4 The Twentieth Century

After the great developments of Chicago, the external expression of retailing in the first part of the 20th century is a disappointment. In Europe the involvement of the pioneers of modern architecture in distributive buildings was on a small scale, confined generally to shop conversions, interiors and boutique-like experiments. *Art Nouveau* was, after all, christened by a shop of that name for modern art in Paris, and its Italian name, 'Stile Liberty', came from the draper's shop in London which adopted *Art Nouveau* fabrics in the 90s. Thus the Mackintosh tea-rooms in Glasgow, Van de Velde's barber shop in Berlin, with its outrageous expression of piped services, and Loos' first work, a shop interior in Vienna, are all minor, if interesting, contributions, entirely peripheral to the larger movements in retailing. The success of *Art Nouveau*, and its close relationship with specialised shops, does however point to the existence of a new fashion-conscious middle-class market, with a taste for the advanced designs of Tiffany glass-ware and Heal's furniture.

In the larger field, Burnham's store for Selfridge's in London of 1908 marks a reaction to the Chicago architecture parallel to that which occurred in New York, with a return to the habit of hiding the structural frame in a classical mask, just as Nash had done in the Regent Street quadrant 90 years before. The result was that one can read a standard work on the history of the Modern Movement, such as Banham's *Theory and Design*,[7] without finding a single example of modern architecture for the retailing industry, although that other commercial objet-type, the multi-storey office block, formed a significant battle ground for the new movement.

New developments were, however, taking place in retailing organisations during the first part of the 20th century. The strengths and weaknesses of the 19th century innovations became more apparent and new systems emerged, eventually leading, after the Second World War, to construction programmes on the scale of the Chicago boom.

Consumers

The social changes of the 20th century have been well charted, and their technological causes and symptoms as widely identified as those of the 19th. The individual consumer transport provided by the automobile led to a new migration of populations into the suburban areas, exposing the dependence of the city centres on the railways. The development of domestic packages for refrigeration, as well as transport, extended the channels of distribution directly to each consumer, enabling a restructuring of distribution itself. The popular press, radio and television, as well as highway-directed advertising, allowed a much more effective monologue from manufacturer and consumer than previously, while rising living standards and labour costs created new markets and new problems for the distributive trades.

Some of these changes were extensions of trends established in the previous century, and some were quite new, but on the whole, and with the possible exception of the USA, the retail industry was remarkably slow to react to them, opposing each new attempt to meet them with the arguments that had been used against the department stores and mail order traders of the 19th century.

Manufacturers

Although the emergence of the manufacturer from the cottages and craftworkers' shops of the 18th century into the factories of the 19th was decisive, production nevertheless remained generally in the hands of small and often under-capitalized enterprises. This situation, which led to the growth of wholesaling as a separate function, had begun to change by the beginning of the 20th century. At that time the tendency towards organisations of increasing size became apparent in retailing with the emergence of the multiple concerns, and was matched by the expanding output of the more efficient manufacturers who supplied them. An important result of this was the 'vertical' growth of some of the larger producers, back into the distributive process, as they became aware of their strength and of the economies that might be achieved by shortening the supply lines to the consumer with greater control of product and market.

The clearest expression of this new development was the direct control of 'captive' or 'tied' outlets by producers in certain fields. In the US, for example, the oil companies have been able to control, through their control of filling stations, the sales of tyres, batteries and accessories. In Britain a similar control of outlets has been achieved by brewers, bakers, wallpaper, pottery and glass producers.

A second and less direct influence of manufacturers upon distribution has been achieved through branding. The practice of branding is extremely old, and was used by the Mediaeval guilds. It was revitalised in the 19th century by the mass production of standard goods, which could thus be guaranteed some degree of uniformity of standard. In Britain the enactment of the basic trade-mark law in 1875 confirmed the practice, which, by the end of the century, covered a wide range of standard commodities. It was soon realised that the effectiveness of branding, from the manufacturer's point of view, was related to advertising. By promoting his brand, the manufacturer could, without depending upon the retailer, create a market for it by appealing directly to the consumer. This process was not resisted by retailers whose role, it has been suggested, was thereby changed from that of a tradesman to that of a business man, being concerned with a knowledge of management rather than commodities and with attracting customers rather than stimulating demand. The implications of branding were, however, opposed by wholesalers, whose middle position was threatened, but by the time they recognised this they were no longer able to compete with like methods. The great expense of modern advertising has had the second effect that it is undertaken on an increasing scale by a decreasing number of large firms.

Wholesalers

The wholesaler's position in 20th-century distribution has been threatened by vertical developments in retailing as well as manufacture. Whether on the initiative of producer or retailer, these movements linking the two parties directly together have deprived wholesalers of some of their larger and most efficient customers, as well as supplies of the better brands. One response to this from wholesalers has been vertical integrations of their own. Several large

wholesale firms have built up considerable retail holdings in the form of small department stores and specialized shops. In Britain perhaps the most successful of these attempts has occurred where a common interest is established with small traders in resisting the power of the multiples. Wholesale sponsored groups of these small traders, with common brand names, such as 'Spar-Vivo', 'Mace' and 'VG', have grown in recent years serving the interests of both parties.

1·5 Retailers

Department Stores

The 20th century has seen the reversal of many of the competitive advantages which encouraged the growth of the department store. Their locations, previously central in relation to the railway networks, became distant from suburban populations and at points of congestion on road networks. Their 'free' services, of deliveries, credit, nursery facilities, etc., caused them, with increases in labour costs, to become among the highest cost retailing institutions. Their buildings, displays and advertising policies, all the most advanced in their day, were overtaken by newer forms of outlet. These trends were not immediately apparent, however, and in the first two decades of the century, with the continued increase in urban populations,

1·08 The Meat Hall: the showpiece of Harrods Ltd., Knightsbridge, London
Architects: Stevens & Hunt, with interior ceramics by W. J. Neatby

improvements in transportation and the availability of electricity for power and lighting in the stores, the department stores continued to expand. They reached their peak in 1929, with sales at 9–10% of total retail sales, and have since declined to around 6% in the USA and 5% in Britain. This relative decline has been modified by a number of steps. In 1924–5 the J. C. Penny Co. introduced the first chain department stores, a trend which was followed by Allied Stores, Gimbel Brothers, Macy, Marshal Field and others, and which was reinforced by the entry of the giant mail-order houses, Sears Roebuck and Montgomery Ward into the field. Between 1929 and 1950 these chain department stores increased their share of total department store trading from 25·1% to 65·6%. Further stores formed 'ownership' or buying groups, such as Allied Merchandisers of Canada, in order to pool financial and buying resources. In Britain this tendency to group has resulted in the major powers of Debenhams, House of Fraser and Lewis's Investment Trust among department stores. A further development, particularly in the US, was the rapid growth during the 1950s of branch department stores to serve the suburban populations.

The Multiples

The grouping of department stores was largely brought about by the pressures arising from the growth of the most spectacularly successful retailing organisations of this century, the multiple or chain stores. These are defined as having at least 10 outlets, and trace their origin to the beginnings of the Great Atlantic and Pacific Tea Company in 1858. In the last decades of the 19th century many of the most famous names were established, such as F. W. Woolworth and Company (1879) and the OWL Drug Company (1880) in the USA. In England Jesse Boot opened his first shop in 1877, and founded the Boot Pure Drug Co. in 1888, while Tom Spencer's 'penny bazaars', later Marks and Spencer, began in 1887, By 1928 some 1,718 companies in the USA owned and operated 87,800 stores, a number which had doubled by 1954.

The chain stores began by serving a different market from that of the department stores. In offering selection rather than price advantages, and service as selling features, the latter successfully met the needs of the rising middle classes. The multiples aimed at the narrower requirements of the working classes where price and convenience were or primary importance. From this beginning the multiples have developed and changed as economic conditions altered. In Britain, for example, Woolworths is the only large group which still conforms to the old variety chain store idea, selling a wide variety of low-priced articles under one roof, without necessarily a clear division between sections. Marks and Spencer, British Home Stores and Littlewoods have moved away from this definition to that of the pure multiple, with a clearly defined commodity group as principal sales volume.

The economies of scale which the multiples could achieve, coupled with their growing share of the market, allowed them to adopt an equivalent vertical development to that which was noted among producers. Their central buying organisations could supplant the wholesale function, and then extend control to the producer by means of specification, bulk purchases of raw material from which suppliers could draw their requirements and standardized accounting, stock handling and marking methods. The confirmation of this control is the use of branding as a retailer's, rather than a manufacturer's, mark.

Despite its origins in the 19th century, the multiple store development has retained its dynamic right up to the present day. Table 1 shows the growth of this sector in the UK in the years from 1961–70, in which, with the exception of mail order houses, the multiples have been the only retail type to increase their share of the market and that convincingly from 28·0% to 36·8%.

Table 1 *Trends in Market Shares of Main Types of Organisation, UK*

		1961	1966	1970
Independents	%	54·2	49·2	46·5
Multiples		28·0	33·4	36·8
Co-operative societies		10·3	8·8	7·7
Department stores		5·0	4·8	4·9
Mail order houses		2·5	3·8	4·1

(Department of Trade and Industry)

Co-operative Societies

The co-operative stores are perhaps the earliest form of multiple, and it is ironic in considering the declining market share of the co-operatives shown in Table 1 to note that many of the techniques introduced by the Rochdale Pioneers form the basis of modern multiple trading. Another field pioneered by the societies was verticalization, with the formation of the Co-operative Wholesale Societies. The advantages of this development were dissipated somewhat by the large number of independent societies involved, and in the competition with the strongly centralised multiples, there has been a move towards amalgamations and the formation of stronger groups. The innovating tradition in the Co-operative movement was demonstrated again in Britain in the 1950s, when it consistently led all other retailing organisations in the development of self-service shops. In 1957, for example, about 60% of all such shops were owned by the societies.

The relative strengths of the Co-operative Societies in Europe may be judged from the following list of per capita sales published in 1958 by the Swiss Co-operative Union (figures in Swiss Francs): Denmark 181; West Germany 48; UK 215; Finland 744; Norway 194; Sweden 321; Switzerland 238.

Discount Houses

Like most of the new retailing methods of the 20th century, the discount house began in the USA and has reached its fullest development there. It is defined as a retail store selling nationally advertised products at prices lower than those available elsewhere. The products sold are generally limited lines of durable or semi-durable goods, such as electrical appliances or records, and a wide range of practices has developed with regard to membership fees and cards.

Originating at the beginning of the century, the discount houses showed some growth after the First World War and again in the Depression with the liquidation of manufacturers' and wholesalers' stock. The greatest growth has occurred since the Second War and was stimulated by rising demand for semi-luxury goods and by the various manoeuvrings over resale price maintenance. By the early 1960s, discount trading accounted for 2–5% of retail sales in the USA and had begun to develop in Europe.

The sudden growth of discount trading in the USA was a shock to the established outlets of durable goods. William H. Whyte's analysis of this effectively summarises the general changes which occurred in the role of the retailer; 'What has been happening is that the consumer has been taking over part of the selling burden historically allocated to the retailer. Just as the consumer has shared in the mark-up on groceries by sharing in the physical burden of distribution, so now with the "big ticket" items; he has worked for part of the mark-up by sharing the selling burden and he wants his cut. Because discount houses give it to him they are often cited as the villains of the piece. But they are not the cause, only the manifestation, and though they are filling the vacuum, it was produced for them. Manufacturers still give retailers a mark-up big enough to justify the missionary work retailers once did. With few exceptions, however, retailers no longer do this kind of work; they *service* demand, but have discarded their former techniques to create demand.'[8]

Supermarkets

The most radical and far-reaching development to emerge

from the conditions which Whyte describes was the super-market. As a retailing method, rather than a retailing organisation like the multiples, it brought together all the separate strands, technological, social and economic, which were tending toward change, and revolutionised the business of selling.

'Defined by operational method, a supermarket could be said basically to operate (a) with emphasis on high turn-over (b) with low unit value merchandise at low prices (c) mass displays of merchandise (d) layout to facilitate large and rapid movement of customers.'[9] The Super Market Institute defines a supermarket as 'a complete departmentalized food store with a minimum sales volume of one million dollars a year and at least the grocery section fully self-service.' The methods exploited to the full all the manufacturing, packaging and customer handling techniques which had become available. These included:

1 The wide use of refrigerated cabinets and self-service freezers as the penultimate link in the 'cold chains' extending from the food freezing plants, cold storage warehouses, refrigerated trucks and railway cars to the domestic refrigerator. The widespread adoption of shop refrigeration also encouraged the development of new food processing techniques such as low temperature vacuum evaporation for frozen juice concentrates

2 The exploitation for self-service purposes of new flexible packaging materials, aluminium foil and transparent polymeric films for example, and of packagings which can be printed with descriptive material, eliminating the need for labels. In this way the side effects of canning seen in the 19th century could be extended to fresh and frozen produce

3 The use of a whole range of gadgets—automatic opening doors, one-way turnstiles, customer trolleys, conveyor belts at check-out points, and cash registers giving change—to handle large numbers of customers

The supermarket began in the 1930s as an answer of the more aggressive American independent traders to the effects of the Depression and the multiples upon their position but its methods have been adopted by all of the forms of retail organisation. A logical extension of this is that, if the self-service, pre-package system works for, say, hardware goods as well as food, there is nothing to prevent the grocer extending his lines into hardware and offering the same cost advantages to the consumer. This has occurred on an increasing scale, as has the parallel expansion of the multiples into food sales, and represents a new 'horizontal' development within retailing. For the retailer in his re-defined role as servicer of demand, the contents of the package become less and less relevant and the traditional specialisations overlap and weaken.

Automatic Vending

The slot machine surely represents a logical conclusion to at least some of the historic trends in retailing. The transfer of goods from producer to consumer through a machine, with a maintenance engineer as the only labour cost item, represents a mechanistic ideal, the realisation of which has been delayed by technical details. The first machines, developed in the 1880s to meter gas, and then electricity and telephones, were so unreliable that for 50 years they were confined to selling items of goods worth less than a penny. This barrier was broken in 1926 with William H. Rowe's dispenser for cigarettes in 15 cent packs, and another 30 years then passed before 'the 99 cent barrier' was passed with the development of machines capable of accepting

bank notes. Automatic vending has thus tended to be a peripheral operation, concentrating on sites and products where convenience and impulse buying have been powerful factors, as in railway stations and in factory and office catering. The idea of much wider applications still remains seductive, however, and fully automated shops have been experimented with in the USA. Rising labour costs, the computerisation of banking methods allowing the substitution of credit cards for cash and increasingly sophisticated forms of packaging, would all seem to favour the machine, and although it doesn't appear to be a particularly low-cost operation at present, time is probably on its side.

Like mail-order trading, automatic vending is a non-building outlet, and so must have a peculiar fascination for those concerned with retailing buildings. It has been suggested in America that mail order trading there has reached its limit of the available market, although recent figures suggest that this is not yet the case in Britain. It may also be that there is some functional limitation on the future penetration of automatic vending. However these systems still basically rely upon the nineteenth century developments of postal systems and mechanics and it is to be expected that even more formidable challenges to shop retailing will emerge from a combination of the motor car, the telephone, television and credit systems.

The Independents

Finally, in this summary of forms of retail outlet, the independents, with less than 10 outlets, must be discussed. The impending demise of this group has been forecast so often that it is perhaps surprising that they remain, in terms of turnover, number of establishments and number of employees, far larger than any other. The figures for Britain in 1966 are given in Table 2.

1·09 Traditional corner grocery shop at Crookes, Sheffield. This became an important trading type in 19th-century industrial England and is fast disappearing because of clearance policies

Table 2 *Organisation Analysis in the UK: 1966*

	Independents	(%)	Multiples	(%)	Co-operatives	(%)
Number of establishments	403,876	(80·1)	73,852	(14·6)	26,684	(5·3)
Total turnover £m	6,278,634	(56·4)	3,837,244	(34·5)	1,015,938	(9·1)
Persons engaged	1,640,446		741,833		173,458	
Sales/establishment £	15,546		51,959		5,857	
Sales/person £	3,827		5,173		5,857	

(Census of Distribution 1966)

1·10 Grocery and off-licence shop at Crookes, Sheffield

The weakening position of the group was shown, however, in Table 1, and the results of this have been for independent retailers either to flourish in areas where the large organisations cannot compete, or else to attempt to compete on more equal terms by forming groups, as was discussed in the sections on wholesalers and department stores.

In the former case, small traders have retained a convincing and unchallenged role as 'corner shops' providing convenience shopping for small catchment areas and providing additional services, such as late and Sunday opening, to compensate for higher costs. The high rents and fierce competition of the high streets, with their larger catchments, can be met by small traders who adopt a highly specialised stance in goods where a high mark-up is not crippling. Such, traditionally, is the case of the jeweller and specialist tailor. More recently, what might be described as a specialised mass market has emerged as an alternative to these narrow fields. In the tradition of the *Art Nouveau* shops, but with a much larger market to draw upon, the boutiques have broken new ground. Selling off-the-peg clothes, with the obsolescence of high fashion, style is an important element in these operations, both with respect to the goods and the shop presentation, in the stimulation of demand.

Between 1968 and 1971 the value of new contracts for the construction of shops and shopping centres in the UK amounted to £451m.[10] This represented 7% of construction work in the private sector and was about the same as that invested in the public sector in hospitals and health buildings and about four times that spent on universities. The results of that investment are considered in the following chapters.

References

1 William Paley, *The Principles of Moral and Political Philosophy* XXth edition, Longman, London 1814, Vol. 11

2 J. M. Keynes, *The General Theory of Employment, Interest and Money* Macmillan, London 1936

3 Lewis Mumford, *The City in History* Secker and Warburg Ltd, London 1961

4 Vincent Scully, *Modern Architecture* London 1961

5 Sigfried Giedion, *Space Time and Architecture* Harvard University Press, Cambridge, Mass. 1959

6 Louis Henri Sullivan, *Autobiography of an Idea* New York, and see Colin Rowe, 'Chicago Frame—Chicago's Place in the Modern Movement', *The Architectural Review* November 1956

7 Reyner Banham, *Theory and Design in the First Machine Age* The Architectural Press Ltd, London 1960

8 William H. Whyte, *The Organisation Man* Jonathan Cape Ltd, London 1957

9 N. A. H. Stacey and A. Wilson, *The Changing Pattern of Distribution* Pergamon Press Ltd, Oxford 1958

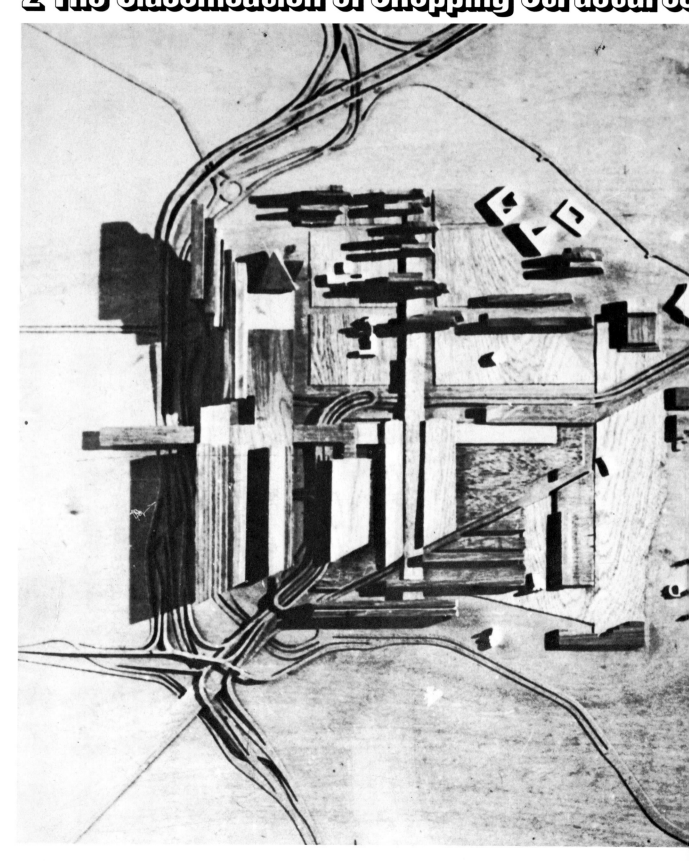

2·01 Project for the redevelopment of Cracow, Poland (1966): air view
of the model showing the medieval existing centre of Cracow
on the right and the new megastructure development on the left
Designers: Zbigniew Gadek, Stanislaw Juchnowicz and Andrzej Skŏczek

2·1 Hierarchy

It would be preferable to be able to base a discussion of current forms of shopping buildings upon an exact vocabulary. A glossary of terms is given in Appendix A, but it must be said that their meanings are more the subject of general understanding than of precise definition.

The basic classification of shopping centres is derived from the size of the area from which they draw their trade. According to the size of this catchment area, three main classes of centre can be recognised:
1 the local or neighbourhood centre
2 the district or community centre
3 the regional or main centre

In the past, this general grouping was sufficient to indicate the size of a shopping centre, the range of goods sold, its geographical location in the urban framework, and its built form. Indeed up until a few decades ago these three terms, local, district and regional, together with a small number of others defining specific retailing operations such as 'department store', constituted a complete and reasonably precise vocabulary. Certainly, shopping centres did not actually fall into just three clear groups, but rather arranged themselves in a continuous range, from the smallest local facility at one end to the great city, with an international catchment, at the other, and planners and statisticians could apply a more specific gradation. Nevertheless the three-tier notion was meaningful and comprehensive enough for general use. The local centre served an area within immediate walking distance and of up to 10,000 people, with convenience goods only. The quality of its shops would have to be very low before its customers would travel elsewhere for these daily requirements, its essential determinant being distance from the customer rather than attraction in terms of assortment or price. At the other end of the scale, the regional centre drew upon a catchment area of at least 100,000 people, and comprised a great number and variety of shops selling convenience goods and competing with one another by low prices and range of assortment. In addition, the centre contained a complete range of shops selling durable goods, and again competing in the sale of these, and it was to make these infrequent purchases that people from a wide area would travel in to the centre. A particularly attractive source of durable goods was the department stores, and these would be strongly represented. The regional shopping centre coincided with the centre of commercial and industrial expansion in that region and transportation investment was directed towards that point.

Between the local and regional centres lay the district centres, with catchment areas of perhaps 40,000 people. These provided for convenience goods more comparison shopping than the local centres, and for durable goods less than the regional centres, so that their draw depended on a balance between travel distance and cost/assortment attraction. In many countries the city department stores established smaller branch stores in these centres, which were located at favoured points on the transport routes and at local concentrations of population.

A feature of the traditional 3-tier pattern is that each level of centre overlaps the functions of those below. Thus the district centre acts as a local centre for the population within walking distance, as well as a district centre for the wider area. Similarly the regional centre provides the needs of a local centre for the workers and residents of the city

centre, and of a district centre for the population lying within a radius beyond, as well as performing its distinctive function as a regional centre.

The classification of shopping centres by the size of their catchment areas is still a valid, but no longer adequate, means of describing the new patterns of shopping. It still tells us the area served by the centre, but no longer defines its location or form, and so a new set of descriptive terms has been coined to supplement the old classification by reference to one or other of these aspects. Regarding location, the new terms—'down-town', 'in-town', 'integrated', 'city centre' on the one hand and 'out-of-town', 'suburban', 'green field' on the other—are concerned with the novel possibilities for siting which have arisen. In a sense, the old regional centres always were 'out-of-town' for part of their catchment population, but this was implicit in the term 'regional centre'. The invention of new names became necessary when the central location ceased to be inevitable. Similarly, terms descriptive of the centre's form, as 'pedestrianised', 'multi-level', 'covered' and 'enclosed', arose when it became necessary to describe families of centre types, each significantly different in their built form.

The result is that a statement such as 'Woodfield Mall is a regional shopping centre' is now of limited value. To communicate a general idea of the centre we would have to say 'Woodfield Mall is an enclosed, multi-level, out-of-town, regional shopping centre', and should probably add that it is American and of the period of the early '70s.

The trouble with these terms is that they are invented to describe a new type as it appears, but do not suggest any classification or indicate the way in which the particular type relates to the overall pattern, so that the proliferation of types appears arbitrary and confusing. The old terms are subtly changed too in their new context. To take the question of overlapping of functions present in the old hierarchy of centres, for example, such a characteristic may or may not occur in new centres of the same type, and it is not apparent from any of the terms generally used whether such a thing does occur, and hence precisely what function the centre is performing. To take the example of four new French centres, all of which would probably be described as 'regional' and 'out-of-town' or 'suburban', Table 3 shows the mode of transport of visitors, and hence indicates the function of these centres within the immediate, 1 km radius, area.

Table 3 *Mode of Shoppers' Transport to 4 French Shopping Centres*[1]

% Visitors	Parly 2	Belle Epine	Velizy 2	Cap 3000
On foot	11	5	9	2
Public transport	10	9	4	3
Motor-car	75	83	85	95
Other	4	3	2	—

While all four centres were planned as 'green-field' developments related to the highway systems, and while the great majority of shoppers in each case arrive by car, it is apparent that Parly 2 serves an important function within the local area and operates on at least two levels, as a local and regional centre. For Cap 3000 on the other hand, the immediate walking-distance catchment is of almost no significance.

Again, the new fluidity in the location of centres, and their independence of the old concentration points of radial routes, means that their function can change in time. An example of this is the shopping centre for Runcorn New Town in the North West of England, for which detailed feasibility studies were undertaken taking into account the status and competitive positions of the existing shopping centres of the region. From these studies it was proposed to develop the new centre in three phases to match the build-up of population within the new town it was to serve. However the first phase was to coincide with the construction of the new town's expressway system linked to new motorway construction in North Cheshire/South Lancashire, and the new centre would thus be in a more favoured position in relation to the region's new highway systems than many competing existing centres. In the event the centre was built immediately, with floor space related to a new town population which would not materialise for some years. The new development was therefore functioning on two levels, both as a main centre for the growing new town population, and also, for a period at least, and in a way which had not been initially anticipated, as a regional centre for a larger catchment area extending along the motorway routes.

Just as with shopping centres, so with individual shops a whole new vocabulary has been called into existence to describe the widening range of new types, as 'supermarket', 'hypermarket', 'superette', 'super store', 'bantam store', and so on. Such terms often overlap and also change in meaning as the type develops. Often the terms are evocative, as in the examples above which, rightly, appear to belong to a common family, but they are rarely precise. Even the distinction between the words 'shop' and 'shopping centre' is no longer quite as clear as it once was. Perhaps the department store, with a variety of concessionary traders operating within one store, first raised this difficulty, although so long as it was in and part of the city centre it could be considered as just a special shop. What happens though when the department store locates, on its own, on some suburban site? Does it not then become a special district centre? Does not a hypermarket selling a wide range of both convenience and durable goods and with small shopping units on its frontage, franchised operations within the store including a restaurant, and ancillary buildings around it on the site selling car and garden accessories, constitute a shopping centre?

In a situation where the meaning of old terms changes and overlaps, and where a variety of new terms, more descriptive than precise, is needed, it would be helpful to postulate a general structure for retailing forms, within which we could locate each new type and understand its transformations.

2·2 Evolution

We have already, in considering individual retailing operations, seen a general tendency for these to modify their low-cost origins. Names like 'Bon Marché' or 'Warenhaus' which sound appropriate for a discount store, betray the extent to which department stores have moved away from their original low-cost operations. Again it was seen that the early supermarkets were competitive in terms of cost, and then, as their number and competition between them grew, how they elaborated their operations with more emphasis on assortment and service.

This principle is also true of new shopping-centre types, as will be seen with the North American out-of-town centres, and it appears to provide a common theme for all new shopping-centre forms. First the new type establishes itself as a low-cost operation; then it increases in size as competition forces it to seek economies in scale and labour costs; next the competition causes it to widen its assortment of goods and finally to offer services. It has now developed away from its low-cost beginnings, and this space is now filled by a new type which opens on the scene. In the meantime, however, external factors have changed. The standard of living has risen, car ownership and highway construction have increased, and the range of staple, mass-produced items has extended from food and convenience goods further into the durable range to include, say, electrical appliances. The new type will therefore occupy the same trading position as the previous type's origin, selling a limited range of goods at low cost, but it will be different from the old type because of the next context, being, perhaps, differently located and selling a different range of goods.

This pattern has been developed by Agergard and Olsen of the Danish Institut for Center-Planlaegning into a general principle which they describe as a 'Theory of Spiral Movement'.[2] They extend the observations made above by demonstrating the effect of this spiral development of trading forms, pictorially the resultant of a circular movement in trading patterns coupled with a linear growth in the standard of living, upon the urban framework with its hierarchy of shopping centres. The effect is one of instability, with shopping centres themselves passing through transformations similar in pattern to those of the shop types. Such an evolution is shown to have occurred in American centres, where a longer history of the new pattern, and the relative absence of planning and space restrictions, provide the clearest examples. There the older suburban department stores, located in the middle-tier district centres, were badly hit by the department store operations in new out-of-town centres, which were bigger and offered a higher level of assortment. The weakening of the district centres' main elements also coincided with the rise of local centre based supermarkets, which, as they developed, grew both in size and assortment so enlarging their required catchment areas. Between 1950 and 1966 the number of items carried by the average supermarket rose from 3,700–3,800 to about 7,000, a significant part of the increase being in non-food items. At the same time the floor space requirement per item rose from as low as $0·1$ m^2 to $0·3$ m^2 and the typical American supermarket of 1966 had a floor space of 1800–2000 m^2 with an annual turnover of $\$1·6$–$1·8$ million. 10% of this was achieved in non-food items which, with intensive competition and lower growth on the food side, were increasingly introduced to maintain net profit levels. The supermarkets had now captured a 75% share of the total food turnover in the USA, and had clearly developed away from their original form with growth in size of units and in costs, prices and gross profits, which now stood at 22% as against 8% for the earliest units.

The supermarket now came to replace the department store as the main store of the district centre and, in those places where this occurred, the centre was reduced to the level of a strong local centre. At the same time some favourably located local centres would grow to the same level through the operations of their new supermarkets. The increasing size of the supermarkets meant that they must draw upon ever wider trading areas with ever reducing opportunities for further growth, until eventually a saturation point and competitive balance was reached. This balance had moved sufficiently far away from the early competition in terms of cost only, that a vacuum was left into which the discount houses, previously dealing solely in non-food items, now moved to start the cycle once more.

The growth of the supermarkets had also however left a gap at a different level, and another new shop type appeared. The widened trading areas of the supermarket-led local centres and the consequent greater travel distances to these facilities, with diminishing cost advantages, gave rise to the bantamstore. This was a reinterpretation of the old corner shop, but writ larger and in a new way. Whereas the corner shop had been typically a family-run business, located in an area of high density housing and provided with little or no parking, the bantamstore was built by the voluntary chains of independent traders and later by the national chains as well, to serve a trading area of 300 to 700 households with high accessibility from that area and with adequate parking. It was designed to complement the more distant supermarket, using its self-service trading methods, and competing in terms not of cost but of convenience and long opening hours. Typically it might remain open from 7 am to 11 pm, as well as trading on Sunday, and, although larger than the old corner shop, was only one tenth the size of the supermarket, in the 100–350 m² range. It carried perhaps 2–4,000 items selected from the supermarket's wider lists, had an annual turnover of $150–200,000, and gross profits 5–10% higher than the supermarket. By 1966 there were about 8,000 bantamstores in the USA and their number was rapidly increasing, as was the 5% share of the market then reached, an overall figure which was much higher in the urbanised areas.

Thus, in the first 20 years of the post war period, the spiral evolution of American trading forms had not only changed the individual forms themselves, but had influenced a similar metamorphosis in the nature and location of the hierarchy of shopping centres. New regional, district and local facilities emerged, with a development in any one producing a gap at another level to be filled in a new way. Although the old three-tier hierarchy could still be held to apply, its usefulness as a classification was diminished. Large local centres might now be larger than small district centres, and similarly with regional/district centres, so that size could no longer be confidently taken as a criterion. Similarly, the composition of a centre was no longer predictable as new trading methods gave rise to new shop types. Finally, as we have seen, the terms of the old static hierarchy no longer specified the location or built form of the centres. The spiral theory then is useful in that it provides a more adequate description of a dynamic situation than the previous fixed pyramidal notion.

2·3 Categories

If we can thus place particular new types in relation to one another, and understand the processes of change, we should then identify the main building groups which emerge and discuss their special characteristics and problems. Certainly size remains an important characteristic, since the building problem changes with changes in scale, but it no longer separates shopping buildings into essential categories. Rather, the considerations of location and content give us a more fundamental grouping of the new building types. With regard to the former, the question of whether a development occurs in an out-of-town location, independent of other centre functions, or is integrated into an urban fabric, would seem to pose two quite separate sets of building problems, and divides the new centres into two species. It can be argued that this is not a fundamental distinction, and that a more important consideration is whether or not a centre is planned in the sense offered by the American Urban Land Institute as 'a group of commercial establishments, planned, developed, owned and managed as a unit: the centre having a planned mix of tenants in relation to the market served and providing on-the-site parking for the customers'. The question as to whether the centre is located in green fields or not is then held to be irrelevant or at most secondary since green fields can rapidly become built-up areas. For the purposes of this study, however, the context of the centre is important in so far as the density of site use and impact of adjacent non-retail uses affects the retailing building. While all of the new shopping forms discussed here would fall within the above definition, the effects of a down-town or out-of-town location upon the centre's built form, and the reverse effects of the planned centre upon its context, are here held to be sufficiently different for the distinction to be a useful one.

The second consideration is concerned with the complexity of the building's content, and is really a matter of the difference between a 'shop' and a 'shopping centre'. For while the functional difference between these may have become confused, the building problem for an essentially single-element, monocellular centre is clearly different from that for a centre comprising an organisation of discrete elements and private and public spaces.

These four categories, out-of-town and integrated, monocell and multicell, divide the new buildings into families of related types, each of which comprises, at least potentially, a range of solutions by size through the local/district/regional scale. Of the twelve possible permutations which this gives, each compounded by national variations, not all will be of importance in this study. This basic breakdown however will be adopted, since the essential similarities between multicellular integrated centres, for example, and the way in which they relate to and have implications for the urban structure, and the way in which these differentiate them from their out-of-town cousins, are of great importance in establishing their built form.

2·4 Out-of-Town

The family of out-of-town centres, whether multicellular like the North American shopping centres, or monocellular like the European hypermarkets, is a product of the internal combustion engine. This relationship is so direct that we can postulate a level of car-ownership in a country, conveniently one car for every 10 people, which must be reached before the new centres will appear. Thereafter they proliferate in numbers and types as car ownership increases. The required level was achieved in the USA during the 1930s, and by 1952 had been reached by only Canada, USA and New Zealand. Ten years later these three had been joined by Australia and seven West European countries.

Coupled with this dependency, the real growth of the out-of-town centres also coincides with the second stage of the highway construction programmes which these countries have undertaken in this century. By 1900, 80 years of railway construction had left European road systems in a state little better than 2,000 years previously, when the Romans had constructed 50,000 miles of first class and 200,000 miles of secondary roads. Some technical developments had occurred, principally the use of concrete for building roads, started in London in the early nineteenth century; tar macadam paving, developed in Britain in mid-century; and asphalt paving which was used in France and Switzerland at the same time.

Towards the end of the century the new owners of bicycles, and then of cars, lobbied for improved road systems, which materialised in all the industrialised countries between the world wars. This first stage involved resurfacing and improvements to existing routes, with little increase in total mileage, and was largely complete by 1940. The start of the second stage, the construction of express highways, was generally delayed by the second war, although it had already begun in some countries. The Italian autostrade, started by private companies in 1924, were the first such express routes, although not yet fully to motorway standards. Then the construction of the German Reichsautobahnen network between 1932 and 1942 established a national system of 1,301 miles of express highways, with controlled access, grade-separated crossings and divided carriageways. Holland also built some mileage before the war, while in the USA the Pennsylvania Turnpike and Merritt Parkway in Connecticut were completed by 1941.

After the war these programmes were resumed. By 1950 eight states in the USA had toll roads of express highway standards, and thereafter almost every state began the construction of mileage. The 1949 Special Roads Act established the beginning of the second stage in Britain, providing for an initial network of 700 miles. In the Netherlands work resumed in 1945, and by 1960 300 miles were completed, giving that country one of the greatest highway densities in the world.

Belgium completed the Ostend–Brussels motorway in 1958 and motorways to all the main cities and border points followed, together with the Belgian sections of the Antwerp–Aachen autoroute in 1964. In Italy the Autostrada del Sole added 500 miles to the system in 1964, while the West Germans resumed construction in 1957 and by 1970 had a network of 2,500 miles, a quarter of the European total. Of the major European countries, France was the slowest to begin the second stage. Several short autoroutes were constructed in the 1950s, but government policy favoured rail travel, and did not start a major highway programme till the '60s. By 1970 600 miles were open and many more under construction.

The most ambitious single programme, and one whose scale overshadows all the others of this period, was the US National System of Interstate Highways. Authorised by Congress in 1944 and apportioned a 90% federal funding of $25,000,000,000 in 1956, the project envisaged the construction of 40,000 miles of express routes within 12 years. This mileage was extended by the Highway Act of 1968 to 44,000 miles and the programme to 1974.

The implications of these intensifying nets of national and regional highways for the urban structure, and in particular for its retailing element, were enormous. At the same time as car ownership made the concentration points of the old routes increasingly congested, large, cheap sites on the outside of the cities were made highly accessible. Since the buildings on such sites need no longer make intensive use of restricted and expensive land, they could be large simple structures of comparatively low cost, with large surrounding areas of car parking again provided cheaply. This combination of size, low land cost and low building cost gave the out-of-town centres a considerable cost advantage over the urban centres, and this coincided with an increasing demand for price competitiveness as standards of living rose. It is paradoxical that this should be so, and that the out-of-town centres should be best placed to meet such a demand originating from precisely that section of the population which could afford the cars to reach them. The reason for this is perhaps that the rise in the standard of living and in the expectations which derive from it do not produce a smooth transition in family expenditure patterns. Rather the requirement at a certain point in income growth for a further range of durable or 'luxury' goods causes the amount of income available for essential items at that time to drop. The out-of-town locations were therefore particularly suited to competitive food retailing operations, and this was reinforced by the growth in ownership of domestic refrigerators and freezers which enabled the consumer to match the new pattern of larger and more distant outlets with less frequent shopping trips. For while the ownership of refrigerators could be expected to alter the shopping pattern for perishable and frozen foods, surveys in the UK suggest that its effect is wider, reducing the frequency of shopping trips for canned and non-perishable items also.[3] Finally, the rise of the out-of-town centres coincided in most countries with general growth of populations and dramatic growth of suburban populations. In the USA for example the suburban populations trebled between 1960 and 1973, from 27 million to 76 million. This meant that a general increase in retailing provision was in any case required, but also that the growth areas requiring these facilities were further removed from the old centres.

All of these factors, the growth of car-ownership, highway systems, land availability, standard of living, cost emphasis, population and suburban development, favoured the out-of-town centres and from the logic of these were their forms derived. So strong were these pressures that it was not necessary for them all to coincide. Thus we shall see that the American centres were able to successfully evolve under the spiral effect away from the low-cost aspect towards more elaborate and expensive building forms and ranges of goods, but remain viable because of their accessibility and site areas. The limitations on the out-of-town centres, and the continued relevance of the integrated solutions, are precisely the limitations on these factors.

2·5 Integrated

Between 1940 and 1970 the population of the USA rose by 55%, that of the UK by 15%. The overall density of population in the USA was 22 persons per km², and in the UK 229. The average American disposed of 2½ times the income of the Briton, and owned 2½ times as many cars, half, in fact, of the world's total. The circumstances which had led to a huge growth in out-of-town centres in the

USA did not therefore apply to the same degree in Britain, nor was it simply a question of the UK being a decade or so behind. This might be the case with car ownership, income or the comparatively modest highway programme, but where population density, and therefore competition for land-use, was intense, the opportunities for a restructuring of the retail pattern on the American scale were more limited. Again, with slower growth of population and wealth, there was a greater resistance to the effects of new facilities upon the existing pattern, and a more frugal attitude towards the investment represented by existing land-use and urban form. Moreover, with wartime bombing, the renewal of this form was made necessary immediately war was over, and before the factors favouring out-of-town locations emerged.

The weakness of this bare analysis can be seen by considering the other European examples. West Germany, for instance, suffered greater bomb damage and, with a population density of 239 persons per km², is comparable to the UK as a whole, although not to England alone at 352 persons per km², yet has developed a large number of out-of-town facilities. France, on the other hand, with the lowest European density at 93 persons per km² and a late but dramatic start in both highway and shopping centre construction, backs the analysis well. Sheer density of population, however, remains a powerful factor, and it is surely not coincidental that the country with the highest gross population density in the world, England, should also have been the slowest of the industrialised nations to adopt the out-of-town solution on any scale. The difference in density of population between England and the USA can be illustrated by the statistic that the whole population of the world could be accommodated in the latter before its density would approach that of the former. The pressure of competing land uses created by English densities is shown by the Financial Times share index between 1959–72 which measured a 662% increase in the price of agricultural land as against a general rise in share prices of 192%.[4]

It is apparent that the two forms, out-of-town and integrated, are not necessarily mutually exclusive, and the political and social attitudes of countries towards their own variation of the circumstances, as expressed in planning legislation, is of major importance. Thus the Scandinavian solutions have much in common with those in the UK, although many of the conditions are different.

If the out-of-town centres are the product of the motor car, the new integrated centres are no less conditioned by it. In order to function at all, whether in competition with out-of-town centres or not, they must provide an equivalent or substitute for the highway interchange and vast parking lots of the alternative location. What is implied by this is a restructuring of the urban cores rather than of the distribution of retailing facilities. Unlike the out-of-town centres, their pedestrian and traffic systems are not 'private' routes, created for their own use and no other. Rather they are but the most public and accessible part of a wider net of urban routes, and their success depends upon this. The decision to renew and retain the retailing element within the urban core therefore means rather more than simply giving the city 'a new heart' as is sometimes said. For that heart to function it will probably mean that the core must be given new stomach, liver and circulation as well, and finish up a somewhat different animal. This is generally a painful business, and certainly expensive. Land and building costs will be greater than in the out-of-town

locations, as will the accompanying infrastructure and car-parking costs. These centre types are therefore not best suited for the low-cost operations with which the out-of-town centres began, and where there is competition with the latter, will tend immediately to compete on a higher level of the spiral. Of course a simple comparison of costs for the two forms is inadequate. The cost consequences of decline in a central area from which the retailing element has evacuated are much wider than those which apply to the retailing element alone, but it has also become clear that the physical consequences of retaining the retailing element are great.

In being so reticent in adopting the out-of-town solution, the UK represents perhaps the opposite end of the spectrum to the USA, with the European countries establishing varying positions between. It is fortunate then that the UK has also adopted a mechanism which conveniently demonstrates the development of solutions to the consequences of the integrated centre. The New Towns are symptomatic of the British attitude towards the factors which brought about the out-of-town centres. They did not prevent suburban growth, nor were they altogether representative of forms of development elsewhere in the country, but their designers have always regarded them as points at which ground should be broken; as prototypes and models for new solutions which could not yet be realised within the constraints of the old settlements. In this they have remained reasonably faithful to Ebenezer Howard's intentions, as also to his location of the main retailing element firmly at the centre of the plan, and since, like the out-of-town centres, they generally begin with a green-field site, the sequence of New Town centres gives us a particularly clear evolution of the integrated centre family. The relevance of these solutions is not academic: many were developed by private capital, employing the same measures of viability as elsewhere.

Of equal importance and more universal impact have been the redevelopment schemes for the centres of existing European towns and cities. Whether brought about by war damage, growth, the need for renewal or simple pressure of competition or the motor car, such schemes have both paralleled the New Town developments and also evolved particular solutions to the problems of integration within an existing frame. The simplification of the retailing pattern into fewer and larger organisations requiring fewer and larger buildings, the widening of the net of accessibility brought about by the car, and the increase in scale of renewal from that of single shop increments to that of whole centres in a few phases, all militate against easy assimilation of the new transplant. The structure is different from that of the old and the circulation systems it generates more elaborate. In some cases it can be accommodated as a graft and absorbed by an existing centre; in others the old centre remains, if at all, as a few fragments embedded in the new.

References

1 International Association of Department Stores: Commissions on Stores in Shopping Centres, Document No. 861, March 1973
2 *The Interaction between Retailing and The Urban Centre Structure—A Theory of Spiral Movement* by Erik Agergard and Poul Anker Olsen of the Institut For Center-Planlaegning July 1968
3 Survey by Birds Eye *What's in Store* 1966
4 *The Architectural Review* October 1973

2·02 The end of an era: interior of the former Biba department
store, Kensington High Street, London
Store designers: Whitmore Thomas Design Associates

3 Out-of-Town Shopping

BURTS SHOES

BURTS SHOES

GRANAT BROS

GRANAT BROS

3·1 North American Regional Centres

Of all the new forms of shopping, the out-of-town centres of North America have been the most dramatic in their novelty, their growth, and their implications for the cities they serve.

Although the first centres recognisably of the type were built in the 1930s, their real growth belongs to the post-war period. In 1949 there were 49 such centres in the USA; by 1965 there were an estimated 11,000, and at the end of 1972, 15,000 of which perhaps 10% were on a regional scale.[1] By the early 1970s they had captured one half of all the retail trade in North America, and were growing at the rate of almost 20 million m² each year.[2] Development on this scale had not simply modified a previous pattern or added a new element to it. It had transformed that pattern, extracting the retailing element from the commercial cores of cities on a large scale and relocating it in isolation from the other elements of city centres with which it had always previously been identified.

The characteristic form of the new regional centres was best captured in aerial photographs, which exercised an ambivalent fascination on European planners and developers, who projected the car ownership and family expenditure patterns of their own countries forward and determined 'lessons to be learned'. The island building, comprising magnet department stores linked by a simple mall arrangement lined by small traders, set in an enormous parking lot adjacent to an intersection on the highway network and on the fringe of a populated area, posed a form of development which appalled some and led others to suggest that here the modern shopping centre was achieving an 'ideal' form, in that it was a form derived purely from the laws which govern the process of retailing, unhindered by the traditional restraints imposed upon development in the urban centres.

Certainly the intensely competitive situation in North America quickly revealed the ground rules for the new shopping centres, and the logic of these has been found to apply equally in different contexts. Thus, the principle of using a few 'magnet' stores, with great attraction for all shoppers, to manipulate pedestrian movements through the centre and past shops of lower individual attraction and thus maximise turnover for all tenants, was soon established, as was the consequent necessity of achieving a correct tenant mix in the planning of the centre. Similarly the principles affecting the siting of centres was clarified, and for the first time considerable effort was spent in estimating catchment areas, patterns of expenditure and the competitive positions of numbers of shopping centres within a region.

Such general lessons are now widely understood, but it is necessary in considering the North American out-of-town centres to remember that they have not produced a constant solution. Rather they represent a continuous mutation as their competitive situation changed along the lines suggested by the 'spiral' theory. Thus what was an appropriate solution for the suburbs of New York in 1955 was not appropriate for the suburbs of Paris or Frankfurt in 1955, and was again inappropriate for the suburbs of New York in 1965. It is therefore worth considering both these aspects of American life which brought about the out-of-town centres and determined their form and also the way in which they have developed and changed. The processes by which they were brought about are relevant and these are illustrated by the parts played by certain key agents.

The Role of the Developer

In order to bring about the new planned shopping centres a new kind of operator was required, the developer, whose primary role was to make the new centre happen; to assemble the finance, land, tenants and professional and building skills in such a way that a complete shopping centre would be produced by a certain date and thereafter function in such a way as to provide a satisfactory return on the capital invested. This role is quite distinct from that of the banker, landowner, retailer, architect or contractor, although it could be undertaken by one of these. Developers of American out-of-town centres have, for example, included insurance companies, contractors, architects and more commonly, department stores, either individually or in combination, as well as companies exclusively concerned with property development.

Since the developer is uniquely concerned with all stages of the shopping centre's life, a catalogue of his activities describes also the processes by which the centre is brought about. These processes are today assisted by an ever-increasing body of statistical method, so that a project in its development stages will accumulate studies analysing traffic patterns, catchment areas and expenditure patterns which will justify the proposed location, size and composition of the development. Nevertheless, the developer's decisions remain speculative and to some extent intuitive.

At the first stage, site selection, he will be concerned not only with the disposition of population within the area of interest, its highway system, patterns of growth, availability of land, and its existing facilities; he must also relate these to the intentions of the department store chains, and their plans for expansion in the area concerned, in order that he can ensure the presence of an appropriate number of these in his development as 'magnet' stores; further he must consider the extent to which particular sites are prone to being isolated by future and possibly unknown changes in any of these factors, or by the appearance of new competing centres. He will typically be assisted by two consultant firms at this stage, who will provide traffic and market analyses for the region, and on the basis of these the developer will prepare his financial analysis and merchandising plan. These can be taken to some considerable detail and may well define specifically the range of shop units, additional to the anchor department stores, which the developer intends, in terms of their type, the range of market served within that type, turnover, area and rental levels. Thus, in a regional centre of, say, 100,000 m² gross leasable area, one half of this area will be taken up by the anchor department stores, and the remaining area will be broken down into a schedule of shop units in the form:

'Men's Shops: One complete line men's wear approximately 1000–1200 m²
One high priced
Three men's furnishings approximately 400 m² each
Two men's tie shops approximately 100 m² each'

and so on, with corresponding financial appraisal. At this point the developer will have determined the range and character of the centre to suit his anchor stores and to meet his interpretation of the potential market, and will have prepared his brief for the design team.

The design problem which arises from this brief is comparatively clear and revolves around the manipulation of anchor stores, mall entry points, servicing arrangements and specialist shop distribution to achieve the greatest trading potential for the centre as a whole. The developer will have his own ideas as to the most advantageous distribution of particular shop types and the extent to which similar types should be grouped or dispersed. What emerges is a sort of chess game, with weightings given to individual pieces according to their 'draw', and rules governing the relationships between them. The architect's difficulty then lies in resolving this with the varying physical requirements of the pieces, with some requiring area but not frontage, and others the reverse. In practice this difficulty may well be overshadowed by the problem of establishing the rules themselves, for these spring directly from the number and nature of the anchor department stores, and should these factors change during the design stage then everything else must change with them.

The composition of the design team and methods of selecting the contractor vary in US practice as elsewhere, but there are general differences of emphasis with UK practice which are worth noting. The 'development team' at design stage, for example, might comprise four central parties, being the developer, the architect, the contractor, and the leasing agent. Structural, HVAC, electrical and soils engineers would also be brought in at appropriate stages, but there would be no quantity surveyor as in the UK, and the contractor would be involved at this stage as a cost consultant. There is also varying practice in the USA regarding the use of HVAC consultants, with an apparently increasing tendency to employ design/build contractors to carry out this function. A further contributor to the development team might also be the Centre Manager of the developer's previous project, to give advice based on management experience.

This pattern is complicated by the fact that the anchor department stores will most probably have their own design teams, retaining the developer's architect as a co-ordinating consultant. The situation may then arise, as when the department stores are acting jointly as developers of the centre, where each must seek the approval of the other stores to its own proposals.

The developer generally acts as leader of the development team, and exercises rigid control in the imposition of freeze dates related to the completion of design stages necessary for bidding and contractual negotiations to proceed. It is general experience that production information is never completed at the time of start on site, and common for site preparation and foundation work to begin at the earliest possible date and while work continues on the production information upon which the main contract will be negotiated.

The 100,000 m² centre will have taken 3 to 5 years in gestation, from site location studies to start on site, and will then have a construction period of about 16 months. During this latter period the developer will seek to lease all of the smaller shop units in accordance with his merchandising plan, and the method of leasing which has been evolved for the North American shopping centres is an essential factor determining the developer's role. This derives from the fact that leasing agreements in North America, unlike those in the UK, relate rental paid by shop units to their turnover. Thus the developer has a direct financial interest in the way in which a tenant operates,

and in the extent to which tenants compete against or complement one another in the centre as a whole. It is for this reason that the merchandising plan, with its detailed tenant mix, is of such importance to the developer, and the implications of the developer's interest in a tenant's turnover extend into all aspects of the centre's design and operation. They are spelled out in the four main provisions of the tenant's lease, the first of which concerns the rental agreement.

The rental agreement provides for a fixed base rent, calculated on a square foot basis as sufficient to provide the developer with a required break even return on the total capital outlay. Once the tenant's turnover rises to the point at which an agreed percentage of that turnover equals the base rent, however, the rental becomes proportional to the rising turnover, although still subject to the guaranteed base level. The percentage of turnover used varies from trade to trade, and base rents will vary in different centres, but the percentages are generally standardised for each trade, varying from perhaps 2% for food sales to 10% or 12% for certain service trades. The anchor department stores may pay turnover rentals on this basis, with percentage fixed at the lower end of the scale, or they may, with their strong bargaining position, negotiate some participation in the equity of the development and contribute a fixed percentage of cost, rather than rental.

Although the turnover rental system theoretically benefits both parties by ensuring their common interest in the success of the whole development, there has been a tendency for developers to increase the base rent at times of lease renewal in order to give the greatest security of income and mortgageability for his asset, while tenants will generally prefer a fixed rental so that their overheads are predetermined. One further implication of the turnover rental system is that, since the developer is concerned not only with leasing space, but also with increasing its yield, he will generally try to persuade tenants to carry out their trading in the least area which is viable, rather than the greatest, since the former will increase the total turnover of a given amount of space. He will therefore wish to check a tenant's own estimates of space requirements as well as the profitability of his business.

The second set of provisions in the lease relates to 'Restriction and Exclusives', by means of which the developer controls the range of goods sold by a particular trader. The purpose of these controls is to extend the intentions of the merchandising plan to cover in detail the operations of the individual stores so that internal competition within the centre doesn't lead to its trading downhill. A difficulty experienced with this, as with all planning controls, is that trading methods and patterns change and shops continually wish to diversify their ranges, so that these restrictive clauses lack the flexibility which the turnover rental system has for accommodating instant adjustments to new conditions.

The lease agreement also provides for strict developer's control of maintenance of premises and stock, and for some measure of approval of displays. Again these logically result from the developer's interest in ensuring the highest possible turnover for any particular tenant and balancing this against the effect on other tenants.

Finally, having established that the merchandising plan is carried through to cover all aspects of tenants' operations, the lease agreement ensures that a Merchants' Association is set up to promote the common interest.

Such associations, with constitutions governed by bye-laws which both developer and tenant covenant to abide by, are felt to be essential to the successful operation of the new centre, their function being to increase the attractiveness and competitive position of the centre, and hence turnover, by advertising, exhibitions and displays in the mall areas, and other promotional gambits.

This broad description of the developer's role gives a general picture of the way in which the North American out-of-town centres have been brought about, and the parameters which have determined their form.[3] However, in considering the number of such centres which have been built, it is necessary to discuss a little further the part played by another key agent, the department store.

The Role of the Department Store

In their appearance, organisation and development procedure, the North American regional centres are literally built around their department-store elements. The crucial role which the anchor stores play at all stages of the development, from site selection and feasibility studies to the detailed form of the merchandising plan and of the building, has already been described. There is however also a sense in which the department stores have been not simply a passive element to be taken into account in creating new centres for which a demand could be argued to exist; they have also, by virtue of competition between department chains, been a party to the creation of that demand.

In the old urban shopping centres, the department stores, along with the other shop types, stood in competition to one another within the one centralised facility. Then, as the first large suburban shopping centres were built, competition occurred between these and the central facility, and between the department stores in each. Finally an increasing number of out-of-town centres became established in competition with one another. The retailing element of the old city had in effect exploded into a ring of satellite regional centres, each dominated by its own pair or trio of department stores and competing not so much internally, as had the old centre, as from centre to centre for the available trade. Thus the situation could occur where a requirement for a new out-of-town centre could arise in an area already served by such centres, by virtue of the need of department store chains not already represented in the existing centres to maintain or improve their competitive position.

The general importance of the strategies of the department store chains to the American development pattern is clearly seen by examining the typical case of North Virginia. This region experienced a dramatic growth in population during and after the Second World War, rising from under 100,000 in 1930 to over 700,000 by 1963. An extensive highway system was also built after the war, and as a result of these factors the shopping pattern of the region, previously dominated by the downtown area of Washington, was transformed. Small shopping centres, based on a branch store of one of the major Washington department stores, were established, and these were followed by the first regional centre on a major highway intersection. In early 1963 the Washington firm of Hammer and Company prepared a market analysis for the developers of an existing suburban centre of 12,350 m² in Springfield Va. which favourably reviewed the possibility of expanding that centre to regional status with three major department stores. However the three key stores decided to locate in a new

regional centre four miles further up the Shirley Highway, and in the latter part of 1963 Hammer and Company produced a second report to determine whether the expansion of Springfield Mall to regional size was still a possibility. Despite the new Landmark centre to be built so short a distance away, the consultants concluded that conditions were still favourable, and the following extract from their report, summarising their analysis of the retail patterns of the region which leads them to their conclusion, gives an insight into the role of the department stores in post-war developments throughout America:[4]

'The growth of retail facilities in Northern Virginia is following a pattern seen in Northern New Jersey years ago. First came expansion of the traditional retail districts in Clarendon and Alexandria which was followed by the development of small shopping centers built around a single branch unit of a major Downtown Washington department store—Parkington (Hecht's) and Virginia Square (Kann's), both near the Clarendon complex, and then Shirlington (Lansburgh's). Then came the big regional shopping center—Seven Corners—with two small department stores and a large number of supporting stores. Now the three-department-store center—Landmark—has emerged with S. Klein and Korvette nearby. All this retail development has followed the growth of population along the major corridors from the older urbanized areas of North Virginia.

Each of the major shoppers-goods firms in the area has had to adopt its own pattern of coverage, taking into account the physical shifts in the market, the moves of competitors, and the availability of sites at strategic locations and with compatible neighbors. Each locational decision of each company has influenced the decisions of the other companies; perhaps more important, each locational decision of each company has been a determining factor in each subsequent decision of the same company as it attempts to get maximum coverage and maximum competitive leverage with minimum impact upon its existing outlet or outlets.

When Hecht's and Kann's moved early into the Clarendon district, for example, they effectively eliminated themselves from a subsequent location in the area's first regional center—Seven Corners. These stores now must obviously leapfrog the primary market area of Seven Corners to reach new expansion areas beyond. The same is also true of Sears. When Woodward & Lothrop built a relatively small store in Seven Corners, as noted earlier, a pattern was set for this company calling for one or more additional units of the same size in other parts of the overall market in order to get adequate coverage. Montgomery Ward sought a central market location when it put its first large store at Seven Corners. Its next logical move would be to leapfrog the Landmark development (Sears-Hecht's-Woodward & Lothrop) to the south and move eventually into the heavy growth area to the north. Lansburgh's, Garfinckel's, Klein's, Penneys—all major shoppers-goods units attempting to reach the Northern Virginia market—must adapt their own particular strategies to meet their own particular needs. . . .

Several important shoppers-goods stores—specifically Ward's, Kann's, Lansburgh's and Penneys, among others—are not represented in the fast-growing southern part of the Northern Virginia market nor are they slated for sites in the Landmark center. Clearly these stores must eventually get representation in this market. They have alternate ways of doing so, either from free-standing locations or as part of a major retail complex. Whatever their individual choices, each clearly must take steps to get coverage of the market, out-flank the competition, and put itself in a position to expand its sales as the market grows in the future.'

Evolution

The number of the new American regional shopping centres is so great that the choice of examples is necessarily arbitrary. It is possible though to use a few such examples to illustrate a general evolution of the centres through three distinct stages. Historically these three stages fall roughly within the '50s, the '60s and the '70s, and could be said to correspond to the pattern of spiral growth in that they represent a development, very like that of the department stores previously, in terms of increasing customer attraction by comfort and services matched by increasing costs of building and of the range of goods sold. It is also interesting to see that, as each new stage was reached, many of the 'rules' governing the building form of the previous period, which had been held to be inviolate at that time, were reversed and their opposites adopted as universal principles of shopping centre design.

Stage 1

The centres of the first stage established two characteristics which were not to change. The first of these was size. By the mid 1950s, a number of suburban growth areas in the USA had regional centres with leased areas in excess of 100,000 m². Parking ratios ranging from 4 to 8 car spaces per 100 m² produced overall site areas for the centres of over 40 ha. The second 'permanent' characteristic established at this time was the clear separation of the various forms of circulation. Pedestrian shopping streets were separated from traffic areas and goods service bays from general parking areas, so that, in contrast to the old urban centres, there was a clear sequence from the highway, through the parking area, to the pedestrian precinct in the centre.

The malls of the precinct were open to the weather at this stage, with canopies extending out from the shop fronts, and the mall layout often elaborate. Roosevelt Fields, LI, illustrates this complexity with its double main malls between the magnet department stores and multiplicity of cross malls and small squares. This development was opened in 1955 on the site of a disused airfield and adjacent to the Meadowbrook Parkway in Nassau County. Its total site area is 49 ha, accommodating 11,000 cars as well as the shopping centre itself. This was typical of its period in comprising two department stores and a supermarket as major elements, together with over a hundred small shops in blocks defining the malls. It was not yet therefore a single building, although conceived and developed as a whole.

Old Orchard, at Skokie, Illinois, is a similar example of the period with 111,000 m² GLA provided in a 38 ha site,

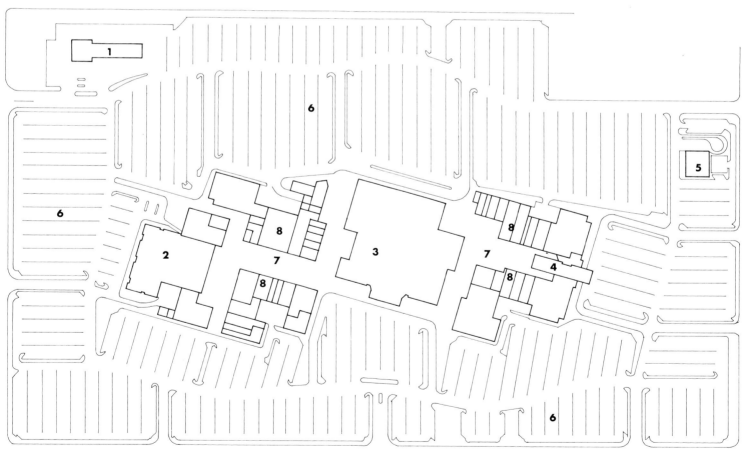

3·02 Old Orchard shopping centre, Illinois, USA: main-level plan
Architects: Loebl, Schlossman, Bennett and Dart

Key:
1 Ward's T B A
2 Ward's department store (4 levels)
3 Marshall Field department store (4 levels)
4 Office building
5 Bank
6 Parking
7 Mall
8 Shops

Scale: 1 : 4000

and a comparison of the two plans illustrates the variety of mall arrangements which were experimented with at this time. Both centres illustrate too the use of trucking tunnels below the centre for goods access to shops, and particularly to main department stores, which was widely adopted in the Stage 1 centres. Old Orchard also shows the introduction from an early stage of secondary uses on the regional centre sites, with a bank, a TBA (tyres, batteries and car accessories) centre, and professional offices. At Bergen Mall, for example, a cinema and theatre were similarly adopted by the regional centre. This case demonstrates a further phenomenon which showed itself in this early period. Located in the strong growth area of Northern New Jersey, Bergen Mall was opened in 1956 within a year of, and only ¾ mile away from, Garden State Plaza, a second regional centre. Between them the two developments provided nearly 300,000 m² of shopping space, occupied almost 120 ha, and could accommodate about 17,000 cars for a catchment of 0·9 million people within 25 minutes and 1·6 million within 40 minutes driving time along the new highway systems of the region.

To summarise then, the regional centres of this first period were characterised by a variety and complexity of mall arrangements, as if the discipline of traffic management had been removed from the old main street pattern of development, but no clear alternative pedestrian-based system found to take its place. They also experimented with more sophisticated solutions in terms of levels than had been possible with the old main streets, by the use of underground servicing and two level malls. They were already enormous, both in rental area and land-take, and had begun to realise the mutually advantageous incorporation of secondary retail and even non-retail uses within the site.

In terms of their built form, however, they were still a grouping of isolated buildings on individual plots, even if those plots had been simultaneously planned and developed. Skidmore, Owings and Merrill's classical disposition of elements at the Short Hills centre in New Jersey is perhaps the most perfect statement of this position. That centre was opened in 1961, but already 5 years previously, the first fully enclosed, all-weather centre had been built at Edina, a suburb of Minneapolis where the annual temperature variation is from −30° to +42°C.

Stage 2
The enclosure of the malls marks a fundamental change in the development of the centres. Its implications are wide and were only gradually worked out through the second and third stages of their growth. For the developer it means that the section of his capital costs for which he will not directly gain rental is greatly increased, and particularly in the field of services costs, since a very large volume of landlord's space is now to be heated and air-conditioned. For the tenant it means a corresponding increase in rental levels, but also a much larger increase in maintenance charges. The relationship between the mall and the shops is now dramatically changed. Instead of being a gap between buildings, the mall is now the central, most densely used space of a single building. The natural environment stops at the building perimeter, and all shops turn in upon this central space, from which they need no longer be separated by glass walls and doors. The department stores are simply extensions of this space, for now the whole centre is like a department store. Despite the additional costs of enclosing the malls, the increased attractiveness to shoppers was such that all new centres

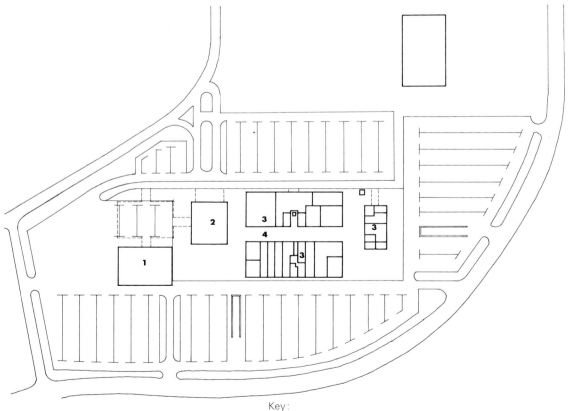

3·03 Short Hills shopping centre, New Jersey, USA: mid-level plan
Architects: Skidmore, Owings and Merrill

Key:
1 Bloomingdale's department store (4 levels)
2 Bonwit Teller's department store (3 levels)
3 Shops
4 Mall

Scale: 1 : 4000

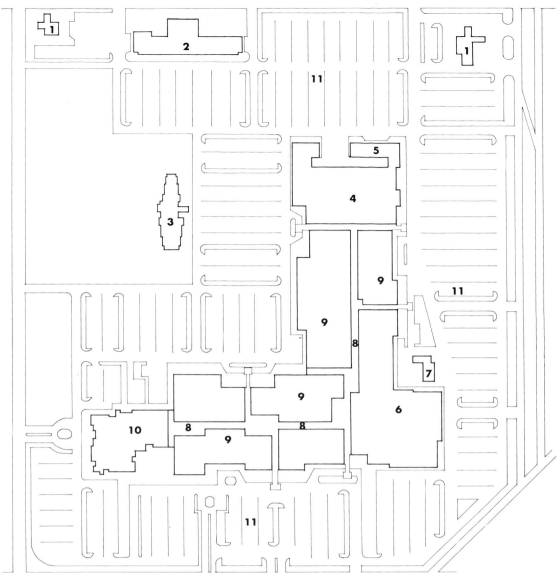

3·04 North Park shopping centre,
Texas, USA: main-level plan
Architects: Harrell and Hamilton

Key:
1 Service station
2 Convenience centre
3 Twin cinema
4 Penney's department store
   (3 levels)

5 Penney's T B A
6 Titche—Goettinger department store (3 levels)
7 Titche—Goettinger T B A
8 Mall

9 Shops
10 Nieman—Marcus depart-
    ment store (2 levels)
11 Parking
Scale: 1 : 4000

begin to be developed in this way, and many of the Stage 1 centres were forced to carry out 'modernisation' programmes, to roof in their malls at considerable cost and inconvenience. The increased costs did however persuade developers and architects away from the more complicated experiments of the Stage 1 centres. Trucking tunnels under the building were less frequently used, servicing taking place in screened areas at the rear of the shops. This had the effect of reinforcing the introspective nature of the building. Except in the case of the department stores, the outside wall ceased to have any function as a shop window, and shops presented their blank back sides to the car parks. The multi-level schemes were also abandoned, since it had been found that the secondary level, not being a part of the main pedestrian flow, was isolated and therefore unable to support rental levels appropriate to the covered centres. Finally the basic layouts of the centres were simplified into a few standard patterns. As previously, the Stage 2 centres were usually built around two or three magnet stores, and these were arranged simply to draw shoppers along a single main mall. The size of the centres was unchanged, and the frontage/depth ratio for the smaller shops could not be

greatly modified, so that the arithmetic governing the centres' form was correspondingly simple. A regional centre of 100,000 m² GLA would have half of this area occupied by magnet stores. The remainder would be in the form of a central mall with a bank of shops on each side interrupted at intervals by side malls leading in from the surrounding car park. The width of this cross-section of shop/mall/shop would be about 100 m, so that the 50,000 m² of smaller shops would require a mall about 500 m long. The effective range of a magnet is only 90–120 m, however, so this length of mall could only be sustained by at least three magnets, otherwise a weak zone would occur in the centre, and the circulation would tend to occur in two independant circuits within the zones of each magnet. The 100,000 m² centre therefore required at least three magnet stores, typically with one at each end and one in the centre. To break the monotony of a quarter of a mile of mall, this sausage could be broken at the point of the centre magnet to form an 'L', and this arrangement emerged as one of the classic forms of development in this period. North Park, Dallas, with a total pedestrian circulation length of 790 m and the largest air-conditioned mall area of any centre at the time of its opening in 1964, is a good example. *The Architectural Record*[5] eulogises on the new form in an article of the time:

'Not a "street of stores" but a flowing series of naturally lighted plazas is the enclosed mall of North Park. There are six such plazas, each with direct access from parking. The three largest, with programmed fountains and plantings, mark the entrances to major stores but also provide visual contact with mall fronts of smaller tenants. Turning the 'L' are two contiguous plazas which break the long vistas.'

And the architect, E. G. Hamilton of Harrell and Hamilton describes his intentions as '. . . to answer the problems of diverse, assertive occupancy and gigantic scale by recognizing that we are dealing with one building. Our solution has attempted to create a sense of unity by the use of a single, simple palette of material (white brick, cast stone and concrete), and to manage the scale by variations in the form—establishing visual areas to which one can respond pleasantly at any point.' This quotation illustrates very well the new preoccupation with the building unity and the function within it of the mall. Certainly the malls at North Park, with their subdued range of materials, controlled bronze anodized aluminium framed shop fronts, immaculate planters and seating units and 'programmed fountains', are of a piece with the high quality department stores they connect, and are some distance removed from the asphalt and concrete tiles and shrubbery beds of the Stage 1 centres.

The high cost/quality aspect emerges most clearly at this time with the development of centres catering for more exclusive trading lines. Paramus, New Jersey, the location of the two Stage 1 giants Bergen Mall and Garden State Plaza, was provided in 1967 with a third regional centre specializing in this way. At 42,000 m², of which 30,000 was occupied by two department stores, Fashion Mall could appropriately adopt the 'dumbell' arrangement of one magnet at either end of a straight 180 m mall. With a site area of just 14 ha some car parking was located on the roof of the central zone of small shops and mall, and giving direct access into the upper levels of the end department

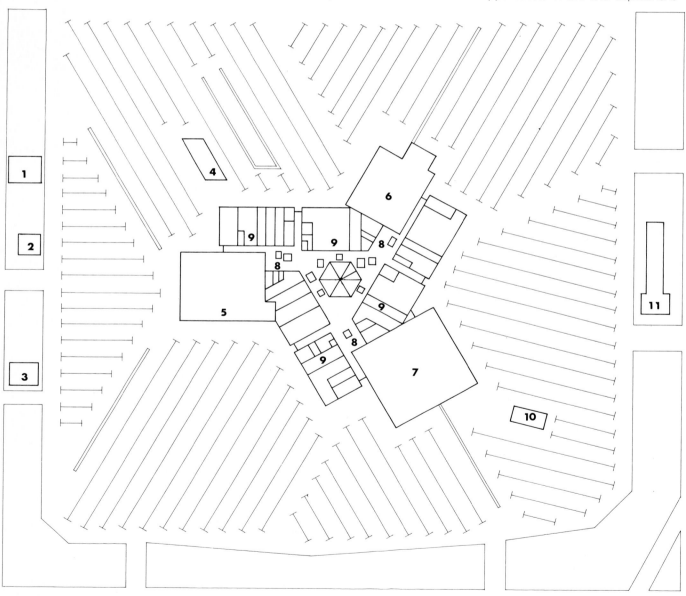

3·05 Randhurst shopping centre, Illinois, USA: main-level plan
Architect: Victor Gruen

Key:
1 Convenience centre
2 Cinema
3 Weiboldt's T B A
4 Bank
5 Weiboldt's department store (3 levels)
6 Carson Pirie Scott department store (3 levels)
7 Ward's department store (3 levels)
8 Mall
9 Postal unit
10 Ward's T B A
11 Restaurants over shops
Scale: 1 : 4000

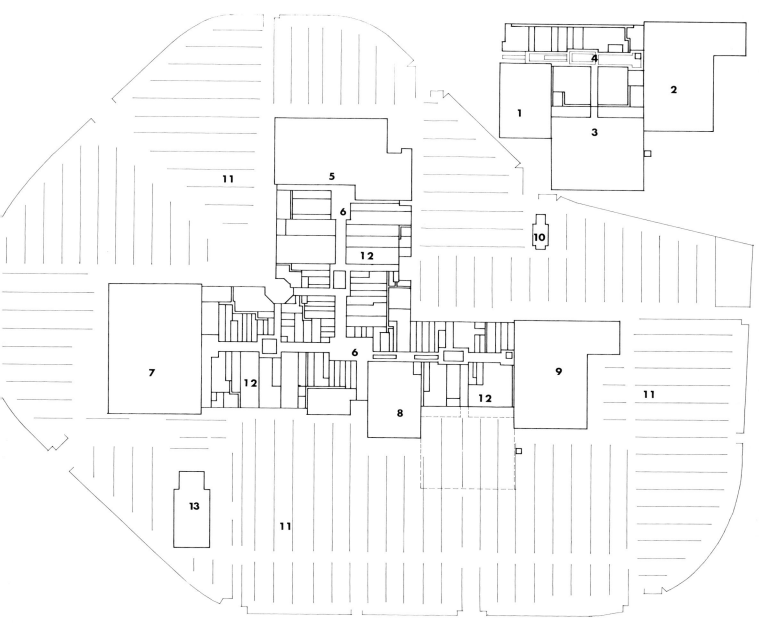

3·06 Willowbrook Mall shopping centre, New Jersey, USA: main- and upper-level plans
Architects: Welton Becket and Associates

Key:
1 Ohrbach's department store (upper level)
2 Stern Bros department store (upper level)
3 Upper-level car parking
4 Gallery
5 Bamberger's department store (main level)
6 Mall
7 Sears department store (main level)
8 Ohrbach's department store (main level)
9 Stern Bros department store (main level)
10 Bank
11 Car park
12 Shops
13 Sears T B A
Scale: 1 : 4000

stores. The centre accommodates exclusive stores, bringing Fifth Avenue to the suburbs, and the mall is fully air-conditioned, artificially lighted apart from a central top lighted feature, and partially carpeted.

The 'rules' which were established for the design of the covered centres in this period thus ran as follows:

1 Mall circulation should be as simple as possible, concentrating pedestrian movement along a single linear route and on one level only

2 The simplicity of the straight mall should be broken only so far as to avoid monotony. Otherwise set-backs and other variations in the shop-front line should be avoided so that each store is visible from the greatest area of the mall without being masked. For the same reason columns and other visual obstructions should be avoided in the malls

3 Malls should be wide (12 m plus) and brightly lighted

There were, however, some interesting exceptions to the general pattern, Randhurst, at Mount Prospect, Illinois, being an early instance. Designed by Victor Gruen for Victor Gruen Associates as developers, this enclosed centre retains some of the complexity of the Stage 1 centres. It has an underground service loop, for example, one-half mile long, and a secondary lower level mall without direct access from the car parking areas. These features are brought together in a new way by virtue of the strongly centralised plan. Instead of disposing the three magnet stores along a linear route, they are used to generate a triple-arm pinwheel about a large central domed space at which point access is gained both down to the secondary mall and up to a restaurant level. The malls, although at 27 m very wide, have small kiosks scattered down them, and the department stores at the ends of the arms are visible from the central space. The geometric clarity of this scheme

3·07

3·08

with its concentration in both plan and section upon a central place, equidistant from the magnet stores, foreshadows many of the developments in Stage 3 and this geometrical completeness illustrates better than any other centre so far considered an essential characteristic of all these schemes. This is their closed-endedness, their inability to grow or to accept major programme changes, as, for example, in the number of magnet stores, without complete redesign. They are complete entities, made up of a specific range of components, and in the linear mall schemes the potentially extendible sausage is stopped off by the end magnet stores. In such circumstances the centralised plan form of Randhurst seems particularly appropriate.

Occurring towards the end of the second stage of development, Willowbrook Mall in Wayne, NJ, opened in 1969, offers a transitional example into the third stage. The main problem with the second generation centres, as we have seen, was the long mall lengths resulting from the simple arithmetic of providing a certain area with a length of section of fixed width. Willowbrook Mall attempts to overcome this difficulty in a number of ways.

Firstly the basic 3 magnet arrangement is based upon a 'T' rather than an 'L' mall form. Since the crossing of the T is closer to the ends than is the angle of an 'L' of the same area, this device shortens apparent mall lengths from the mean point. In other words the arrangement is centralised, reading as a cross with the fourth arm omitted, and in this case a fourth department store, smaller than the three end magnet stores, is located by the centroid, as if the fourth arm had failed to grow.

Secondly, the width of section of the sausage is increased to 120 m plus, decreasing the mall length necessary to produce the required rental area. With fairly fixed frontage/depth ratios for most stores this means the location of some shops with frontage to side malls only and a corresponding drop in passing customer traffic, and hence in turnover and rental potential. It also has the effect of greatly increasing the amount of service movements necessary across mall areas in order to reach units isolated within the depth of the section and particurly in the internal corners of the T form.

The third device used to compress the plan form of this large centre was the use of an upper mall level. Although this is still essentially secondary to the main ground level malls and confined to one arm of the T, it is much more firmly integrated into the pedestrian system than in the stage 1 centres. Despite a site area of 52 ha, a section of two-storey car-parking structure is provided, feeding shoppers directly in to the secondary mall at the upper level. This mall is divided into perimeter routes along the shop frontages by large voids into the lower mall, providing visual connection between the two levels and accommodating escalator and stair connections between them. The upper mall also has a satisfactory circulation of its own, since it lies between one of the end department stores and the small central one, so that it conforms to the 'dumbell' arrangement between two magnets.

3·07 Interior of Connector Court in the Willowbrook Mall, Wayne, New Jersey

3·08 Interior of the Central Court at Willowbrook Mall

3·09 Exterior view of Bamberger's department store at Willowbrook Mall

Stage 3

The introduction of a second mall level in balance with the first, seen at Willowbrook in embryo form, is the most common mark of the third generation of centres, as enclosure was of the second. Along with a tendency to centralised plans and more intensive site use, it is similarly a symptom of the spiral effect, for, by taking this next step in increased costs, the centres were able to grow still larger without falling apart through sheer inconvenience and without absorbing more of the site area, which in many regions was becoming increasingly expensive and difficult to obtain in competitive locations. Again the arithmetic of this problem is straightforward. A new centre of 150,000 m² GLA occupies perhaps 14 ha with the building itself. At 6 cars per 100 m² it requires another 26 ha for parking, and with ancillary buildings, road junctions and inefficient parking layouts in the irregular areas between site and building perimeter, the total land-take will probably be in excess of 50 ha. In the same issue of *The Architectural Record* referred to earlier, this concern, at a time when the Stage 3 centres were beginning to come on to the drawing boards, is reflected in an article by Laurence J. Israel, of the architectural firm of Copeland, Novak and Israel. He proposes that 'where the one-story shopping center is no longer economical—as it is not now in many regions—the multi-level center is its logical and perhaps inevitable successor', and goes on to suggest three alternative types of solution in which both shopping and car parking are on many levels and are piled on top of one another. Sections of this complexity have only been possible to date in urban areas of highest land costs and would have been inexplicable to the developers of the early out-of-town centres. Nevertheless his comments illustrate the general realisation at this time of the problem, and of Laurence Israel's own heightened awareness of it through his firm's involvement in one of Europe's first regional suburban centres at Woluwe, with a site area of just 6 ha.

The Stage 3 centres were not confined to such tiny sites, and their multi-level solutions generally comprise just two levels of shopping equally served by a single level of car parking. This is simply achieved on a site with a steady cross fall by feeding the parking areas on the higher land into the upper mall on one side of the building, and those on the lower areas into the lower mall on the opposite side. An elaboration of this pattern is seen in an early example of 1967, at Sun Valley in Concord, California, where the 'restricted' site area of 42 ha has also meant the addition of a second car parking level on the lower side of the site in order to reach the 6 cars per 100 m² figure of 9,000 spaces. The upper mall therefore has side malls feeding in from both natural ground level on the west and a parking deck on the east, while the lower mall has access from the east only, from parking areas half cut into the slope. The form of the centre is linear, with a magnet store at each end and one in the centre. Because of the double-level arrangement, however, the central mall length is kept to 335 m, with a 120 m distance from the limit of Macy's frontage in the centre to either of the two end stores. The relative size of the second level puts Sun Valley into the third generation of centres, but as yet the two levels are not in balance, the lower being curtailed at its southern end. The openings between the two levels are also more limited than was to become usual and the mall shopfront geometry more straightforward.

A sequence of three Victor Gruen centres takes us through into the developed Stage 3 solution. The first of these is

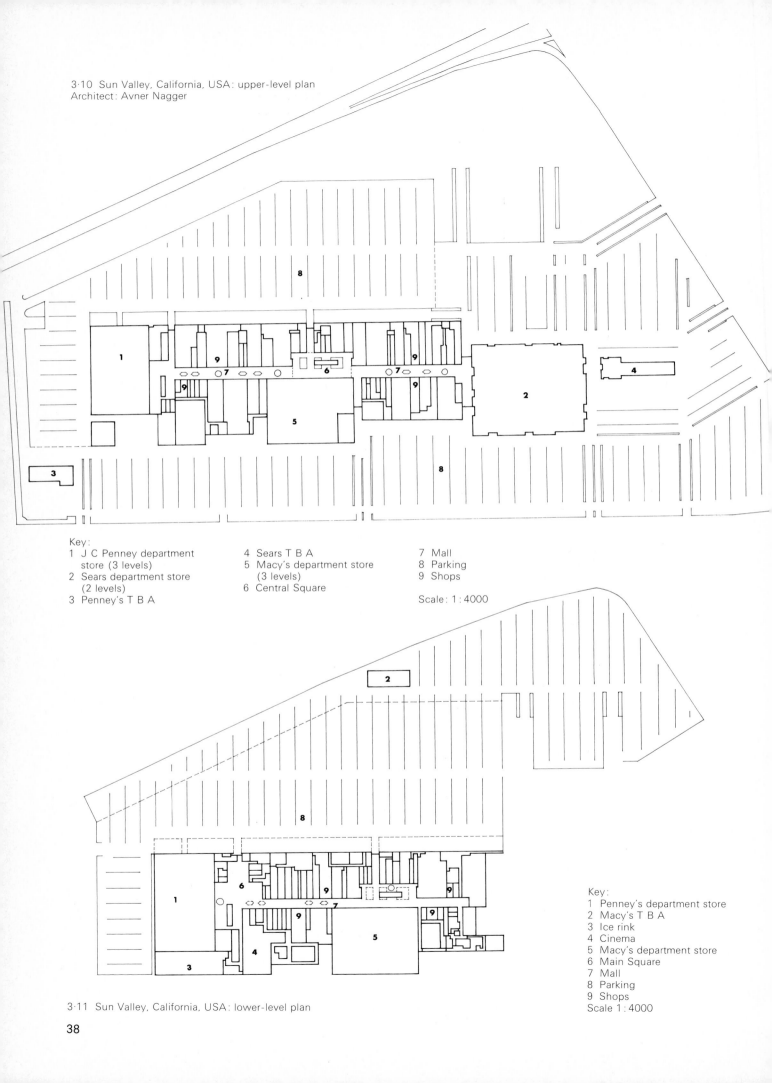

3·10 Sun Valley, California, USA: upper-level plan
Architect: Avner Nagger

Key:
1 J C Penney department
   store (3 levels)
2 Sears department store
   (2 levels)
3 Penney's T B A

4 Sears T B A
5 Macy's department store
   (3 levels)
6 Central Square

7 Mall
8 Parking
9 Shops

Scale: 1:4000

Key:
1 Penney's department store
2 Macy's T B A
3 Ice rink
4 Cinema
5 Macy's department store
6 Main Square
7 Mall
8 Parking
9 Shops
Scale 1:4000

3·11 Sun Valley, California, USA: lower-level plan

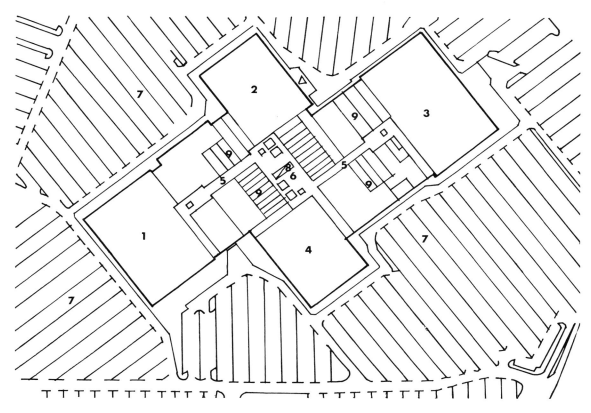

3·12 Yorktown shopping centre, Illinois, USA: main-level plan
Architect: Victor Gruen

Key:
1 Ward's department store
2 Carson's department store
3 Penney's department store
4 Westclot's department store
5 Mall
6 Central Square
7 Car parking
8 Escalators to upper level
9 Shops
Scale: 1 : 4000

Yorktown at Lombard, Illinois, of 1968. This uses the straight split-level idea, and, with 52 ha of site, needs no parking deck to accommodate its 9,000 cars. It is also the first scheme we have discussed to have four full-strength magnet stores, each in the 20,000 m² region, and this increase in the number of magnets is a common feature of the Stage 3 centres, being a reflection of the general tendency towards the 150,000 m² GLA figure without a corresponding increase in the size of the individual department stores. The result of this four equal-magnet programme is a struggle between a linear solution, like Sun Valley, with axis lying along the 'fault' line between the two levels of parking, and a cruciform plan generating a central node space.

The latter alternative is adopted in the second scheme, the Lakehurst centre at Waukegan, Illinois of 1971. Here the central space, previously the east-west mall made flat, becomes a separate double storey volume at the heart of the cross and equidistant from the department stores at the ends of the arms. The fourth arm is in fact allocated to

future expansion, in itself a new feature, but the plan is developed around the assumption of four magnets. The previous conflict arising from the division of the site into halves is now resolved by its division into quadrants of alternating upper and lower level parking feeding symmetrically into both malls and department stores. The malls then run in pin-wheel formation into the central square where escalators connect the two circulation levels.

The orderliness of this plan is given a mall design of corresponding conviction in the third Gruen example, that of La Puente on the Pomona Freeway in California, where the quadruple symmetry is applied with a precision which makes previous examples of mall layouts appear arbitrary. This symmetry produces not two escalators in the central space as at Lakehurst, but four, related to each arm of the cross. The central square is indeed a square, rather than a rectangle, and is twisted through 45° to set up a shop-frontage line geometry of splays and set-backs which not only breaks the Stage 2 tenet of straight shop-front lines, but also establishes the malls as a discrete spatial entity, independent of the structural and planning grid applying to retail areas, and imposing its form upon these areas. It is said that the modulating shop front line breaks down visually the length of the malls and gives a useful variety of store depths, but it must also be said that the central cruciform section of this building, containing the malls and small store units, achieves a remarkable degree of geometric exactitude for a shopping centre, and it is only with the

somewhat inconsequential forms of the end department stores that the consistency breaks down. This is a result of the practice of treating such developments as a series of independent department store buildings stuck together by the central tenant building, and in this case the five elements each had their own architect, with that of the tenant building, Victor Gruen, retained jointly by all parties in a co-ordinating role, and with some design control exercised in common by the four stores in the development partnership

3·13 Lakehurst shopping centre, Illinois, USA: main-level plan
Architect: Victor Gruen

Key:
1 Wiedolot's department store (2 levels)
2 Carson, Pirie Scott department store (3 levels)
3 Penney's department store (2 levels)
4 Central Square

5 Mall
6 Upper-level parking
7 Lower-level parking
8 Future expansion
9 Penney's T B A
10 Bank

Scale: 1 : 4000

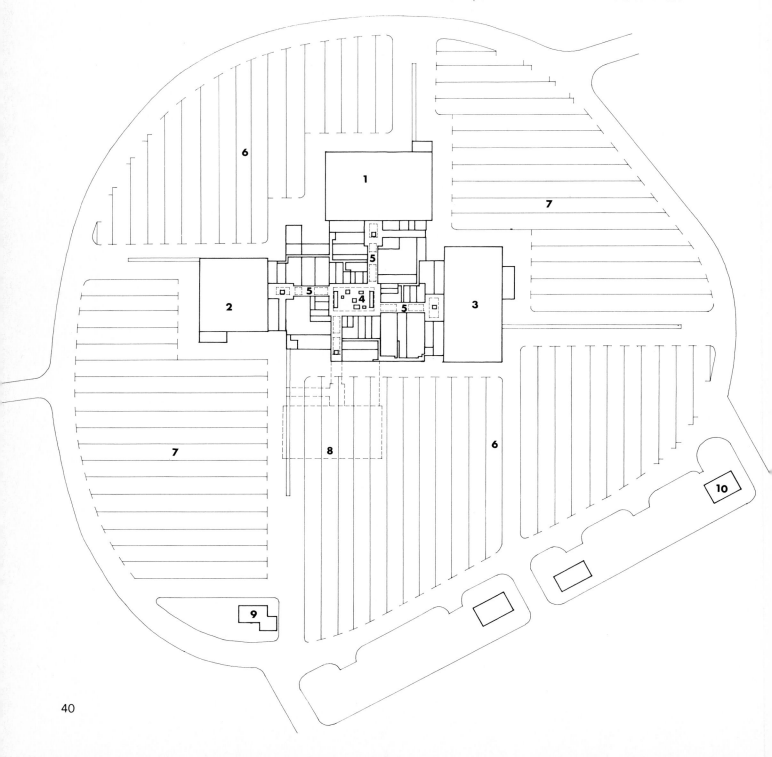

upon the intentions of each one.

The impression of the malls at La Puente as spaces determined by their own internal requirements rather than by the pressure of rental areas upon a boundary line, and hence as an ordered sequence carved out of the Greek Cross plan, is seen again in the section of the building. A comparison between this and that of an early Stage 2 centre, such as Yorkdale, effectively illustrates what has occurred in the intervening period. The latter case is still close to the open malls of Stage 1, and its enclosure is more simply an environmental device. Natural light floods in through continuous high clerestoreys in an intensity which diminishes that of the illuminated shop fronts below. This solution is made to appear somewhat bland by the section at La Puente, where the ceiling repeats the splay modulation of the plan, accommodating air-conditioning and artificial lighting slots and restricting daylighting to a series of skylight shafts.

3·14 La Puente shopping centre, California, USA
Architects: Gruen Associates

Key:
1 Drug store
2 Penney's department store
3 Central Court
4 Upper-lever mall
5 Escalators
6 Restaurant
7 Shop units
8 Robinson's department store
Scale: Plan: 1 : 4000

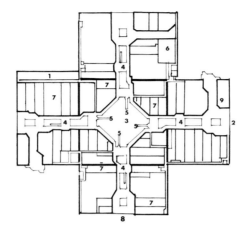

Diagonal section
Key:
1 Translucent plastic skylights
2 Air-conditioning slot
3 Upper-level
4 Lower-level
5 Escalators
6 Fountain
7 Plastic luminous ceiling
Sections: 1 : 2000

Cross section
Key:
1 Translucent plastic skylights
2 Air-conditioning slot
3 Upper-level
4 Lower-level
5 Fluorescent tubing light
  band with white acrylic lens

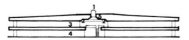

3·15 Exterior of East Side, Eastridge shopping centre

3·16 Eastridge shopping centre, California, USA: main-level plan
Architect: Avner Nagger

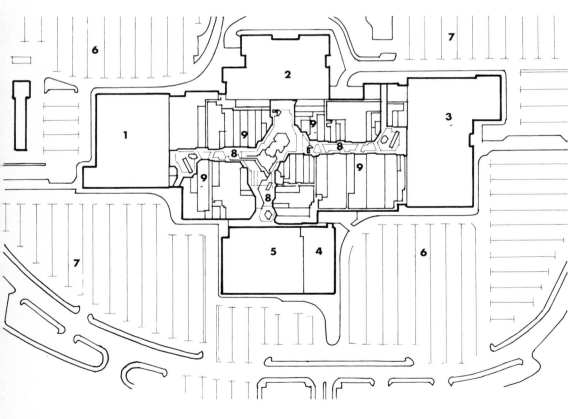

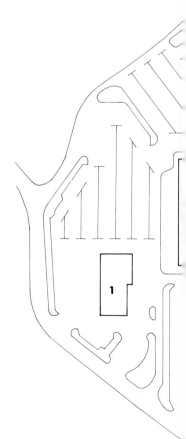

Key:
1 Sears department store
  (3 levels)
2 Macy's department store
  (3 levels)
3 Penney's department store
  (2 levels)
4 Ice rink
5 Liberty House department
  store (3 levels)
6 Upper-level parking
7 Lower-level parking
8 Mall
9 Shops
Scale: 1:4000

The Eastridge Centre at San Jose, California, and Woodfield Mall at Schaumberg, Illinois, both take the same basic 4-magnet organisation as La Puente, with car parking quadrants feeding upper and lower mall levels in rotation around the scheme. They do not, however, attempt to maintain a similar geometric determinism but instead relish the arbitrary, producing mall layouts which resemble cave or grotto formations on plan. The latter case is very large indeed, providing, with the opening of its fourth department store in 1973, more than 190,000 m² GLA. Despite this great size, its dense plan form keeps the maximum mall length, from east to west magnets, below 300 m. As noted at Willowbrook Mall, the very deep width of shop/mall/shop section, 150 m in this case, together with the concentration of mall routes requires the use of every available area of frontage, including side mall frontage, and also means that the smallest stores tend to group around corner and central square locations where frontage on two sides allows a large number of small units to be packed in. Since these units can function with minimum ceiling heights, this allows the introduction of a mezzanine level between to the two main mall levels about the central square. The density of small units in these locations also requires some of them to be trolley serviced from the mall.

The great plan depth at Woodfield, and consequent need to utilise every foot of mall frontage, takes this scheme away from the Stage 2 manipulation of a linear shopping band in 'L', 'T' or cross formation, with clear articulation of the hierarchy of pedestrian routes. Instead, its mall arrangements resemble tunnelling operations through dense blocks of retail space, with the tunnel walls so facetted and carved out that the distinction between squares, malls and side malls is blurred, allowing as many units as possible either to face directly onto the areas of densest traffic or to be visible from them.

All shop fronts are open to the mall, which is as highly profiled in section as in plan, with modelled soffites preventing the dilution of shop display lighting by the natural light allowed into the mall. The mall ceiling is now an environmental control element of some sophistication, with deeply modelled rooflights containing also air-conditioning units and computer control of artificial lighting to complement changes in the daylight entering the mall. The mall floor plane is also broken with changes of level and at one point is formed into a bowl of carpeted steps which act as amphitheatre seating for fashion parades and similar promotions in the central space.

3·17 Woodfield Mall shopping centre, Illinois, USA: lower-level plan
Architects: Jickling and Lyman Architects Inc.

Key:
1 Sears T B A
2 Sears department store (2 levels)
3 Marshall Field department store (4 levels)
4 J C Penney department store (3 levels)
5 Future expansion
6 Upper-level parking
7 Lower-level parking
8 Mall
9 Shops
10 Penney's T B A
Scale: 1:4000

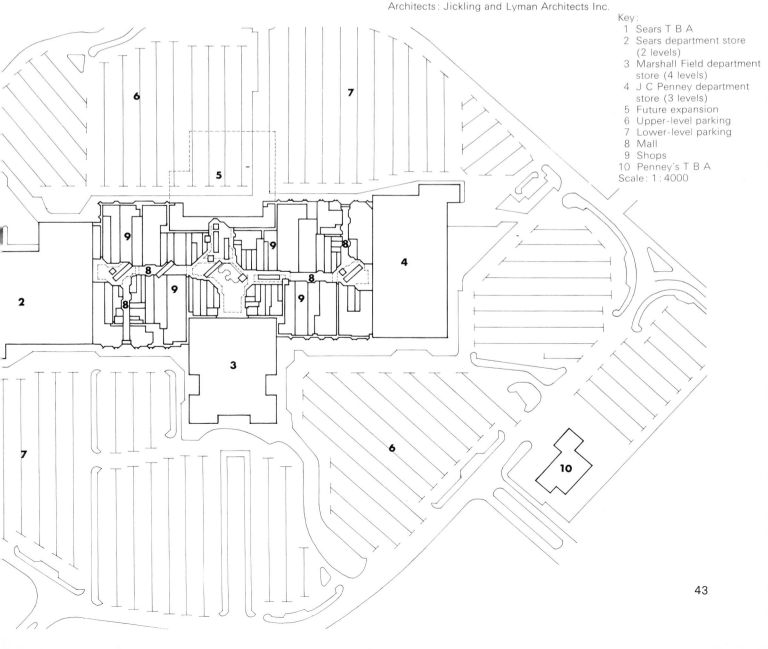

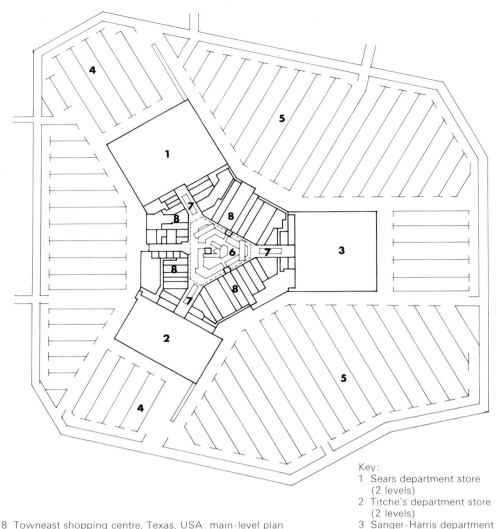

3·18 Towneast shopping centre, Texas, USA: main-level plan
Architects: Omniplan Architects and Harrell and Hamilton

Key:
1 Sears department store   4 Lower-level parking
   (2 levels)   5 Upper-level parking
2 Titche's department store   6 Central square
   (2 levels)   7 Mall
3 Sanger-Harris department   8 Shops
   store (2 levels)   Scale: 1 : 4000

The triple-magnet equivalent of the compact and centra-lised Stage 3 cruciforms discussed above is illustrated by the Towneast centre at Mesquite, Texas. The geometric form resembles closely the earlier Gruen Randhurst centre, but the residual Stage 1 elements of that scheme are now translated into their Stage 3 form. The two mall levels are each served by a level of the surrounding grade car parking, the trucking tunnel is omitted and the central tenant building area treated less as blocks of standard shop unit depth than as solid rental area formed between the geometry of mall and external wall and subdivided as conveniently as these shapes allow. The malls in fact read as appendages of the dominant central space from which most of the centre is visible and which is as big as a baseball diamond and enclosed by a cable roof structure suspended from a central mast.

An interesting exception to the multi-level and centra-lised pattern of development at this period of the early 1970s is provided by Sherway Gardens in Toronto. Being a smaller centre than those discussed above, with 75,000 m² GLA and 4,860 parking spaces on a 26 ha site, it has just two magnet stores and a single mall level. However the appeal to geometric models which marks the Stage 3 schemes here produces a novel mall layout and one which accommodates later growth. Like a molecule diagram, the figure-of-eight mall pattern creates the possibility of two main malls running from magnet to magnet in the form of two circuits connected at a central square, and with just

one linkage formed in the first phase. The travel distance along either route of 365 m from department store to department store appears to stretch the zone of attraction which the magnets must exert to maintain shopper flow, but this is presumably assisted by the attraction of the central square and by the mall form itself which, in its completed form, allows shoppers to cover the whole centre in a circuit without repeating any section. In this way Sherway Gardens provides a single level equivalent to the two circuit levels of the larger schemes.

The third generation of out-of-town centres has therefore evolved towards denser, more complex and more highly ordered solutions, and in the process has reversed many of the Stage 2 tenets of effective design. Multi-level mall systems are now possible and the straight, uninterrupted shop front line discarded. At the same time the internal content of the centres has undergone a further shift as development has progressed up the spiral.

The supermarket, which was a major element of the Stage 1 centres and actually formed an end-mall magnet for the Stage 2 Yorkdale centre, is generally absent by Stage 3. With the low margins operating in general food sales, and with competition from the district and local centre based supermarkets, it was unable to meet the rental levels of the enclosed, two-level centres and was either given an independent location elsewhere on the site or omitted altogether.

On the other hand, small stores of ever more exotic

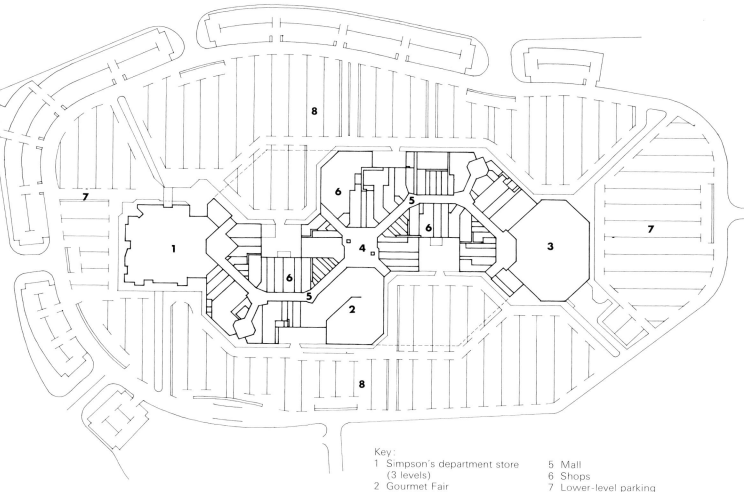

3·19 Sherway Gardens shopping centre, Toronto: main-level plan
Architects: Fleiss and Murray

Key:
1 Simpson's department store   5 Mall
   (3 levels)   6 Shops
2 Gourmet Fair   7 Lower-level parking
3 Eaton's department store   8 Upper-level parking
   (3 levels)
4 Central square   Scale: 1:4000

specialisation were eagerly sought by developers to enhance the variety, interest and hence attractiveness of the later centres to an ever more affluent consumer. Woodfield Mall, for example, has no supermarket, but instead sixteen delicatessen, health food and other speciality food shops. Its tenants' schedule also lists 15 women's and 7 men's speciality apparel shops in addition to 26 women's and 13 men's general clothing shops. There are 13 restaurants and 22 speciality shops which do not fall within other categories of books, fabrics, shoes, jewellery, furnishings, music, gifts, pets and so on, and all of these, it must be remembered, lie within 365 m of four major department stores. It is apparent that the Tie Inn, Morrow Nut Shop, Schaale Electronics, Parkway Fashions Imports and Unique Interiors by DeAngelis, are providing the half million within a ten mile radius with something more than the basic necessities of life, and their position in the retailing spectrum mirrors that of the Stage 3 centres generally. Sun Valley, the first Stage 3 centre discussed, incorporates within its structure, at the lower mall level, a health spa with pool, a 1,100 m² skating rink and a 1,500 seat cinema, and Eastridge similarly includes an ice rink and community hall. The symbiotic relationship between such non-retail uses and the primary function of the centre is simply a reflection of what pertained in the older urban centres. The huge draw of the regional shopping facility enables the secondary uses to become at least marginally viable, while increasing competition between centres encourages the introduction of

leisure, recreation and service uses as additional attractions. The emphasis on service facilities as a corollary of the increased sophistication and cost of buildings and tenant uses is exemplified by Woodfield Mall, which provides lockers for shoppers' parcels and coats, a small nursery school for their children, an auditorium which can be booked for meetings and classes, as well as public telephones, lavatories and information kiosk.

Woodfield Mall also has two cinemas in an independent building in the surrounding parking area, and in this is typical of many contemporary centres. The introduction of non-retail uses on the edges of the centre sites was noted in the early developments of the '50s, and this feature continued through the second and third stages. North Park Centre also included a twin cinema of 250 and 350 seats in a separate building on the site, together with a Convenience Centre of 2,800 m² and two service stations. In addition the developer, Raymond D. Nasher, set aside 8 ha of site to be grassed and later developed with office and medical buildings, apartments and recreation facilities. This pattern is matched to some degree in almost all the centres discussed. Department stores commonly developed independent TBA buildings in the parking areas, and a four-magnet centre might well have two or three such buildings on its site. Banks, restaurants, cinemas, offices, discount centres, hotels, motels and pizza parlours are all represented on some or other of the sites of the Stage 3 centres discussed.

The increased land values generated around a regional centre thus has encouraged developers to buy surrounding land areas at the same time as the centre site itself, and to consider their development on an increasingly ambitious scale, and while a drive-in bank, TBA centre or restaurant may be considered as a secondary and almost accidental growth attached to the regional shopping centre, the development of office blocks, hotels and even high-rise apartment buildings implies something different. By the generation on the one hand of internal leisure and entertainment 'lures', and on the other of external empathic commercial and residential uses, the shopping centre reasserts its traditional fertility as a growth point for the whole urban ecology. No longer a free-wheeling, lone element, locating opportunistically in isolation from the other core uses, it now draws those uses to it, and the term 'out-of-town centre' becomes ambiguous and paradoxical.

There is then a general tendency of development which brings the design problems of the down-town and out-of-town centres closer together. At the same time, the American experience has begun to force attention back to the problems of the former. The changing preoccupations of the last ten years are charted in the technical literature of the period. Four years after its articles of 1966 on North Park and the Stage 2 centres, the *Architectural Record* devoted a second issue to shopping centres, with particular attention to a group of new Stage 3 projects by the same architects, Harrell and Hamilton, including Town East, then under construction.[6] These articles effectively summarise the evolution of the species. In 1966 'the new forms have come a long way from the street of stores, to the asphalt-encompassed sprawl of the open mall, to the roofed-in closed rectangle of the early air-conditioned mall, to the culmination of the horizontal concept of the single building on the fringes of open country serving both city and surrounding regions. Such a peak of development is North Park . . .' In 1970 we have '. . . a newer, richer, more exciting architectural concept . . . Music endlessly oozing from loudspeakers is out, and many other current practices and ideas as to what the shopping experience is all about have been scrapped . . . . The previous, long corridor-type mall becomes a centralised multi-level giant court filled with many activities, that facilitates, by the way, quicker and easier access to the stores . . . . Harrel and Hamilton also encourages the developer to buy and build on the land surrounding the center. The building containing the stores clustered about the center court becomes itself the core of a larger whole, a community; an urban sub-center.' By 1973, in a third set of articles on the subject,[7] the out-of-town centres are no longer the point at issue. Instead it has become apparent that of the newest centres 'a sizeable proportion will be located in the urban cores of this country, on sites that are small, expensive and in the centre of dense development. Although regional shopping centres will continue to be important as retailing centres and as a building type, it is clear that a new glamour has begun to develop around downtown as a place to shop and as a place to be.'

The Stage 3 centres which have been discussed are all recognisably of the same out-of-town family which included Roosevelt Fields and Old Orchard. Their forms are generated

above all by the logic of their own internal disciplines. Contemporary with them are other centres in which the role of urban sub-centre and density of development have reached a point where their organisation becomes a function also of a wider frame. Because of this, and whether or not they are located in existing down-town areas, they are considered in this study as integrated centres. We reach, therefore, a convenient point at which to turn to the development of the original out-of-town idea in a different habitat, that of Europe.

3·2 European Regional Centres

European regional out-of-town centres have been heavily influenced by the North American example. Since they date only from the mid 1960s, when the American centres were already well into their second stage of development, it is natural that this should have occurred, both indirectly through the force of existing examples upon a virgin situation, and directly through the employment of American consultants. Copeland, Novak and Israel of New York, for example, quoted in connection with the 1966 issue of the *Architectural Record* and responsible for the design of shopping centres in Phoenix, New Rochelle, Smithtown, Salt Lake City and elsewhere, acted as consultants for the Woluwe Centre and as architects for Rosny 2; Lathrope Douglas, architects for Fashion Mall, were retained as consultant architects at Parly 2; traffic studies for Rosny 2 were prepared by Freeman, Fox and Wilbur Smith Associates, with extensive American experience; and market analyses for Woluwe, Parly 2, Velizy 2 and Rosny 2 were compiled by Larry Smith, according to M. Jean-Louis Solal, Director General of la Societe des Centres Commerciaux, 'the most notorious among the notorious in the shopping centre world.'

It has not however been an altogether simple matter to decide just how the European versions should relate to an American pattern which had evolved through a variety of solutions. Since the retailing spirals on each side of the Atlantic were out of phase, the problem arose as to whether the European centres should repeat the process of development, knowing that each solution would shortly become obsolete, or else go straight to the contemporary American model and risk a premature response to the condition of the market. A year after the opening of Parly 2, doubts were being expressed that developers 'suffered from the sin of pride' in projecting 'more of a luxury character than was desirable' to a French public which 'seemed to think that it was only in a souk that one could make purchases at reasonable prices. The dirtier it was, the cheaper it was'. The developers, La Société des Centres Commerciaux, obviously did not share this view, since they proceeded to build further centres on the Parly 2 model, yet these are themselves special cases of the American Stage 3 type. For, in transplanting the form across the Atlantic, certain strains have been so far selected and some new variants devised to suit the conditions of the adopted soil. The European centres are small by American standards, only recently approaching 100,000 m² GLA, and site areas less generous. This has in itself led to unconventional solutions, as in the particularly restricted case of Woluwe. The composition of centres does also not generally correspond to the American Stage 3 model, with variety stores and super-

3·20 Interior views of Sherway Gardens shopping centre, Toronto

markets retained as important elements, and the tenant mix in each case is modified by the inclusion of locally important multiples, as Prisunic in the French centres and Migros in the Swiss. And while the GLA range of the European centres would suggest the adoption of two-magnet solutions, which is generally the case, CAP 3000 at Nice provides an aberrant example of a 50,000 m² centre based upon a single magnet department store. Since there have been so comparatively few regional out-of-town centres built in Europe so far, perhaps 1% of the American total, such variations become unduly prominent. In comparison with the American situation, where we can retrospectively trace a smooth development, progress in Europe necessarily appears patchy, producing solutions which can be referred to the American sequence but are not a part of it.

The uncertainty surrounding the form of the European centres in relation to American precedent, and the viability of solutions in a European situation, is reflected in the attitude of the department stores, for if the American pattern was to be adopted then the department store groups must play an essential role. The condition of these groups was therefore an important factor, and while the continental groups were generally much stronger than those in the UK, having diversified into 'popular' shops and taken at least part of the market served in the UK by the large multiples, the situation varied greatly from country to country. In Germany, for example, the department stores were extremely healthy, with the largest group, Karstadt, achieving sales of $1,500 million in 1971 in 140 stores. For Kaufhof, the second largest group, the corresponding figures were $1,350 m. and 142, and both had opened up chains of out-of-town cheap discount stores which accounted for 20% of sales. Hertie, with sales of $1,325 m, and Horten, $750 m., formed two further large and successful groupings in Germany. In France, however, the development of out-of-town centres in the late '60s and early '70s corresponded with a period of difficulty and reorganisation for the department store group. Both Galeries Lafayette and Printemps were having difficulty earning enough to cover depreciation and the former was having to raise money by selling off valuable city centre properties, such as its store in Regent Street, London. In the case of the latter the situation had not been eased by efforts during the '60s to build up the expanding Prisunic chain, and in 1971 Printemps-Prisunic became part of the Swiss Maus group. In Belgium this period saw also the merger of the Innovation and Bon Marché groups to form the Inno stores.

In such circumstances the opportunity and risk presented by the development of new regional centres was a mixed blessing, and by 1973 the department stores were reflecting that they were not 'a miracle way of making money. In fact, the results in all cases so far are negative, or nearly negative.' A review in 1970 of the principal new centres opened by that time in Europe indicated why this was so.[8]

Comparing the average figures for these first centres with corresponding figures for enclosed American centres, it was found that land costs were higher in Europe, averaging 13% of first capital costs as against 9·5%. Costs excluding land were also higher, at $311 per m² instead of $300 per m². On the other hand, department store sales per m², which American experience suggested should be typical of the centre as a whole, were actually estimated to be 10% higher than in the USA, at $650 per m² of GLA as against $583.

From the figures it was concluded that the cost of a department store built in one of the new centres was perhaps 20–33% more than the cost of a new store built on an independent location, and while American examples could give the former a 15% higher sales figure than the latter, the estimated sales per m² for the stores in the new centres were universally lower than those for other stores in the same group, and in come cases less than half. By 1973, an examination of the performance of seven department stores in the new regional centres showed only one; Bon Marché at Woluwe, producing higher sales per m² than the corresponding main stores. The fact that Woluwe was the earliest of the enclosed out-of-town examples, and the only one which had been operating at that time for more than four years, made it impossible for definitive conclusions to be drawn from these figures. All that could be said for certain was that, in the early years at least, they did not offer a miracle solution to the department stores' problems.

One factor regarding the new centres which the department store operators were sure about was the necessity for maintaining the American standard of parking places. The American Urban Land Institute in 1965 produced a norm of 5·9 spaces per 100 m² of GLA as being 'adequate to meet the parking needs of a shopping centre for all but ten highest hours of demand during the year'. This figure is generally matched by the European centres, and where it is not, parking is felt to be inadequate. Indeed the department store operators felt that the main limitation on sales at peak times in the new centres was the limitation on parking and since comparatively few families had two cars, the congestion at those times appeared to be more marked than in North America. In an effort to match shopping hours to the periods of availability of the family car for shopping trips, the European centres have universally adopted late opening hours throughout the week, with centres closing at either 9.00 pm or 10.00 pm in roughly equal proportions. The pattern of sales that emerges is again common to most centres and is an interesting one. Taking the distribution by days of the week, about one third of all sales are made on Saturday, and one half on Friday and Saturday together. The remaining half is evenly spread over Monday to Thursday, with a slightly greater volume occurring on Wednesday. The peak towards the end of the week is matched on a daily basis by a build up in volume towards the latter part of the day, the percentage sales occurring during the four three-hour periods 9 am–noon, noon–3 pm, 3 pm–6 pm and 6 pm–9 or 10 pm, being approximately 10, 20, 40 and 30% respectively.

The readiness in Europe from the mid '60s on to try the new American form of regional centre, coupled with the differences in conditions on the two continents, produced then a pattern of development which reads as a distortion of that American evolution which has already been discussed.

Evolution

The pattern begins in West Germany with the opening between 1964 and 1966 of open-malled, single-level centres, at Frankfurt, Bochum, Hamburg and Munich. The first of these, the Main Taunus Zentrum, located near the intersection of two autobahnen 10 km west of Frankfurt, illustrates the type. Although, by virtue of the open mall, this centre corresponds to the first generation of American centres, the very simple mall layout and servicing arrangements identify it as a special case. The retailing elements are

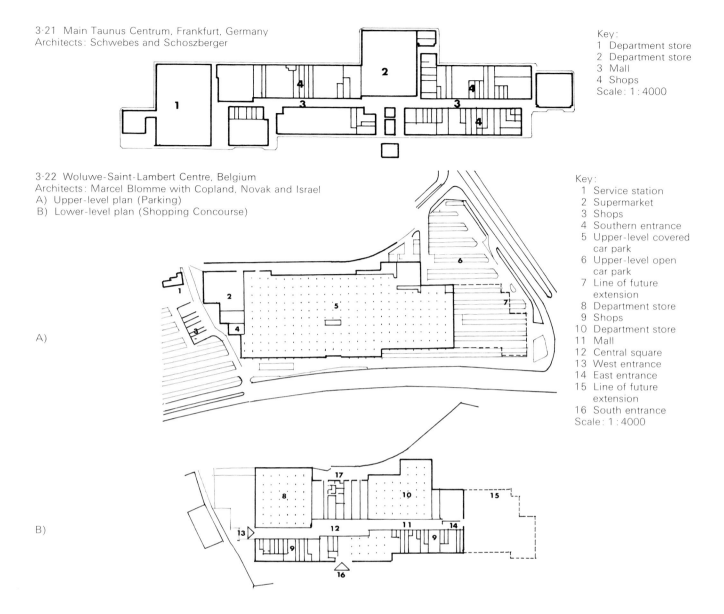

3·21 Main Taunus Centrum, Frankfurt, Germany
Architects: Schwebes and Schoszberger

Key:
1 Department store
2 Department store
3 Mall
4 Shops
Scale: 1 : 4000

3·22 Woluwe-Saint-Lambert Centre, Belgium
Architects: Marcel Blomme with Copland, Novak and Israel
A) Upper-level plan (Parking)
B) Lower-level plan (Shopping Concourse)

A)

B)

Key:
1 Service station
2 Supermarket
3 Shops
4 Southern entrance
5 Upper-level covered car park
6 Upper-level open car park
7 Line of future extension
8 Department store
9 Shops
10 Department store
11 Mall
12 Central square
13 West entrance
14 East entrance
15 Line of future extension
16 South entrance
Scale: 1 : 4000

grouped along a single straight mall, about 350 m long, with projecting canopies down each side. The main department stores, Hertie and Horten act as end- and mid-mall magnets, with a supermarket serving as the other stop end to the mall. Side malls then feed in to the central mall from the surrounding parking areas, with emphasis given to the entry point opposite the central department store, where a pedestrian route leads in from a bus stopping point on the main road. The site also contains the usual complement of TBA facilities, filling station and car-wash, together with a drive-in movie screen, an element which one might have expected to see more frequently associated with the out-of-town centre as a natural counterpart to the large grade parking areas.

The prosperity of Frankfurt, the banking centre of West Germany and a city in which 60% of the working population are office workers and only 30% employed in industry, together with the presence of US forces in the area, make this a natural starting point for the development of the out-of-town centre in Europe, to be followed by the Ruhr Park centre at Bochum in the same year and the Elbe-Einkaufszentrum, Hamburg in 1966.

The form then spread west and south, and in 1968 an enclosed centre was opened at Woluwe-Saint-Lambert,

7 km to the east of the centre of Brussels, on the third city ring road and near the Liège highway. The extremely restricted site area for a development of this kind produced here a solution unlike any of the American forms discussed. As an enclosed, single main mall layout on one level it corresponds to the second stage American centre, but with the whole building raised up 3 m to allow the site car parking to extend through below it. Unlike the contemporary American solution at Sun Valley, where site limitations produced a second parking level which in turn suggested the possibility of a second mall level, the car parking at Woluwe maintains its ground station, forcing the building up and isolating the mall from the access level. A supermarket, a row of small shops and a service station are located at the ground level, and three escalator positions give access up to each end of the mall and its centre. A single side mall also occurs in the middle, running east to a flight of steps on the edge of the building where a car drop-off point ramps up to meet it. The mall section, with its straight profiles and long runs of deep clerestorey lighting, corresponds to the American Stage 2 pattern, as does the simple mall layout, although the location of the two department stores along the mall rather than as stop-ends to it, leaving open the possibility of longitudinal growth, is less usual.

The relationship of mall and ground levels which was tried at Woluwe was not repeated. Instead the European centres now adopted the American Stage 3 form as their organisational model, with two equally weighted mall levels doubling the retail site use. The first of these was Parly 2, opened in 1969 in the suburbs of Paris 19 km west of the city. Again the site area was restricted by American standards, with about 9 ha available as against Woluwe's 6, but with a proportionate increase in the GLA from 37,000 m² to 59,000 m² and a greater increase in the parking provision to improve the parking ratio from 4·6 to 5·1 spaces per 100 m². The solution adopted was the Sun Valley form, with a second deck level of parking formed over about half of the site car parking area to the south and east, and serving two levels of shopping based on a single straight main mall arrangement. The folded site formation was used to the utmost in this way, with a service station tucked under the upper parking level in the extreme north corner, and lower retail areas elsewhere spreading out under that parking level to give two levels of development over the greater part of the site.

The shopping elements are organised into a simple dumbell arrangement, with a central 'sausage' of small units on two levels stopped off at its ends by two clusters of space users. At the north-west end of the mall these comprise the department store Printemps, together with Sum and a 'drugstore', 'Drugwest', at the south-east and the department store BHV (Bazar de L'Hotel de Ville) and Printemps' partner store Prisunic, and at each level one of the mall ends is allowed to penetrate out to the car parking area, giving one end-mall and two side-mall entrances to the centre at each level. The central sausage is 65 m wide, matching the band width adopted for the Stage 2 American centres, and has servicing direct from the car park sides to the two ranges of small shops which face a 16 m wide mall, punctuated at the upper level by voids to the lower mall and with natural lighting restricted to just three areas of rooflighting corresponding to the principal points of vertical circulation between the two mall levels.

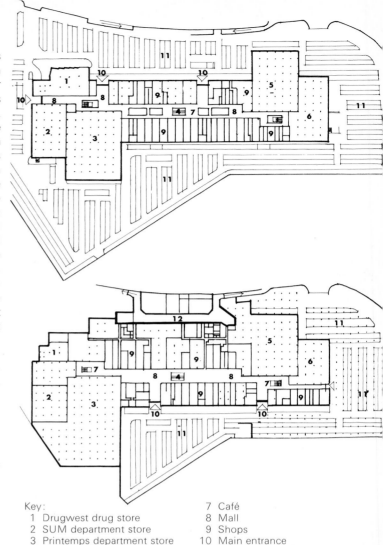

Key:
1 Drugwest drug store
2 SUM department store
3 Printemps department store
4 Central escalators
5 BHU department store
6 Prisunic department store
7 Café
8 Mall
9 Shops
10 Main entrance
11 Car parking
12 Underground service road
Scale: 1 : 4000

3·23 Upper and lower-level plans of the Parly 2 shopping centre, near Paris, France
Architect: Claude Balick

3·24 Upper-level interior views of the Parly 2 shopping centre, Chesnay, near Paris. Note the absence of shop fronts
Architect: Claude Balick

By opting for the full two-level solution, Parly 2 achieved a 50% increase in rental area over Woluwe while decreasing the mall length from end to end from 240 m to 225 m. Another centre opened in the same year near Nice produced an even more dramatic reduction in mall travel distance to 120 m on each level with a GLA of 50,000 m². The great compactness of the CAP 3000 plan is made possible by the presence of only one magnet department store against which the mall and other stores can be tightly arranged. Developed by the department store group itself, La Societe Francaise des Nouvelles Galeries, this unusual single magnet base is reflected in the building form in which, unlike almost all multiple magnet centres, the department store does not express an aggressive independance of the general envelope. Instead the department store simply occupies the eastern zone of a two-level cube and the whole building becomes an extension of it. By this coincidence of interests of developer and single space user, the building thus approaches the homogeneity of a monocellular centre, in which all the parts are complementary rather than competitive, and comes close to an aspiration of Stage 3 centres generally, that by the elimination of shop-fronts and concentration of plan form, the distinction between public and private space, between mall and shop, should become blurred and the whole become a more unified and continuous shopping place. At CAP 3000 the name on a fascia line may declare the territorial limits of the department store, but the continuity of surfaces from the mall into the store and the option of entering the building via either mall or department store space, reduces such signs to a formality and it becomes unclear and unimportant whether common facilities, such as the swimming pool and sun terrace on the upper level, 'belong' to the main store or the centre as a whole.

Although the square plan form of CAP 3000 is unusual, it employs the device common to Stage 3 centres of site falls to give direct access from the surrounding parking into both shopping levels. With the department store occupying the eastern zone against the west bank of the River Var, the lower mall forms an 'L', with access from north and west parking areas. In addition to Nouvelles Galeries and 24 small shops there are two larger units at this level, a drugstore 'Drug 3000' and a self-service food shop 'Super 3000'. At the upper level the mall is straight, running from the southern parking area in front of the sea directly north to a two-level square corresponding to the corner of the 'L' below and thence to the sun terrace with swimming pool, children's pool, bar and area for open-air displays. The development also includes a 420-seat cinema, a garden centre in a pavilion linked to the main building, and an auto centre.

Despite such atypical flowerings as CAP 3000 and Woluwe, the Parly 2/Sun Valley solution clearly emerged as the typical form of European out-of-town centres in the late '60s and early '70s, and all of the remaining centres considered here represent variations on this type. Although a Stage 3 solution in its two-level organisation with each mall level served directly from the car parking areas, this type retains the mall plan form of the Stage 2 centres, the squares disposed along a linear route linking magnet stores. It could therefore be regarded as the simplest form of third generation centre, in effect two Stage 2 plans laid on top of one another and without any of the centralising geometry of the later American models, and, perhaps because they are generally 2-magnet centres, has been adopted as the most appropriate formula for the European

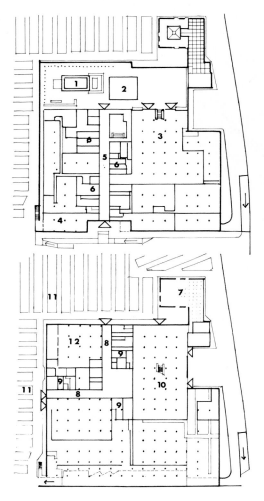

Key:
1 Swimming pool
2 Show podium
3 Nouvelles Galeries department store (upper level)
4 Snack (restaurant)
5 Upper-level shopping concourse
6 Shops (upper-level)
7 Garden centre
8 Lower-level shopping concourse
9 Shops (lower-level)
10 Nouvelles Galeries department store (lower level)
11 Car parking
12 Drug 3000 drugstore

Scale: 1 : 4000

3·25 Cap 3000 Centre, Nice, France: upper-level and lower-level plan
Architect: Antoine Dory

centres of this period.

The Spreitenbach Centre near Zurich followed Cap 3000 in 1970 and conformed to this pattern, with its lower mall level served by car-parking areas on three sides of the building and the upper level by that on the fourth side. This centre achieves a parking ratio of 7·8 spaces per 100 m² and despite its comparatively small size includes a third, underground, service level with central service road corresponding in position to the malls above. The main space users, comprising two department stores, Vilan and ABM, and a Migros cooperative store, flank each end of the mall, rather than blocking them, but the possibility which this suggests of future growth by linear extension is precluded by the emergence of the access ramps to the service road just beyond the building perimeter.

Although by no means a common preoccupation of out-of-town centres, a second development in Paris, near Orly, does allow such a possibility. Belle Epine is also the first of the European centres to show a tendency towards increased size of centres with a GLA of 99,800 m² as against 59,000 m² at Parly 2, the largest previous example. In American practice this area would probably be sufficient to generate three department store magnets, but this does not occur at Belle Epine, and the resulting length of sausage required to accommodate the smaller units becomes, even on two levels, rather long for the standard dumbell arrangement. The solution adopted was to add to such an arrangement a spur mall at one end of the mall, running off at right angles to it, and open-ended allowing its later continuation or else completion with a third magnet. In other words the classic stage 2 solution to the problem of too much mall by bending it into an 'L' is applied to a two-

level, Stage 3 scheme.

In two German centres opened in 1970, at Bergen-Enkheim near Frankfurt and at Hamburg, compact plans were achieved by pursuing the single dumbell plan arrangement onto three levels, giving axial mall distances of only 150 m in both cases for centres of 54,000 and 61,000 m² GLA respectively.

Finally, Velizy 2 in 1972 and Rosny 2 in 1973, two sister centres to Parly 2 in the suburbs of Paris, continue the variations on the pattern of the earlier model, and at 82,000 and 83,000 m² respectively, they stretch this pattern without resource to Belle Epine's 'L' shaped mall. In both cases the magnet department stores block squarely the

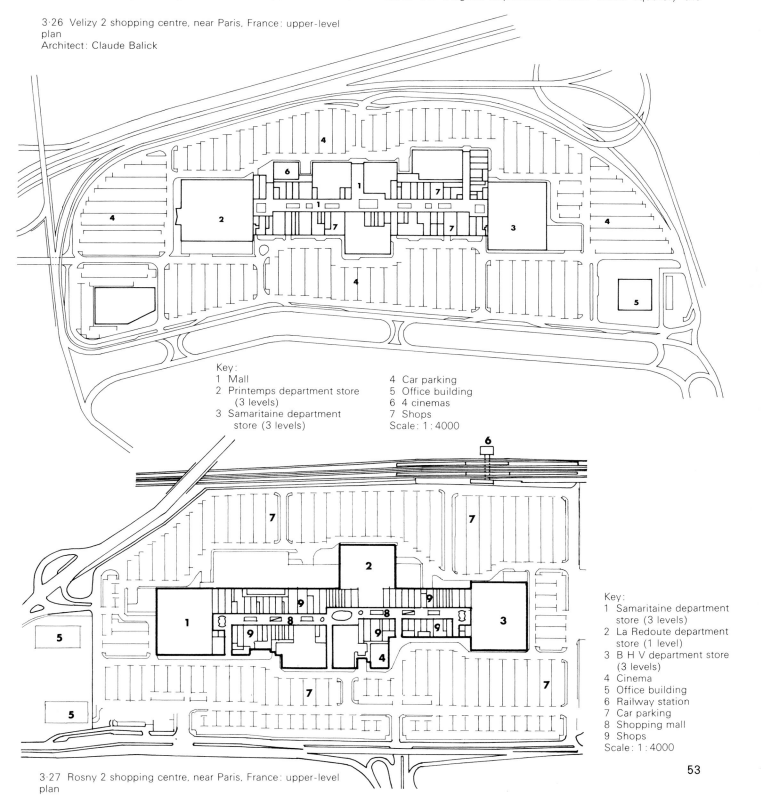

3·26 Velizy 2 shopping centre, near Paris, France: upper-level plan
Architect: Claude Balick

Key:
1 Mall
2 Printemps department store (3 levels)
3 Samaritaine department store (3 levels)
4 Car parking
5 Office building
6 4 cinemas
7 Shops
Scale: 1 : 4000

Key:
1 Samaritaine department store (3 levels)
2 La Redoute department store (1 level)
3 B H V department store (3 levels)
4 Cinema
5 Office building
6 Railway station
7 Car parking
8 Shopping mall
9 Shops
Scale: 1 : 4000

3·27 Rosny 2 shopping centre, near Paris, France: upper-level plan

53

ends of the malls and define a central band which begins to distort under the pressure of rental area to be contained. The axial mall lengths of the two schemes are 245 m and 275 m, and both therefore beyond the 180–240 m range considered maximum for travel distance between magnets in American centres. To compensate this the secondary multiple store magnets, C & A, Prisunic, Drugwest, etc, which at Parly 2 were grouped with the department stores at the ends of the mall, are now located in the central sector of the mall to strengthen this potentially weak zone beyond the range of the two end magnets. The increased mall lengths also produce a larger number of side malls leading out to the car parking areas, and in both schemes a few of these side malls are stretched to give secondary frontage to rows of small units. This has the effect of thickening the band of small units, precisely as had occurred in the development of the American centres. The plans of these two centres thus appear to hover on the limit of the Parly 2 form. Further increases in rental area would first thicken the sausage still further and then surely cause one or more of the side malls to develop to full mall stature and grow an end magnet, turning the centre into a multiple magnet configuration. The quasi-magnets formed by the multiple store groups in the centre of the two schemes seem to prefigure such a growth outwards at this point and at right angles to the main axis, allowing the two outer magnets to draw closer together and eventually stabilise into the centralised Stage 3 plan form of the American centres.

The above description of the evolution of plan forms of the new European centres, soon to be followed by increasingly sophisticated examples, as at Ulis 2 and Barentin, does not adequately convey their impact.

The success of the American transplant has been accompanied by its other connotations, and while the European developers' 'sin of pride' in offering the French housewife a glossier alternative to the souk has not yet brought the more exotic specialisations of California to the Ile de France the intentions have been clearly stated. It is appropriate that Parly 2 should have been sited between SHAPE and the palace of Versailles, for it carries a social content additional to the utilitarian exchange of cash for groceries which leans both on the American dream and on the aura of quality surrounding the older indigenous and aristocratic culture. The shopping centre indeed is part of a wider new development, almost a small new town, described in its publicity as 'an extraordinary conjunction of incomparable and distinct elements: the palace of Versailles, Printemps, 8 swimming clubs, BHV, a garden city of 100 ha, a Prisunic and a supermarket, the giant Drug-West open at night, schools, 2 cinemas, the view over the 220 ha of the Musée de l'Arbre, 100 shops, 8 tennis clubs, a discotheque 'Le Paryland', 2 banks, an equine club (where 'the most French and noble of sports is practised') and 3 large forms of apartments for sale with modest service charges. Each day the many Parlysiens already installed play tennis, ride horses or bathe in the swimming club of their choice. By evening they can dine at the Drug-West and see a film in one of the two exclusive cinemas of the Commercial Centre. Their life has been transformed since they exchanged Paris for Parly 2'.

This is a description of the good suburban life, the idyllic environment within commuting distance which turns a Parisien into a Parlysien, glimpsed also on the sun terraces of CAP 3000 and in the swimming/dancing/bowling and restaurant complex incorporated at Spreitenbach. Jean-

3·28 Entrance to main hall at Les Ulis shopping centre, near Paris, France
Architect: Jean Lasny

Louis Solal, developer of the 'Deux' series of centres, in a paper to the conference of the Royal Institute of Chartered Surveyors in Amsterdam in 1973[9] described the relationship between the shopping centre and its suburban area as follows:

'Regional shopping centres are something more than simply retail and trading hubs. They consist of two, three or four department stores and scores of smaller shops and services. More and more they are becoming miniature downtowns. The new regional shopping centre is becoming an urban centre. Regional shopping centres have developed the same kind of ambiance and personality that was previously found in what the US developers call CBD, the central business district.'

Thus although the evolution of the European centres has been more spasmodic than the American, leap-frogging and modifying some of the stages of development that were experienced there and omitting altogether the second stage, the general progress has been the same. Each new centre attempts to improve on its predecessor in terms of size, quality of mall and shop treatment, and range of surrounding facilities, and thus climbs a little higher up the spiral. The speed with which this spiral is mounted is partly dependant on the success of other retailing forms operating at other levels of the market, for the strong growth of low cost forms will force the higher cost operations to develop away from their mixed beginnings and concentrate on a narrower trading band. The development of the regional out-of-town centres is therefore linked to that of those retailing forms competing equally in terms of their out-of-town location but occupying differing positions or more specialised functions within the market. Whether or not there is some economic law that enables only the developments of higher capital commitment and cost range to assemble the multiple tenancies of the regional centres, it happens that the other out-of-town forms are largely monocellular, dominated by a single large operator, and these types are the subject of the next part of this study.

3·3 Hypermarkets

The new out-of-town shopping centres represent one major part of the revolution in shopping forms which has occurred on the continent of Europe. Designed to supply a complete range of durable goods, they are complemented by the hypermarket, an equally novel type which is primarily concerned with the sale of convenience goods. Adopting the same logic as the shopping centres in relation to location and massive car parking provision, their main trading parameter is that of price, rather than those of service and variety which characterise their centre cousins. Their name comes from the French 'hypermarché', implying their origin as supermarkets writ large, and their form does appear as a development of the supermarket idea, extending the techniques of self-service and making as direct as possible the line from the manufacturer to customer. This principle is demonstrated by Carrefour, the major French hypermarket operators, in this description of their operating methods,

'Carrefour has no central warehouse. All goods sold would be delivered direct from the supplier, thereby the store saves the cost of central warehousing and transport. Large warehousing areas are directly associated with the store and are located principally to either side of the selling area. This arrangement enables the maximum use to be made of mechanical aids such as fork-lift trucks and the rate of productivity achieved is exceptionally high.'

With gross areas ranging from 10,000 to 50,000 m², the hypermarket becomes a large, simply organised volume for the transfer of goods from bulk to individual transport, operating with the minimum capital and running costs, and handling as wide a variety of goods, probably between 25,000 and 35,000 stock items, as may be conveniently dealt with in this manner. Upon this bare formula some embellishments can be made, as with the introduction of service functions, such as restaurants and hairdressers, often occurring as lettings within the building envelope, but the basis of the enterprise remains as the single-level, single-volume transfer shed, and, as with the supermarket, its symbol is the wire shopping trolley.

The distribution of hypermarkets throughout Western Europe by 1973 is given in Table 5, from which it can be seen that the major impact of this form of trading to date has been in Germany, France and Belgium, and to a lesser extent Switzerland, being precisely those countries from which examples of the new shopping centre types were drawn in section 3·2.

The contrast between conditions in those countries and in the UK, which has been least affected by the hypermarket, are most vividly demonstrated in the case of France, where the development of hypermarkets, as with out-of-town centres, occurred somewhat later than in Germany, and where the growth of the new form has been most dramatic.

This growth has appeared all the more spectacular by contrast with the condition of the retailing industry in France prior to its occurrence, for whereas in Britain there had been a steady development of the multiples during the inter-war period and of supermarket operations in the '50s, France had largely retained a more archaic structure with a high percentage of small traders. By 1966 only 7·6% of all retail trade in France had been captured by multiple stores as against 34·5% in Britain, and including department and cooperative stores, the trade shared by all large scale retailers totalled 19·3% in France compared with 43·6% in Britain. The distribution of main retail centres was also quite different in France, and more remote from the suburban populations which had grown up.

The position in the capital city, itself unusually dominant in the country in demographic terms, is described by Clout as follows:

'Apart from Versailles there is no urban service centre in the whole agglomeration between the 30,000 population

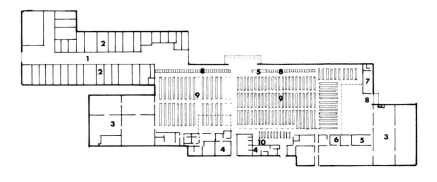

Key:
1 Shopping gallery
2 Shops
3 Reserved space
4 Food preparation
5 Information
6 Staff
7 TBA
8 Checkout points
9 Hypermarket sales area
10 Bar

Scale: 1:4000

3·29 Carrefour Hypermarket, Vitrolles, Marseilles, France
Architects: George Briere and André Gouaux

level and the Ville de Paris itself. Greater Paris possesses one real centre, which has no parallel in France and few in Europe, and a number of minor centres which are little better than overgrown villages. This comment applies not only to pre-1940 development but also to post-war suburban growth.'[12]

Again, the growth in prosperity which produced the supermarkets in Britain in the '50s and early '60s, occurred later in France. The disposable income per head in that country grew by 125% between 1961 and 1972, to a level some 30% higher than that in the UK, and the combination of this, the late commitment to major highway programmes, and an unprecedented population growth rate since the war, produced pressures on the existing retailing pattern which particularly favoured the introduction of revolutionary, rather than evolutionary, changes to that pattern in the late '60s. Symptomatic of this has been the growth of hypermarkets, demonstrated in Table 4.

Of the 115 hypermarkets which had been opened in France by the end of 1972, 57 were operated by multiple groups, such as Carrefour, Casino and Docks de France, 14 by department stores and 39 by independents. The response of independent traders in the USA and the UK to the growth of the multiples by forming groupings around central buying organisations has similarly occurred in France, and the relative strength of the independents in the hypermarket field is reflected in the size of such organisations, as for example Paridoc, with an annual turnover of between £400 and £500 million and serving 29 hypermarkets trading under the group name of Mammouth.

The largest group of hypermarkets in France is that operated by Carrefour, who have also opened stores in Belgium, Switzerland, Italy and the UK. Their units range in size from the smaller end of the scale at around 5,000 m² net selling space, to the giant stores at Vitrolles near Marseilles, and Portet sur Garonne near Toulouse, with selling areas of 20,000 and 23,000 m² respectively. In the case of the smaller units, the net area generally represents half of the total building area, with the remainder occupied by warehousing, food preparation rooms and offices, while in the larger stores the proportion of net to gross increases to about 3:5.

Car parking provision varies considerably over the range of Carrefour stores but the standard of 5·9 spaces spaces per 100 m² GLA quoted in connection with the out-of-town centres is generally greatly exceeded, with levels of parking provision twice and even three times this figure not uncommon. Treatment of the parking areas, like that of the buildings themselves, is utilitarian and contrasts with the attempts at landscaping of the huge tarmac zones made in the regional centres. This sparseness is a reflection not only of the low-cost nature of the operations, but also, in many cases, of their intended short life, since many of the hypermarkets built in France have building permission limited to a 10- or 15-year period. In the case of the hypermarket at Creteil, for example, one of five built by Carrefour around Paris, consent to the development in a new residential area in course of construction was conditional upon the site being cleared at the end of a 10-year period. Such restrictions inevitably heighten the priority of the cost parameter and the necessity to achieve high turnover rates, which in the large stores can exceed £20 million per annum. The normal breakdown of turnover is in the order of 54% food, wines and spirits, 22% household goods, 12% clothing and textiles, 9% car services and 3% restaurants.

Another of the Carrefour Paris units, not far from Parly 2, provides a typical example of the middle sized hyper-

Table 4 *Growth of hypermarkets in France*[13]

Date	Total number of hypermarkets	Additional number of hypermarkets per annum	Total selling area (m²)	Additional selling area per annum (m²)	Average selling area (m²)
January 1st 1963	0	—	—	—	—
January 1st 1964	1	1	2,600	2,600	2,600
January 1st 1965	1	—	2,600	—	2,600
January 1st 1966	1	—	2,600	—	2,600
January 1st 1967	4	3	19,400	16,800	4,800
January 1st 1968	12	8	61,700	42,300	4,800
January 1st 1969	28	16	138,000	76,300	4,800
January 1st 1970	73	45	408,900	270,900	5,600
January 1st 1971	115	42	665,400	275,100	5,800
January 1st 1972	161	46	940,500	275,100	5,800
January 1st 1973	212	51	1,332,700	392,200	5,800

Source: L'Institut Français du Libre Service et des Techniques Modernes de Distribution; MPC & Associates Limited

market.[14] The Montesson store was opened in March 1970 and occupies some 10·5 ha of site area about 9 miles (15 km) north-west of the centre of Paris, and with an estimated 100,000 population within a 2½ mile (4 km) radius. The main shed has a total area of about 13,000 m², of which 7,000 m² is selling space, and is set at the rear of the site with a 1,300-space car park laid out between it and the main road. An independent auto centre and car wash building is located at the front of the site between the two entry/exit points from the highway. The main building incorporates a frontage of small shop units, behind which lies the major sales floor, serviced as far as possible on pallets by fork-lift trucks from the storage and preparation areas fed from the unloading points along the rear side of the building.

A 275-seat restaurant and 60-seat snack-bar are incorporated in the store, which carries a wide variety of lines, including some durable items, such as colour television sets and cameras, which can enjoy a high turnover in a situation where a 15% discount on non-food items is claimed.

Opening hours are 3 pm–10 pm on Monday and 10 am–10 pm from Tuesday to Saturday, with peak sales on Friday night and Saturday morning, when it is estimated that about 60% of trade is done.

A butchery and bakery, where bread and delicatessen items are cooked, are included in the preparation areas, and the hypermarket employs some 350 people in all, including 80 assistants working in two shifts on the checkout points, where the cash registers are linked to a central computer which controls the stock level of non-food items.

This description should not, however, give the impression of a high precision in the functioning of the hypermarket building itself, for with a turnover of £12m in its first year, the pressure of use has made itself felt in an un-planned extension of activities beyond the building envelope. It is perhaps an indication of a healthy business that this should be so, but the stacking of goods 6m high within the shed and the overspill at Montesson and elsewhere of specialist trading activities into the forecourt areas, of refuse and storage into the service areas, and of the all-important giant trolleys, or 'chariots' everywhere, reinforces the impression of the hypermarket buildings themselves as being intended to accommodate an industrial process, and, in some cases, with a degree of impermanence not far removed from the plastic sheeting which improvises additional storage shelter at their rear.

The form and trading methods of hypermarkets in Belgium is similar to that in France, with GB Bazaars a major operator. This company was an established multiple with shops and supermarkets throughout Belgium, and began developing hypermarkets in the early '60s around the major cities, Brussels, Liege, Bruges and Antwerp, under the title of Super Bazaars. The earliest of these was the Mervann store at Auderghem, some 6 km from the centre of Brussels, and built in 1961. With its suburban, rather than truly out-of-town, location, the unit has a comparatively low level of parking provision for a hypermarket, with 810 spaces for 7,800 m² of sales area. It does, like the Carrefour Montesson store, include a few small service shop units, such as a bank, dry cleaners and restaurant. An unusual feature of this early hypermarket was the inclusion of a small branch unit for the department store 'Innovation' in the car parking area. At first sight, and in view of the quasi-industrial image of the later French hypermarkets, this seems anachronistic. Yet the notion of attaching an essentially durable goods trader to the magnetism of the discount convenience goods store has a logic which was to be exploited elsewhere. For just as the shopping centre as a whole traditionally acted as a major draw for the city centre, so its convenience goods traders, supplying the day-to-day needs of large numbers of people, ensured passing trade for the less frequently visited durable goods shops. Thus, just as the new regional shopping centres have attracted non shopping uses around them, turning out-of-town sites into something like new 'Central Business Districts', so the hypermarket is potentially capable of drawing to itself something like a new shopping centre.

At the Schoten Centre near Antwerp, built in 1966, GB Bazaars tried a variant on this approach, though with less commercial success. The site contains secondary uses common to hypermarket developments, such as car and garden centres and a restaurant, but in addition the main hypermarket building was designed to have about one quarter of its total floor area devoted to a furniture store. Although it was found that this use did not lend itself to cash and carry methods in that case, the success of the Ikea furniture stores in Sweden shows that trading in more ambitious durable good lines could be successfully carried out using hypermarket techniques. These stores, together with similar examples operated by Habitat in the UK, are discussed in Chapter 5 as special trading forms, but the possibility of physically relating such durable goods operations to hypermarkets is demonstrated in another example, this time in Germany.

The first European out-of-town centre to be discussed was the Main Taunus Zentrum, near Frankfurt, a development which included the first discount store on hypermarket lines by the Wertkauf organisation. Although not truly a hypermarket, being both too small, at 3,000 m², and also firmly embedded as a secondary magnet within a regional centre, the group went on to develop true hypermarkets around Frieburg, Munich and Karlsruhe. In addition the Wertkauf organisation operates a chain of furniture stores, Mann Mobilia, and at Rhein-Main near Weisbaden they opened in 1970 an out-of-town development comprising both a 'Wertkauf Center' hypermarket and a Mann Mobilia furniture store, each of about 15,000 m² gross area, and together served by 2,000 parking spaces. Between the two giant stores the small service traders found in association with hypermarkets are grouped into an arcade with landscaped open mall, described in the advertising brochure as follows:

'All around the delightful green courtyard with its outdoor cafe, there is a whole group of marvellous shops: the travel bureau, the hairdressers', the pet shop and the quick cleaning, where your clothes are cleaned while you shop.'

What has emerged is a version of the classic dumbell shopping centre pattern, with a mall of small traders set between two major magnet stores.

In arriving at this position one suspects that the Rhein-Main Wertkauf Centre has shifted away from the minimal-cost hypermarket idea, and that the term 'Wertkauf', literally 'value buying', may be undergoing the same metamorphosis as the term 'Warenhaus'. Although the operational methods of the hypermarket are those of the French examples, the buildings appear less transitory, and there is a greater emphasis on service. The difficulties of operating the furniture store on a cash and carry basis are overcome by providing a cheap van-hire service, and the organisation provides a private bus service for shoppers without cars. Cost advantages remain important, but these are held to result from the efficiency of the operation, rather than from cost-paring at all levels.

The cooperative Society in Sweden, KF, a major operator of hypermarkets in Scandinavia, places a similar emphasis upon the nature of this form of trading. Regarding it as an industrialised method of retail distribution, KF relate it to new methods developed throughout the Swedish economy since the Second War in response to technical and social changes. They maintain that, by building large, rationally planned units on cheap land, their Obs stores are able to sell products at prices on average 11% below those in traditional shops. In achieving this, an important factor is the high level of sales per employee, resulting in operating costs less than half those of other shops.

As in the German case, however, minimal building costs do not figure so prominently in this formula. The Obs stores at both Varby and Rotebro, for example, are two storey structures, with ground and basement levels linked by travellators. Their plan forms are triangular, with the row of check-outs along one side, and service access, stores and preparation rooms along another. These hypermarkets were opened in 1963 and 1967, with gross floor areas of 15,000 m² and 16,280 m² respectively.

Carrefour describe their stores as selling 'Food as in a large supermarket; clothing as in a chain store; household goods as in a department store', while both Wertkauf and Obs hypermarkets are referred to by their operators as 'self service department stores'. The idea that the hyper-

market might be simply a rebirth of the department store in its original low-cost, 'Warehouse' form, is suggested also by one of the most recent Obs stores, opened in 1974 in the centre of the new Danish town of Høje Tastrup. For this store, a unit of 26,000 m² gross area, is in fact the first phase of the new town centre, to be complemented at the end of 1975 by a further 55,000 m² GLA of shopping floor space of conventional mix, ie supermarkets, specialist stores, service traders and entertainment uses on pedestrian shopping malls. The store therefore begins life as an independent hypermarket on a green-field site, and then becomes the major magnet of a complete shopping centre. While the building may be said to display the virtues of good industrial architecture, its design also pays considerable attention to the service aspects of its role as a town centre structure. Much care, for instance, is devoted to its use by handicapped shoppers, for whom are provided special parking bays, check-out points, lavatories and rooms for trying on clothes. The store also provides a nursery which dispenses free disposable nappies, and some 2,100 m² of floor area is taken up by a customer service department, which deals with information, claims, exchanges, etc.

These examples show that the range of environments in which hypermarkets can operate is wide. If all of these do indeed fall within a useful definition of the term 'hypermarket', then it may be that minimum building-, or even land-, cost is not a vital part of that definition, but that size, method of trading and car accessibility are. Like the out-of-town centre, the hypermarket may then, as the Høje Tastrup example indicates, prove too irresistable an attraction to maintain its separateness from other urban uses.

3·30 Exterior of the Carrefour Hypermarket at Les Ulis, near Paris

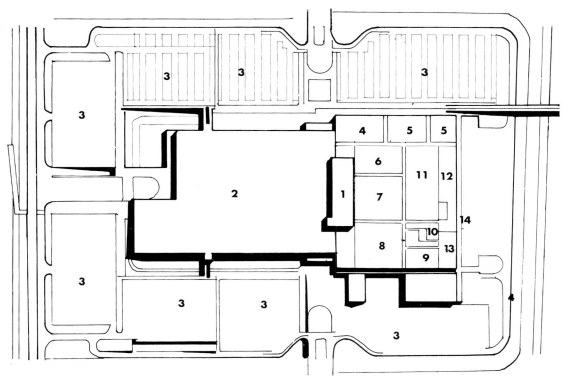

3·31 OBS Hypermarket, Høje Tastrup Storcenter, near Copenhagen Denmark: block plan
Architects: Jorgen Staermose and Grae & Helger

3·32 OBS Hypermarket, Høje Tastrup Storcenter: model of
development giving a plan view

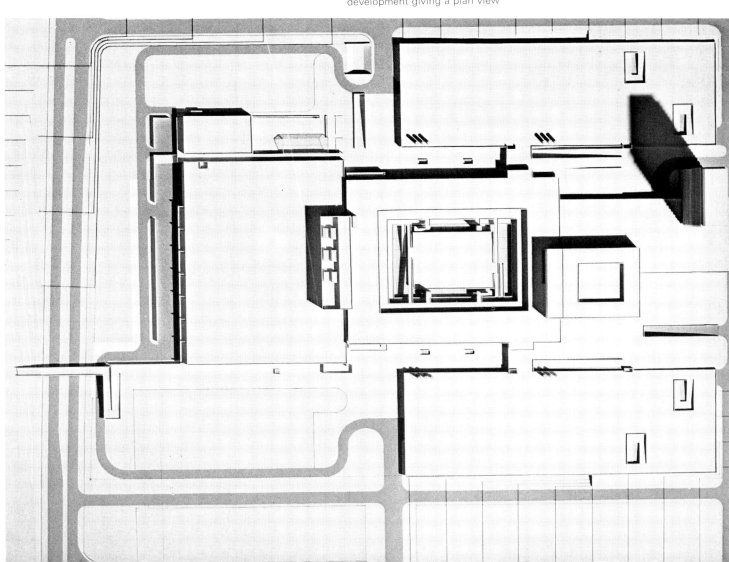

3·33 Interior of the OBS Hypermarket showing food and
pharmaceutical sales area
3·34 Checkout point at the OBS Hypermarket
3·35 Exterior showing loading bays at the OBS Hypermarket
3·36 Exterior of the OBS Hypermarket with garden centre in the
background

3·33

3·34

3·35

3·36

3·4 Superstores

Table 5 indicated only one hypermarket in the UK in 1972, this being the Carrefour store at Caerphilly. A variety of functional explanations have been offered earlier for the comparative paucity of out-of-town shopping forms in Britain, and yet it is difficult to establish these as being conclusive. Density of population is cited, and yet the out-of-town forms first took hold in Europe in two of its most densely populated countries, Belgium and West Germany. Again a low level of economic growth may be proposed, but in the key area of car ownership Britain has not been behind, and in 1972 had a higher level than either Belgium or West Germany. As regards this argument it is also strange that the new forms, when they have appeared in the UK, did so in the less prosperous regions, and not in the South-East where the greater party of the country's disposable income is concentrated. In 1973 Russell Schiller, an economist specialising in the economic aspects of retailing, described the situation as follows:[15]

'All the main forms of new retailing have taken place predominantly outside the South East. The first two Carrefour hypermarkets are in Wales and Shropshire, for example. Asda, a leading superstore operator, has no branch south of a line from Bristol to the Wash. Other leading food discounters such as Kwik Save and William Morrison are unknown in the south. Of eight Woolcos, only the Hatfield store is in the Home Counties. Similarly, out of eleven covered Arndale Centres only three (Wandsworth, Luton, and Poole) are south of Birmingham. The West End of London cannot even boast a main pedestrianised shopping street.

'The paradox lies in the fact that development has not occurred where market potential exists. Southern England has a high, even alarming proportion of the nation's population (nearly half) and an even greater concentration of its wealth and of new growth industries. And yet, in retailing development, it is a backwater.'

This picture contrasts sharply with the situation in the corresponding area of France, for example, where the

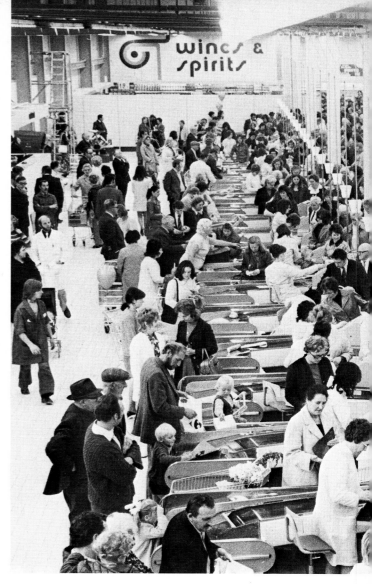

3·37 Checkout points at the Carrefour Hypermarket, Caerphilly, Wales
Architects: Peter Black and Partners

Table 5 *Hypermarkets in Western Europe at the end of 1972*[11]

	Belgium	Denmark	France	Italy	Nether-lands	Switzer-land	West Germany	United Kingdom
Number of hypermarkets	46	2	212	3	7	10	406	1*
Total selling area (m²)	307,000	21,600	1,239,300	28,200	33,800	58,700	2,596,900	5,200
Average selling area (m²)	6,700	10,800	5,800	9,400	4,800	5,900	6,400	5,200
Average car parking area (m²)	19,900	34,700	33,900	41,500	14,900	27,100	18,600	26,800
Average number of employees	140	195	205	165	78	108	142	240
Percentage of total retail trade	4·6	<1	4·8	n.a.	<1	1·5	6·8	n.a.

Source: MPC & Associates Ltd

*This is the Carrefour hypermarket at Caerphilly, opened in October, 1972. Superstores, eg Asda, Fine Fare, etc are not counted

3·38 Woolco Superstore, Hatfield New Town, England
Architect: Woolco Architect's Department

3·39 Sainsbury Superstore, Bretton, England
Architects: Scott, Brownrigg and Turner

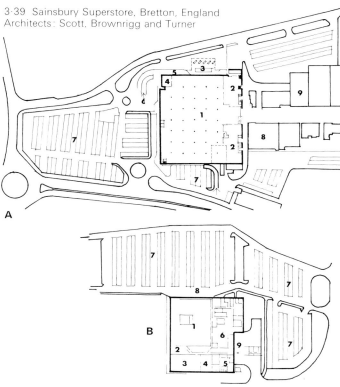

Key A)
1 Sales area
2 Storage (2 levels)
3 Service station
4 T B A
5 Ramp down from roof-top car park
6 Ramp up to roof-top car park
7 Ground-level car park
8 Tesco Food Supermarket
9 Fine Fare Food Supermarket

B)
1 Sales area
2 Wimpy coffee bar
3 Boots sales area (pharmacy)
4 Holding area
5 Staff, stockroom etc.
6 Bulk stock
7 Car park
8 Customers pick-up area
9 Truck area

Scale: 1 : 4000

3·40 Exterior of the Woolco Superstore, Hatfield New Town,
England from the road interchange
Architects: Woolco Architect's Department

Paris region has six hypermarkets by Carrefour alone, and ten regional shopping centres by 1975, with a further six planned into the 1980s. The phenomenon suggests that that there is some special factor, other than broad social or economic considerations, operating upon the form of retailing developments in the UK and one which operates less strongly in the regions where new investment of all kinds is less easily attracted and more keenly sought. By the early 1970s, the instigators of the hundreds of outstanding planning applications for out-of-town shopping developments had identified this factor as being the almost unanimous opposition of planning authorities to these forms. In a paper written in 1973, T. J. Hoggett of Peter Black and Partners noted four main reasons given by planning authorities as grounds for refusal of such applications.[16] The first of these is the effect which the proposal is likely to have upon other existing shopping centres, although this would seem to be based on a general apprehension rather than specific information as to precisely how these centres would be affected. Secondly the out-of-town solutions are held to generate traffic, although in fact they only bring about its redistribution, arguably with advantage. The third basis for opposition is the effect of the proposal upon existing amenities, this being a long-standing objection dating back to the restriction of ribbon development in the 1930s and establishment of Green Belts around cities. Fourthly, approval of the proposal would have the effect of distorting current planning policies, which are invariably framed around the assumption of a central location for main retailing facilities.

Where this last reason is cited it suggests that the planning process itself must resist change which is, or appears to be, at all radical, and it has been the general experience that, even where out-of-town developments have been eventually approved, the route to that approval has been a long and expensive one. While in France a small Carrefour hypermarket might have a construction time of 4 or 5 months, and a large one 6 months, the period between the hearing of the planning appeal for the Carrefour store at Eastleigh and the announcement of the result alone took almost 18 months, and the whole operation from preliminary site investigations to start of trading a total of 5 years.

Whatever the reasons for resistance in the UK to the out-of-town forms, and the machinery by which this resistance took effect, the result by the early 1970s had become sufficiently divergent from the situation elsewhere for it to become a subject of wide debate. Whether one looked to the 'free market' situation in North America or to the 'socially advanced' countries of Scandinavia, the out-of-town solution in one form or another seemed to have gained such widespread acceptance abroad that the British position appeared increasingly odd. It became the subject of numerous articles, reports and conferences organised by business groups[17] and local authorities, and from February 1972 it became mandatory to refer all applications for stores of over 5,000 m² to the Department of the Environment while central planning policy on the question underwent painful review.

Yet the general antipathy in the UK had not entirely excluded the out-of-town solutions, examples of which, in accordance with 'Schillers Law', were to be found in places remote from London. There are exceptions to this and notably the Brent Cross regional shopping centre, providing some 100,000 m² GLA at the junction of the North Circular and the main radial approach to the M1

from Central London. Long before this, however, multiple groups had been opening large out-of-town outlets on the hypermarket principle in the provinces. These units are generally referred to as 'Superstores', although whether the difference between this term and hypermarket is more than semantic is arguable where units over 5,000 m² are involved.

One of the first examples of the type was the GEM Supercentre at West Bridgeford, near Nottingham, which was opened early in 1965.[18] As a large American retailing organisation, GEM based the operation upon its successful experience with similar supercentre developments in the USA. In this the West Bridgeford store differed from what was to become the normal trading form of the hypermarket/superstore, since the operating pattern resembled that of a shopping centre, with GEM acting as developer of the building and trading within it being undertaken by licensees or concessionaires who might be local traders or national multiples. Whether for this reason, or else because retail price maintenance was not yet abolished in the UK, the store was not at first as successful as had been hoped, and in 1967 GEM sold the majority of its interest in it and in another supercentre it had built to Associated Dairies. This multiple now incorporated the GEM stores into the ASDA group of discount stores, a rapidly growing participant in the new centres which within the following five years had 27 hypermarkets and superstores in operation during which time the company's annual turnover increased from £19m to £95m. The original West Bridgeford GEM store shared the industrial characteristics of the new discount forms, with a simple, neatly detailed envelope cladding to a steel frame structure, 8 bays by 4 at 15·25 m each, providing a total 7,400 m² of artificially ventilated and illuminated space. Only 25% of this was devoted to storage and ancillary uses however, and a further 2,800 m² of warehouse accommodation was later added by ASDA, at the same time reducing the importance of the concessionaire form of trading in favour of the main discount operation.

In 1965 another American based company, F. W. Woolworth, took steps to emulate in the UK the success of the parent company in operating superstores in the USA and Canada, and formed the Woolco Department Stores division. The first Woolco superstore was opened in 1967 at Oadby near Leicester and has been followed by further units at the rate of about one per year since then. Like other superstore operators, 'Woolco does not call itself a hypermarket, but it could probably be termed a superstore, or department store which is geared for the motorised shopper. The locating and establishment of a Woolco store has proved a difficult task due to strong planning objections, which are now well known throughout the Country'. It could be that this difficulty has contributed to the hesitancy of operators in using the term hypermarket, but it is also significant that many of the Woolco stores, such as those at Killingworth (1970), Hatfield (1972), Washington (1973) and Cumbernauld (1974) are integral parts of New Town centres, in which the department store aspect of their nature fully asserts itself. In the first three cases they act as single major magnet stores within the development in much the same way, though on a smaller scale, as Obs at Høje Tastrup. It is also apparent that such a location can force the superstore away from the simple industrial ideal, with more restricted and expensive sites leading to more elaborate solutions for car parking. At Cumbernauld undercroft parking is incorporated, while at Hatfield there is car parking both below the superstore and on its roof, and in addition shop storage on two levels with flats built above.

In the UK the development of these 'edge-of-town' or semi-integrated superstore/hypermarkets has reached the point where the traditional department store groups have entered the scene, as with Debenham's Scan superstores. The majority however have been developed by established food or supermarket trading groups, as Morrisons, Kwik Save and Brierley, and among the larger multiples Fine Fare, Tesco and J. Sainsbury. The Sainsbury Bretton store provides an example of another way in which the superstore has found an acceptable role within a New Town development. This unit does not form part of a main town centre as in the earlier examples, but provides in itself a district centre for one of the townships within Peterborough. About three-quarters of the floor·area is occupied by the Sainsbury store itself, and the remainder by a Boots chemist unit and a Wimpy Bar, with future expansion to include service trades. Planning restrictions specified 'that the building was to be square in shape, single storey in height and approached by a covered way 'as well as the location of the building on the site and its orientation.[19] Within these restraints, the architects, Scott Brownrigg and Turner, felt the major design problem to be 'to stop the building looking just like a factory or a warehouse'. perhaps a debatable ambition for the superstore at this stage of its development. Internally the space is modified by variations in the suspended ceiling height, from 2·75 m to 4·00 m to suit the variation in uses within the envelope.

In the case of the UK, and perhaps also of Denmark, it is difficult to be sure how much the attempts at integration reflect a commercial or a planning priority, and the degree to which the New Town locations represent a particular situation where the interests of both may be made to coincide without actually adopting a true out-of-town location. In this context the superstore developments in the UK may be seen as a special case of the hypermarket principle, burgeoning in an unreceptive environment. That this hesitation over the acceptability of hypermarkets can produce novel solutions is shown by two projects designed by Foster Associates in which unusual mixes of retail and non-retail uses are proposed by the clients. In both of these projects for the Knowsley Pavilion in England and the Badhoevedorp Pavilion in Holland the commercial operation is combined with a wide range of social and recreational uses offered in mitigation by the developers. In the former case, proposed for a site of 20 ha at the junction of the M57 and the Liverpool Road some 7 miles east of the centre of Liverpool, an Asda superstore occupies 12,000 m² gross (9,300 m² net) of a total building floor area of 47,000 m². 41% of that total area is taken up by a swimming pool, sports hall, roller skating, golf, archery, bingo and snooker areas, squash courts, bars and restaurants as well as a library and adult education and medical centres. Outside this main building the site also contains a riding school, soccer pitches, and athletics and cycle tracks, and a dry ski run. Among the reasons given for the introduction of such facilities were:

1 To ensure that the commercial strength of a hypermarket was employed in such a way that it could act as a catalyst for more social facilities, thus giving more to the community/catchment area

2 To give more credibility to the social acceptance of a hypermarket'[20]

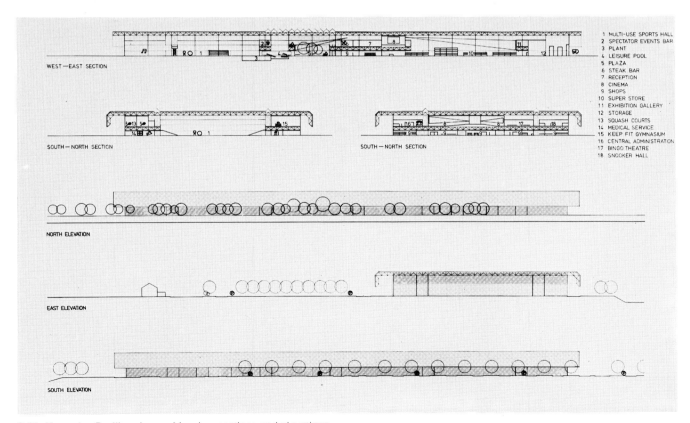

3·41 Knowsley Pavilion, Lancashire: key sections and elevations of the main building, showing leisure facilities associated with shopping functions
Architects: Foster Associates

At Badhoevedorp a similar, though less ambitious, recreational element is combined with a hypermarket operated by Miro, a leading multiple group in Holland. The proportion of retail: recreational: circulation and ancilliary uses in this building is given as 50:22:28%, as against 32:41:27% for the Knowsley Pavilion, and again the reasoning is seen as being that 'The mix aimed at retranslating the hypermarket as an individual building operating solely for commercial gain, into a centre for all the family. The recreational facilities might well be subsidised by the hypermarket operation.'[21]

In both of these projects the design of the main 'pavilion' building elevates the industrial or neutral character of hypermarket structures to a principle. At Knowsley it is described as an 'umbrella', 288 m long × 126 m wide × 15 m high below which the large units of accommodation—hypermarket, sports hall and central plaza—are located in a central full height band, with the smaller spaces ranged in two storeys along each long side. On the south long face of the pavilion the wall is held back to form a broad sheltered arcade below the overhang of the umbrella roof facing the car park. Servicing to the superstore takes place at the end of the building, and on the north side for the restaurant and other functions.

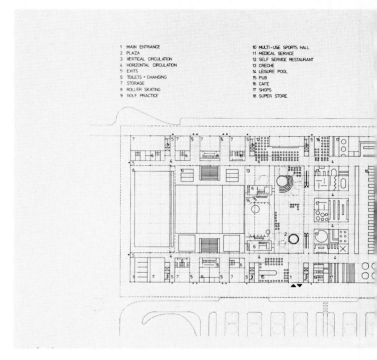

1 MAIN ENTRANCE	10 MULTI-USE SPORTS HALL
2 PLAZA	11 MEDICAL SERVICE
3 VERTICAL CIRCULATION	12 SELF SERVICE RESTAURANT
4 HORIZONTAL CIRCULATION	13 CRECHE
5 EXITS	14 LEISURE POOL
6 TOILETS + CHANGING	15 PUB
7 STORAGE	16 CAFE
8 ROLLER SKATING	17 SHOPS
9 GOLF PRACTICE	18 SUPER STORE

3·42 Knowsley Pavilion, Lancashire: ground-level plan

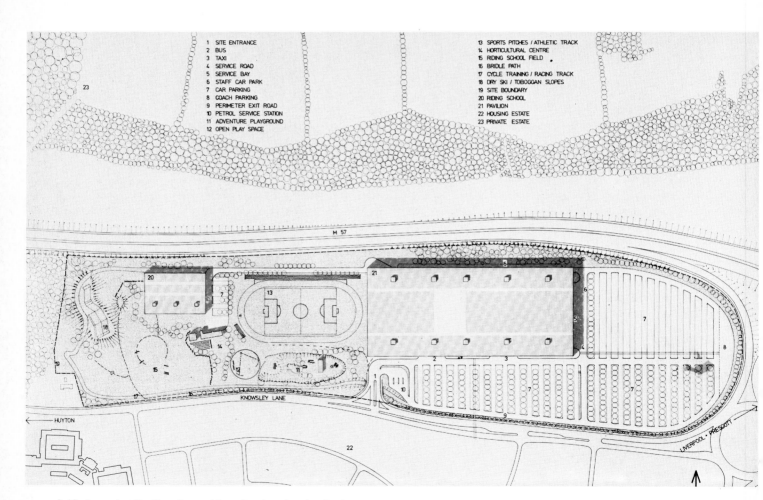

1 SITE ENTRANCE	13 SPORTS PITCHES / ATHLETIC TRACK
2 BUS	14 HORTICULTURAL CENTRE
3 TAXI	15 RIDING SCHOOL FIELD
4 SERVICE ROAD	16 BRIDLE PATH
5 SERVICE BAY	17 CYCLE TRAINING / RACING TRACK
6 STAFF CAR PARK	18 DRY SKI / TOBOGGAN SLOPES
7 CAR PARKING	19 SITE BOUNDARY
8 COACH PARKING	20 RIDING SCHOOL
9 PERIMETER EXIT ROAD	21 PAVILION
10 PETROL SERVICE STATION	22 HOUSING ESTATE
11 ADVENTURE PLAYGROUND	23 PRIVATE ESTATE
12 OPEN PLAY SPACE	

3·43 Knowsley Pavilion, Lancashire: site plan showing land use with adventure playground, riding school, athletic tracks and horticultural centre

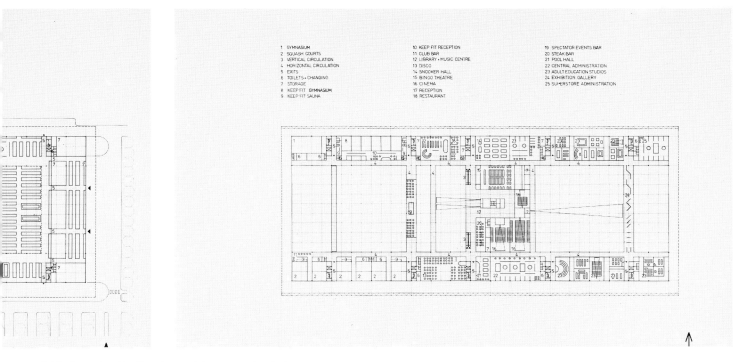

1 GYMNASIUM	10 KEEP FIT RECEPTION	19 SPECTATOR EVENTS BAR
2 SQUASH COURTS	11 CLUB BAR	20 STEAK BAR
3 VERTICAL CIRCULATION	12 LIBRARY + MUSIC CENTRE	21 POOL HALL
4 HORIZONTAL CIRCULATION	13 DISCO	22 CENTRAL ADMINISTRATION
5 EXITS	14 SNOOKER HALL	23 ADULT EDUCATION STUDIOS
6 TOILETS + CHANGING	15 BINGO THEATRE	24 EXHIBITION GALLERY
7 STORAGE	16 CINEMA	25 SUPERSTORE ADMINISTRATION
8 KEEP FIT GYMNASIUM	17 RECEPTION	
9 KEEP FIT SAUNA	18 RESTAURANT	

3·44 Knowsley Pavilion, Lancashire: upper-level plan

3·45 Internal Perspective of the Central Plaza Area at the
Knowsley Pavilion, Lancashire

3·46 External perspective of the Knowsley Pavilion, Lancashire
from the Adventure Playground

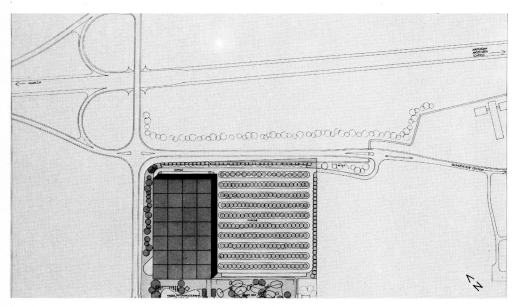
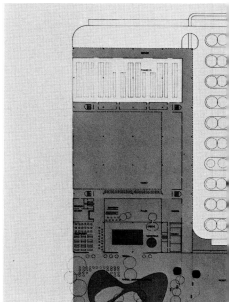

3·47 Badhoevedorp Pavilion, Holland: block plan showing
landscaped car parking; ground-floor plan and cross sections
Architects: Foster Associates

3·48 Internal perspective of the entrance area at the Badhoevedorp Pavilion

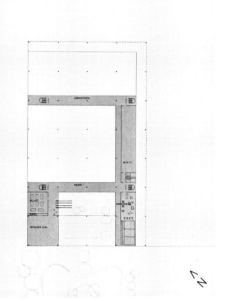
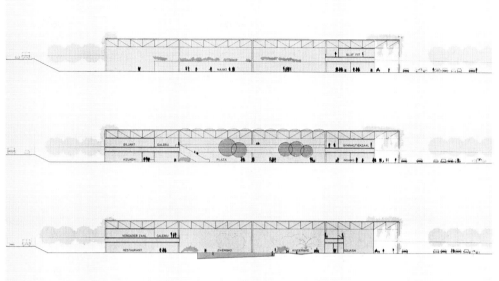

In the Dutch example, which lies 2 km north of Bad-hoevedorp centre near Amsterdam on the Badhoevedorp/Amsterdam-Haarlem motorway, a similar organisation is proposed within a 168 m × 96 m envelope set out on a 24 m structural grid and with an 8 m clear internal height. Again the external wall is held back from the roof perimeter to provide a covered entry from the car park along one long side and covered service bays along a short side, and the plan organisation follows an ordered sequence along its length from service area to hypermarket storage, hyper-market sales, plaza and recreational uses, with first floor galleries defining these major areas.

The novelty of the briefs for these two projects, together with the lucidity of the building solutions proposed, makes them exceptional among the examples discussed and suggests the architectural quality which the hypermarket building type is capable of generating and the wide variety of relationships it can establish with the non-retail functions of the community.

References

1 *Architectural Record* March 1973
2 *Design for Shopping* published by Capital & Counties Property Co Ltd
3 See also four recent publications by the International Council of Shopping Centres, New York:
   Shopping Center Strategy: A Case Study of the Planning, Location and Development of the Del Monte Center, Monterey, California by William Applebaum 1970; *Case Studies in Shopping Center Development and Operation* by William Applebaum and S. O. Kaylin 1974; *Shopping Center Management* by Horace Carpenter Jr. 1974; *Shopping Center Promotions* by William W. Callahan 1972
4 *Market Analysis of Springfield Mall* Hammer & Co Associates, Washington
5 *Architectural Record* April 1966
6 *Architectural Record* March 1970
7 *Architectural Record* March 1973
8 International Association of Department Stores: *Commission on Department Stores in Shopping Centres* No. 833, July 1970
9 RICS Conference, Amsterdam, 1973: 'Regional Shopping Centre Development in France' by Jean-Louis Solal, published in *Chartered Surveyor* September 1973
10 See article 'Retail Planning in France' by B. A. Smith
11 Source: MPC & Associates Ltd, Marketing & Planning Consultants, *The Changing Pattern of Retailing Western Europe 1973* Worcester, England, 1973
12 H. D. Clout, *The Geography of Post-War France: A Social and Economic Approach* Oxford 1972
13 Source: L'Institut Français du Libre Service et des Techniques Modernes de Distribution; MPC & Associates Limited. Cited by B. A. Smith *op cit*
14 See *Recent Shopping Developments in Europe*, Corporation of Glasgow, March 1971, for further information on some of hypermarket examples
15 Article 'Retailing and Planning', by Russell Schiller of Hillier Parker May & Rowden
16 'Report on the Future of Hypermarkets', T. J. Hoggett of Peter Black and Partners
17 eg Glasgow Corporation, Conference on *Discount Trading and Hypermarkets* April 1972: Bolton Chamber of Trade, Conference on *Hypermarkets and Out-of-Town Shopping Centres—The Need for Planning Strategy* March 1972
18 See building appraisal in *The Architects' Journal* 5 May 1965 and reappraisal in *The Architects' Journal* 28th July 1971, both by Brian Foyle
19 Article 'Shopping in the Future', by K. E. Gilham, partner of Scott Brownrigg & Turner
20 Source: Foster Associates, Architects and Engineers
21 *ibid*

4 Integrated Shopping

4·01 Model of the shopping building at Milton Keynes New Town, England showing roof-top servicing
Architect: Derek Walker

The evolution of North American out-of-town centres through a sequence of types which, for a time seemed appropriate and were then superceded by new forms, is paralleled in the development of European integrated, or down-town centres over the same period. Yet while the general tendency towards forms of greater size, cost and complexity has been the same, the sequence has not. An earlier emphasis upon the development of more complex arrangements in section, springing from the problem of accommodating similar programmes upon smaller and more expensive sites, is one major factor in the evolution of the integrated as against the out-of-town centres. Another has been the particular consequences of their contexts. For while irregular and constrained sites may be held to have simply distorted an 'ideal' shopping centre arrangement, in practice the consequences have often been more far-reaching. The new centre may itself be only a part of a wider system of movement and must therefore be open-ended, pragmatically reacting to the influence of magnets outside itself. The degree of constraint imposed by the urban context is crucial, and the results of building in an existing city distinct from those in a new settlement. Because of this it is useful to consider these two groups of solutions separately, the former constituting an evolution through a wide variety of special cases, the latter a development through 'model' solutions in 'model' contexts.

These models related to contemporary developments both in out-of-town and integrated shopping, and in fact two species of New Town Centres are apparent, referred to here as 'precinct' and 'megastructure' solutions. Their development forms an independent commentary upon the line of shopping development in the old cities, sometimes coinciding with it, sometimes proposing new models for it, and sometimes diverging from it in response to the alternative models appearing in the out-of-town locations. The evolution of the New Town strands thus provide a useful reference for the necessarily more constrained cases of development in existing towns, and a link between them and the out-of-town forms discussed in the previous chapter.

4·1 New Towns I: Precincts

The first generation of European New Town Centres established with reformative enthusiasm two notions of a town centre and its shopping content which arose from pre-war planning philosophies. The first was the idea of the centre itself as a discrete element or zone within the town, generally in the English examples as the highest in a three-tier arrangement of shopping facilities serving an overall plan itself developed in hierarchical form. The second was the separation of traffic circulations within the centre, and in particular the pedestrian, again as the most articulated case of a general principle to be applied to the town plan as a whole.

These two ideas, which became universally recognised in New Town planning during the 1950s, corresponded closely to the principles of development of the first American out-of-town centres, yet their virtue, and particularly that of pedestrianisation, was by no means apparent to retailers unfamiliar with them and who at first argued strongly against them. They differed also from the American examples in remaining part of a town structure, though a town developed at suburban densities with space both for the segregation of categories of traffic and for the planned provision of

4·02 View of the Main Concourse at Vällingby New Town, near Stockholm, Sweden
Architect/Planner: Sven Markelius
Architects: Svenska Bostader

surface car parking.

The centres of Stevenage, Harlow and East Kilbride in the UK exemplified variations of solutions of this centre type, with the central area defined by a main distributor road feeding a ring of car parks and a service road system to the mix of town centre uses, arranged along pedestrian streets and squares themselves connected outwards to adjacent zones.

In Sweden, where the New Towns were conceived as radial extensions to Stockholm rather than as independent satellites, an additional element was the underground railway link to the city. In the case of Vällingby, for example, the centre, opened in 1954, effectively formed a bridge deck across the rail line which passed below it. In other respects the Vällingby centre shared many of the characteristics of the British examples. The scale of development was low, generally 2-storey, in contrast to that of the surrounding housing blocks; its form was of independent building blocks of mixed use, defining and separated by the circulation routes for pedestrians and vehicles.

The diffusion of the shopping element through the town centres of this period produced a pattern similar to that of the more elaborate mall layouts of the first American out-of-town centres, with considerable lengths of secondary malls and frontage. And just as this was abandoned in the next stage of American development, so also in the Scandinavian New Towns the shopping element of the town centre began now to be condensed around a more simple precinct pattern. The centre plans of the '50s had also experienced difficulty in reconciling the conflicts between the various circulation systems on grade, and this also was reconsidered, together with the level of car parking provision.

The Farsta centre, opened in 1960, illustrates the next step made in response to these considerations. Although still in the form of independent blocks with open malls, the arrangement is now concentrated around a single, lozenge-shaped main space with short side malls leading directly in. Describing this area, the architects Sven Backström and Leif Reinius wrote 'This consists of a rectangular space having the form, in principle, of a broad shopping street where the show-windows of the one side support the other, great care having been exercised in dimensioning the street space. In order to afford a contrast to the open space with a maximum breadth of 38 m and a minimum breadth of 20 m, all the converging streets have been made narrow, measuring no more than 9 m across (by way of comparison it may be mentioned that the corresponding breadth in Vällingby is 10 m).' Non-retail uses are either excluded from this space or confined to areas where they will not break the shopping frontage, which is disposed about 3 magnet department store blocks, and it is noticeable that descriptions of the Farsta Centrum refer to it as a 'shopping centre'. Thus O. Enghvist in 1971, 'In presenting Farsta, the latest and biggest shopping centre in Sweden, we have had the advantage of studying and learning from its American forerunners.'[1]

In concentrating upon how the shopping element of the town centre should work, and from this core accommodating non-retail elements in spurs or independent elements, Farsta also offered an alternative solution to the question of servicing. The centre is located at the foot of a valley which it spans, to accommodate at a basement level below the deck not only the rail station, as at Vällingby, but also a service road loop and shop storage areas. Pedestrian routes running down the sides of the valley from the housing areas are picked up at each end of the centre, while side malls along its length lead out to car parking areas on either side. 1,600 car spaces were provided at grade, with an additional 300 spaces in a parking garage. Serving a gross retail area of 40,000 m², this contrasted with the earlier Vällingby centre where 500 spaces had been provided for 20,000 m² GLA.

4·03 Aerial view of the shopping centre and surrounding housing at Farsta New Town, near Stockholm, Sweden
Architects: Sven Backstrom and Leif Reinius

4·04 Farsta New Town Centre, near Stockholm, Sweden: plan showing the ground floor with market-place level

4·05 Longitudinal section through buildings on north-west side of market-place

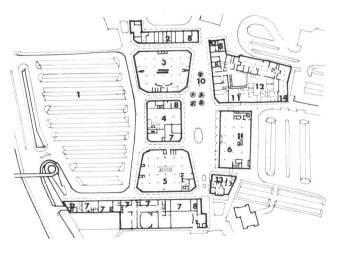

Key:
1 Car parking
2 Building D, shops, offices, Baptist church
3 Kvickly Department Store
4 Building B, shops, branch library, offices
5 Tempo Department Store
6 N K Department Store
7 Shops
8 Banks
9 Police station
10 Central Square with pond and fountains
11 Chemist
12 Post office
13 Restaurant
14 Depot for sale of wines and spirits
Scale: Plan 1 : 4000
Section 1 : 2000

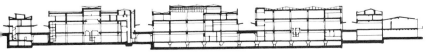

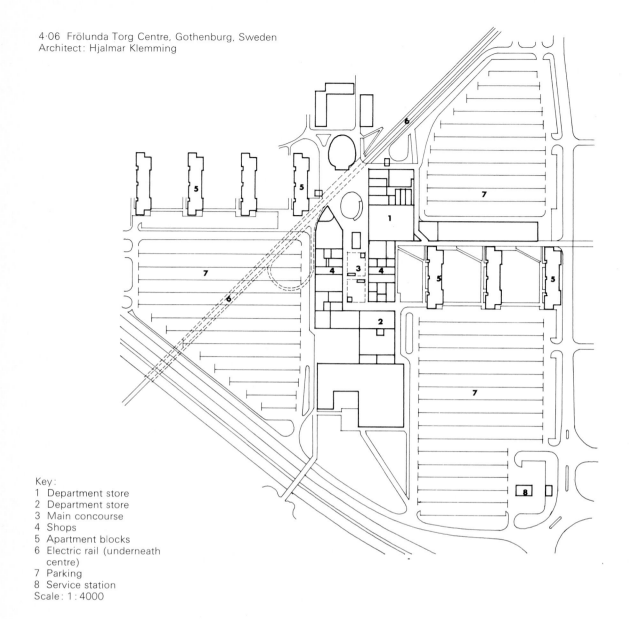

4·06 Frölunda Torg Centre, Gothenburg, Sweden
Architect: Hjalmar Klemming

Key:
1 Department store
2 Department store
3 Main concourse
4 Shops
5 Apartment blocks
6 Electric rail (underneath centre)
7 Parking
8 Service station
Scale: 1:4000

Having established the shopping centre as a separate entity within the central area of the New Town, and having established its special requirements for layout and circulation, the next step was to enclose it and make of it a single building. Adopting a very similar topographical solution to Farsta, the Frölunda Centre, some 8 km south of Gottenburg, did this. Again the centre spans a valley floor, with pedestrian routes entering at north and south ends and with the rail station below the former. A service route runs below the length of the centre, which again is flanked to east and west by parking areas. These however now provide 3,000 spaces for a similar GLA, and are formed at two site levels to generate two levels of malls within the shopping building. The main core of this has sales areas disposed around a large central space rising through the two levels and includes 3 large shop units balancing a main department store magnet which abuts on the north east corner to form one side of an open square over the underground station.

Although the Frölunda Centre remains connected by pedestrian routes to its town, and non-retail central area uses encroach upon its surrounding site, the scale of its grade car parks and the way in which these relate to the balanced circulation of the internal organisation, relate it

closely to the contemporary out-of-town forms of N. America. The New Town shopping precinct had now become, by the mid '60s, a self-contained and complex island building, complete with by-pass pedestrian routes to allow its closure at night.

Although not stricly speaking a New Town Centre, the Rodovre Centrum corresponds closely to this type. Completed in 1966, it was designed to serve as the main centre for a new suburban area to the West of Copenhagen. It was initiated by a planning committee comprising equal representation of the local authority and the developer, with participation by the Danish Ministry of Housing's commissioner in urban planning and by the Institute of Centre Planning. This latter body, referred to in Chapter 2 in connection with its theoretical work on shopping forms, was set up by retailers and the Cooperative movement in Denmark and is subsidised by direct grant from the government. Employing architects, planners and economists, it acts as a research and data centre for questions related to shopping, providing advice to local authorities such as the Rodovre municipality, and has been the model for similar institutes now established in Sweden and Norway. At Rodovre it 'strongly expressed to the committee the necessity of not only making the centre a commercial

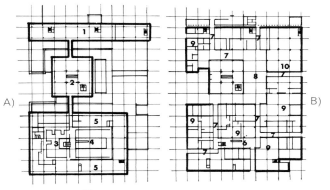

Key: A)
1 Offices
2 Banqueting rooms
3 Restaurant
4 Escalator down
5 Upper-level shops

B)
6 Garden court with removable glass roof
7 Shopping concourse
8 Piazza with removable glass roof

9 Shops
10 Department store/supermarket
Scale: 1 : 4000

4·07 Rodovre Centrum shopping centre, near Copenhagen
A) Upper-level plan
B) Ground-level plan
Architects: Krohn and Hartvig Rasmussen

4·08 View of the central concourse with escalator to upper-level shops at the Rodovre shopping centre near Copenhagen. Note the removable glass roof

4·09 View of the Side Mall with glazed roof at the Rodovre shopping centre

4·10 Central escalator at the Rodovre shopping centre

4·11 Exterior view of the Rodovre shopping centre

75

centre, but to construct it to include a combination of shops, offices, entertainments, and more or less official public institutions.' Its site was close to that for the town hall and the main library building so that they might together 'create a town-centre with both commercial and cultural activities.' While the centre does include an hotel, bowling alley and similar non-retail uses on its site, and while it is geographically located in a 'central area', the building solution is nevertheless a self-contained island structure on the lines of Frölunda. The elementarist nature of the central area, with its buildings set apart on a town centre 'campus', traversed by the Rodovre Parkvej and Tarnvej dual carriageways, is reflected in the design of the shopping centre itself. Set out on a 12 m² structural grid, the building occupies a rectangle 10 bays × 13, which supports three separate elements at first floor level; a full width band of single storey offices on the eastern side, a department store cube in the centre, and a large rectangular upper shopping level hall to the west. At ground level the full building area is taken up by the main shopping floor which acts as a podium for the three upper elements and is organised around the single magnet of the department store, 3 bays square on plan, a large single height square in front of it, 5 bays by 2, and a second double height square in the centre of the two storey shopping hall. Side malls lead into this arrangement from all sides of the building, which is flanked by the Rodovre Parkvej and its bus layby on one side, and by car parking, up to a total of 2,000 spaces for the 30,000 m² GLA, on the other three sides. At basement level the building rectangle is occupied by shop storage areas, the bowling alley, and a service road loop.

The design of the Rodovre Centre is unusual in a number of respects. In its organisation, the area of upper shopping, although not supported by any direct pedestrian flow, yet works well, with its central high square acting as a focus of attraction in balance with that of the single department store. In its detail design the architects, Krohn and Hartvig Rasmussen, have carried the orderliness of the plan into a simple and effective language of parts and materials. The roofs to the malls are glass or corrugated plastic carried on timber beams supported on exposed steel columns, and can be rolled open over the squares in summer; mall furniture, planters, seating etc, are timber; shop fronts are continuous glass planes unbroken by obtruding cross-walls between units. Finally Rodovre is unusual in the quality and profusion of the indoor planting with which the developer, A. Knudsen, who formerly ran a market garden on the site, has filled it.

The idiosyncratic elements in the organisation of the Rodovre and Frölunda island buildings were resolved in the classic form of the final Scandinavian New Town example discussed here. Symmetrical in plan and balanced in section, Taby Centrum stands as a complete and self-contained element in its central area. A simple rectangle on plan with two 2-storey department stores located at diagonally opposite corners, it forms a simple envelope within which two levels of shops are ranged around a large double-height central space. The upper level is accessible from the car parking areas to the east and pedestrian routes from housing and other central area uses to the north, while the western car parks feed into the lower level which also connects to the underground station to the south. Travellators link the two mall levels in the central space which is air-conditioned and used for trading promotions as well as exhibitions, concerts and festivals. Despite its town centre location, pedestrian feeders and bus and rail links, the Taby

Centre, with 1,800 car parking spaces serving 32,800 m² GLA almost exactly meets the recommendations of the American Urban Land Institute for a norm of 5·9 spaces per 100 m² for the out-of-town centre, and its form is also as appropriate to such a location.

There has thus been one line of development of European New Town centres in which the shopping element has been first drawn together into a compact entity, then enclosed as a single building element and organized according to its own internal logic. In a New Town Centre where large areas of at-grade car parking could be found, the solutions which this logic produced were entirely compatible with the out-of-town forms previously discussed and might easily be exchanged for them. In building, if not planning, terms, the central area location is almost incidental to these solutions and their evolution is in a sense the reverse of the American experience of the out-of-town centre finding itself at the heart of a new central business district. Here the CBD has found itself harbouring an out-of-town centre, in form if not location.

We refer here to this line of New Town Centres as 'precinct centres' and while examples have been taken from Scandinavia, they have not been confined to that region. In Britain a tendency of this type has expressed itself in New Town Centres in which the alternative out-of-town form, the hypermarket or superstore, has been an important constituent. Such an example, in the Danish New Town of Høje Tastrup, has already been discussed, and in England the centre at Telford similarly incorporates a Carrefour hypermarket making up almost half of the Phase I GLA.

The gradual elimination of wayward and specific elements in the design in favour of internal consistency and organisational logic, seen in the development of precinct centres from Vällingby to Farsta to Frölunda and Taby, reaches a new level in the plan for Central Milton Keynes. Designed to serve a new city population of 250,000 mid-way between London and Birmingham, the scale of this development has been a particular preoccupation of its designers, whose 'scale studies' invite comparison of its size to that of other commercial areas, ancient and modern, from Paris and London to Stevenage, Welwyn and Northlands Detroit.[2] Scale is also a major consideration with regard to built form:

'The necessary requirement of a plot ratio (1:1·5 max.) which controls the density of a development reinforces the concept of Central Milton Keynes as a place where buildings play a subservient visual role. In order that this concept is not prejudiced by tall buildings of inhuman scale, creating micro-climatic problems, a maximum height of 15 m (four storeys) applies to office and other commercial development.'

The central area occupies two grid squares of the Master Plan, an area of about 1·8 × ·9 km., which is subdivided by a grid of east-west boulevards and north-south roads into plots of land 342 × 144 m, two of which are allocated to the shopping centre. The boulevards and roads form broad strips, 72 m and 120 m wide respectively, through the central area, with side parking roads within these strips providing about 1,000 parking spaces evenly distributed around each block and an eventual capacity of some 18,000 spaces in the whole central area. Coinciding with bus stopping points along the boulevards, portes cochère cross the parking roads and set up pedestrian entry points into the city blocks at 90 m centres along their longer north and south sides, alternating with notional entry points for service roads at the same spacing, and the Cartesian grid of

4·12 Lyngby shopping centre, near Copenhagen
Architects: Gunnar Krohn and Hartvig Rasmussen

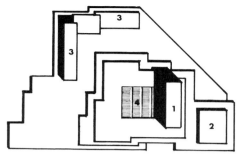

A) Block plan

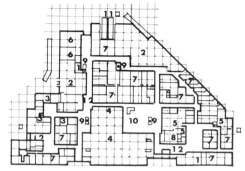

B) Shopping-level plan

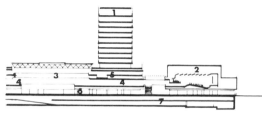

C) Section

4·13 View of the central square with glazed roof at the Lyngby shopping centre, near Copenhagen

4·14 Exterior of the Lyngby shopping centre showing hotel above shopping centre

Key: A)
 1 Hotel
 2 Cinema
 3 Office block
 4 Glazed roof to shopping centre
Scale: 1 : 4000

B)
 1 Banks
 2 Supermarket
 3 Provision/food shops
 4 Department store
 5 Restaurant, pub etc.
 6 Municipal administration
   offices
 7 Shops
 8 Hotel foyer
 9 Escalators to basement car
   parking
10 Central square with glazed roof
11 Ramps to basement car parks
12 Shopping concourse
Scale: 1 : 4000

C)
 1 Hotel
 2 Cinema
 3 Central square with glazed roof
 4 Upper-level shopping
 5 Restaurant
 6 Lower-level shopping
 7 Basement car parking
Scale: 1 : 2000

the infrastructure thus establishes a discipline for the internal planning of the blocks, and further implies a function of a 3 m planning module within them.

The shopping building adopts a 6 m square planning grid and 6 m × 6 m and 6 m × 12 m structural grid, and takes up the full 144 m width of its double block site, with side malls coinciding with the 90 m spacing of pedestrian entries along north and south sides. Within the frame thus established, the shopping accommodation is divided as in the Knowsley hypermarket project discussed in Chapter 3·4, into three longitudinal bands, separated by two large 12 m wide × 14 m high weather protected and naturally lit pedestrian arcades which run the full 600 m length of the first phase building. The central band, 60 m wide, contains space users, a single major department store, and two public squares. The outer bands, to north and south, accommodate standard units, generally 27 m × 6 m, with frontage both to the internal arcades and to the building's perimeter facing the boulevard car parks. The mall circulation is thus entirely at ground level and shop servicing takes place above, on an open first-floor service loop run from the north-south road dividing the two city blocks of the shopping building, and which is ramped up and over the building where it crosses. At this first-floor level storage accommodation is provided for the shops below, and in addition the structure of the central band is sized to allow the expansion of the larger units of that zone to extend to 3 storeys. In all some 100,858 m² of GLA is provided in this building, scheduled to open in stages between 1977 and 1979, with the possibility of further expansion beyond the department store at its east end to a total of 190,000 m².

Referring again to the question of scale, the designers of Central Milton Keynes, under Chief Architect and Planning Officer Derek Walker, relate the 162 ha of the Central area as: '. . . about the same as that in London contained within Oxford Street between Marble Arch and St Giles' Circus, Park Lane, Piccadilly, and Charing Cross Road. This example is given for the comparative purpose only of size: there is of course no suggestion that Milton Keynes Centre would be as intensively developed, or that it would be used in the same way. It is very unlikely that a visitor to the centre would ever be involved at one time with the whole area, but more likely only with a specific part for one or two specific purposes eg work, shopping, or recreation and so on . . .'

The centre is thus a series of semi-autonomous island functions, developed at similar low intensities of site use, linked and disciplined by the circulation grid. If it could be said of Taby that the central area had fostered an out-of-town form for its shopping centre, it might be said of Milton Keynes that the shopping centre has now fostered an out-of-town form for its CBD, in which the unifying element is the highway and the parking lot strip.

4·15 Site plan of the shopping building in the central area of Milton Keynes New Town, England
Architect: Derek Walker

4·16 The shopping building, Milton Keynes New Town: ground-floor plan

4·17 The shopping building, Milton Keynes New Town: first-floor plan

4·18 Perspective of hall in the shopping building at Milton Keynes New Town

4·19 Perspective of a shopping arcade at Milton Keynes New Town

4·20 Perspective of a garden court in the central area of Milton Keynes New Town

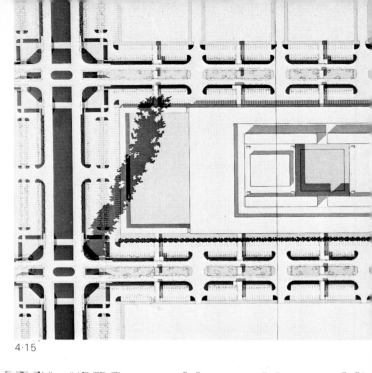

4·15

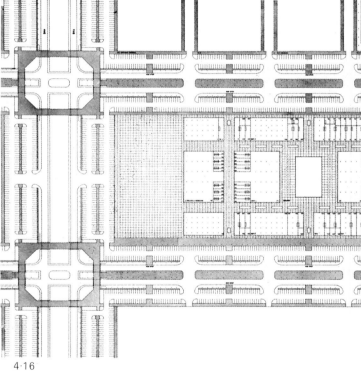

4·16

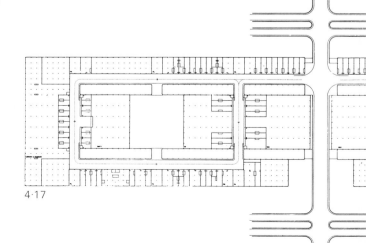

4·17

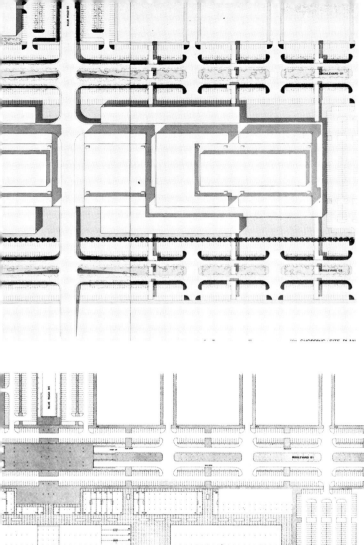

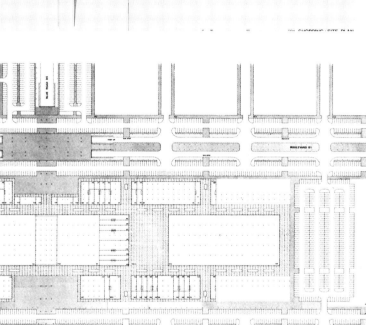

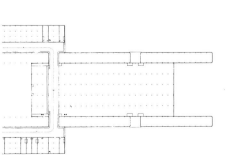

4·18

4·19

4·20

4·2 New Towns 2: Megastructures

From the preceding analysis it can be seen that a point was reached during the late '50s when the specialised requirements of the shopping element of a town centre were recognised in isolation from the general requirements of the central area. Beyond this point the precinct shopping centres developed into independent island buildings which, because of the relatively low intensity of land use of their New Town locations, could closely resemble the corresponding forms of out-of-town centres or even postulate alternatives for them. In a sense this tendency was a natural extension of the premise in the planning philosophy of the first post-war New Towns of 'rigid functional zoning of city plans, with green belts between the areas reserved to the different functions',[3] for if the central area could be isolated as a function of the town so also could its constituent parts be isolated from one another, or at least solved individually, as at Milton Keynes, in independent reservations. As with the shopping precinct, so also the office precincts, the 'City Club' precinct, the 'technocentre' precinct and so on.

This view was challenged by an alternative line of New Town centres which became explicit with the publication of the Hook and Cumbernauld proposals in the UK in 1961 and 1962. The term 'megastructure' is used here to describe the buildings of this second series of New Town centres, because their shopping element was conceived as being a part and major generator of a larger physical urban structure. While the images which they invoked might be various, ranging from the romantic to the futuristic, they began with the same awareness in the late '50s of the increasing specialisation of building types and levels in car ownership which led to the development of the precinct centres. The megastructure centres however, and for differing reasons, proposed high density solutions, and thus offered a set of alternative possibilities more relevant to the problems of redevelopment in the centre of existing cities.

The design for the centre of Nordweststadt, a new town lying 6 km to the north of Frankfurt, formed an early example of the development of the earlier planning principles of the New Town centres in this direction. The result of a competition held in 1961 and won by Apel and Beckert, it represented a concentration of the mixed uses of those earlier centres into a layered complex in which the whole central area, and not just its individual buildings, had a vertical as well as a horizontal organisation. Its extent was defined by a one-way loop distributor road which described a site area approximately 360 × 230 m and served a car-parking floor covering almost the whole extent of the centre at its lowest level and establishing with its planning requirements the structural grid for the decks above. Servicing to the centre, as well as bus stopping points, occur at the next level, above which is the main concourse level, a network of open pedestrian malls and squares between the individual commercial, social and entertainment buildings of the complex, and extending across the surrounding moat of the road loop at five points in bridges connecting with the pedestrian systems of the surrounding housing areas. This character of the main deck, supporting individual buildings on an artificial pedestrian plane and bridging over the surrounding traffic routes, recalls Le Corbusier's plan for the centre of Saint-Dié of 1945. Within the context of post-war New Town plans Nordwestzentrum is in effect

a precinct centre raised on a supporting substructure of those vehicular uses with which, it was now felt, the earlier single-level solutions could no longer adequately cope. Although never implemented, the proposals for a New Town at Hook, Hampshire, published in 1961 by the London County council, formed one of the most imaginative plans produced for a British New Town, and considerably influenced future planning thought. Abandoning the hierarchical arrangement of facilities and radial dispersal of neighbourhood units of the earlier British New Towns, it proposed a town linear in plan, formed around the spine of its central area, itself linear:

'A strong central area was conceived as the dominant focus of the town's social, business and intellectual life, projecting outwards along the main pedestrian routes into the inner residential areas. To effect this the central area would need to be fully integrated with housing in and around it, and designed as the town's main pedestrian meeting-place, served but not dominated by the motor vehicle. This could be done by building over most of the central car parking and service areas and so avoiding the isolation of the central area by a ring of car parks from the remainder of the town.'[4]

As at Farsta and Frölunda, '. . . a multi-level central area of this kind can most easily be sited in an existing valley, where the top deck can be placed like a lid over the valley.' On the pedestrian deck an informal layout appeared to be the aim though there were certain strong determinants in the design. It was stated that well defined pedestrian entries would lead from housing surrounding the centre and converge from either side on focal points along the axis of the centre. The focal points would be the locations of major retail stores, key public buildings and office buildings and, in a general sense, conform to commercial practice in predetermining the flow of pedestrians. It was accepted in the plan that it was vital to maintain continuity of retail shopping frontage. The common link in forming the spine of entertainment areas, quiet areas, market, public, office and governmental areas was to be the continuity of retailing shopping.

Below the deck the vehicular routes, car parking and service areas were to lie along the floor of the valley, based upon a central spine road generating a series of one-way service road loops on either side, between the central spine road and outer parallel distributor roads. Anti-clockwise in their circulation, each of these loops defined in incremental unit of the centre, approximately 120 m × 140 m, by the addition of which it would grow along its length. In the middle of each unit a common service hoist point was located by which the upper deck was serviced, while bus stops, ramps, escalators and stairs were positioned around its perimeter.

The traffic circulation pattern proposed for Central Hook was an important step forward in recognition of much higher levels of car ownership than had been designed for in the earlier New Towns. Since it was not taken beyond the Master Plan stage, however, it did not investigate the difficulties of reconciling a variety of incompatible structures to a single support deck and its car parking and circulation spaces below, nor were the internal requirements of the shopping element, necessary to produce a successful shopping centre and partly instrumental in establishing its separateness in the precinct centres, developed in depth.

The notion that the linear form of the central area, as well as suiting traffic requirements, might also place it

Key:
1 Ichigaya connecting with
  Chuo Line
2 Tokyo Station connecting
  with Keihin Line and subway
3 Office building district
4 1st Cycle in Bay: office
  building district
5 New to Kaido Line and
  underground highway
6 2nd Cycle in Bay: New
  Tokyo station
7 3rd Cycle in Bay: Tokyo
  Harbour
8 4th Cycle in Bay: Government district
Not to scale

4·21 Tokyo Bay Plan: traffic
circulation diagram
Architects and Planners:
Kenzo Tange and Associates

within walking distance of all parts of the town, and thus substantiate its integration and dominance within the plan, was taken up also at Cumbernauld. Of the 70,000 original target population, 70% were to be housed within ½ km of some part of the linear centre, and all within a 20 minutes walk of it. Following the preparation of Hugh Wilson's first planning proposals in 1958, the design for the town centre was published in 1962. Writing in the following year, Geoffrey Copcutt described his scheme:

'On the ridge and upper southern slope of the Cumbernauld hill, 200 ft. above the reconstructed Glasgow–Stirling trunk road, will rise a single citadel-like structure nearly half a mile long, 200 yards wide and up to eight storeys high. Elevated over a unidirectional vehicular system, this multi-level development, with provision for most of the commercial, civic, religious, cultural and recreational uses for a population of 70,000 will be the largest single employment source, traffic generator and land-space user in the town.'[5]

Despite its location on the crest of a ridge, rather than a valley bottom, the basic organisation of Cumbernauld was to be similar to that proposed for Hook, with pedestrian circulation fed from each side of the linear form onto a deck structure below which traffic circulation, parking and service bays would operate. Again the organisation of the lower level was based on a central spine route, with flanking parallel distributor roads and service and parking areas between. The design of the superstructure to the deck was to be much more cohesive, however, with three 100 m long ranges of penthouse structures providing a dominant 'element of visual and physical control'.[5] The seductiveness of the 1962 design produced wide interest and acclaim, matched later, upon the completion of Phase I in 1966–67, with perhaps over-compensatory doubts and criticism.

Key:
1 Service roads and connecting road
2 Distributor road, one-way
  traffic
3 Service roads, two-way
4 Underdeck service zones
  with bus stops, ramps and
  escalator to pedestrian deck
  above
Not to scale

4·22 Hook New Town,
England: traffic circulation
diagram of town centre
Architects and Planners:
London County Council
Architect's Department
(subsequently the Greater
London Council Department
of Architecture and Civic
Design)

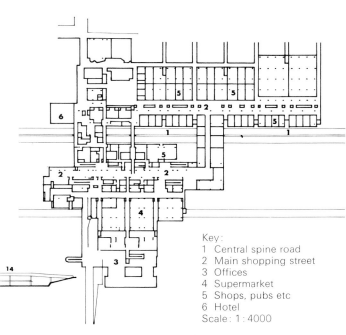

Key:
1 Central spine road
2 Main shopping street
3 Offices
4 Supermarket
5 Shops, pubs etc
6 Hotel
Scale: 1:4000

4·24 Cumbernauld New Town Centre, Scotland Plan: main mall-
level phases 1 and 2
Architects: Cumbernauld Development Corporation
Chief architects: Hugh Wilson, Dudley Leaker, Ken Davie
Principal architect: Geoffrey Copcutt

Key:
1 Restaurant   9 Supermarket
2 Office chamber   10 Storage retail
3 Public house   11 Loading dock
4 Library   12 Penthouses
5 Main shopping street 13 Hotel
6 Offices   14 Pedestrian approach from
7 Central spine road   North
8 Parking   Scale: 1:2000

4·23 North-south section through the first stage of Cumbernauld
New Town Centre, Scotland

A comparatively small part of the total centre, the first stage provided 10,800 m² of shopping space and almost 4,000 m² of offices together with banks, health centre, library, hotel, public hall, 35 of the penthouse maisonettes and car-parking for about 400 cars out of the eventual planned total of 5,000 spaces.

The subsequent criticisms of Cumbernauld centre as a shopping centre arise from the fact that that aspect of its function was overlaid by a series of other concepts which were in conflict with it. Among these were the notion that the centre should visually express its functional dominance of the town, the idea that it should achieve a satisfactory mix of uses by literally piling them on top of one another and should again express this in fragmented forms and circulations, and the adoption of a brutalist aesthetic to clad the complexity thus produced. The application of these concepts to the shopping centre programme gave rise to a number of paradoxical results. Regarding the 'citadel-like' intent, which evoked from others analogies to Italian hill towns and medieval cathedrals, the ridge-top siting had the disadvantage not only of circulation difficulties discussed in the Hook report, but also of maximum exposure to a climate which Geoffrey Copcutt, in the same description referred to earlier, vividly described:

'The climate on this exposed hilltop includes annually one month of snow, one month of fog, 200 raindays and seven months from the first to the last screen frosts. It is in addition an area of high humidity and the Beaufort Force diagram accompanying the general plan illustrates the severity of the winds.'[5]

It was therefore decided to enclose the centre in 'a single envelope wherein all journeys will be free of hazard'. Yet the parallel requirement for a complex and broken external form with voids, openings and terraces, paradoxically produced a covered shopping centre with an inhospitable internal climate. Again, the whole concept of the centre is built around the creation of articulated and rationally ordered circulation systems, yet these were elaborated to the point where they provided an inefficient shopping circulation, with shopping occurring on five different floor levels and short-circuiting occurring between car parks and the phase one magnet store. Similarly the building was given extremely utilitarian finishes, predominantly exposed concrete, and yet it was costly in its resolution of incompatible structures within a common section.

Whether or not these contradictions were inevitable corollaries of the initial concept of Cumbernauld, the complex sculptural expression of its nature as a town centre appeared to subordinate its more limited objective as a shopping centre. While the refusal to isolate the shopping element in a precinct independant of the rest of the centre could be held to be an important virtue, it seemed that the result was in conflict. The next generation of New Towns therefore attempted to find solutions in which appropriate forms for the shopping element could be developed within a megastructure idea as convincing as those of Cumbernauld and Hook. In doing this the shopping centre did become a distinct element within its central area framework, and much of the difficulty, but also potential richness of the Cumbernauld solution was thereby avoided. Before discussing these it is worth considering another, earlier, centre in which the intentions of creating a mix of uses together with a complex internal circulation were attempted.

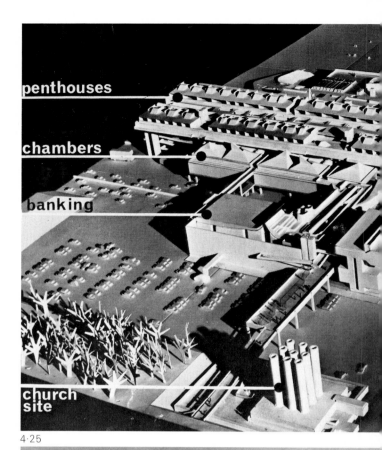

4·25

4·27

retail hall

roads

hotel

4·25 Cumbernauld New Town: aerial view of first phase model of the Central Area from the north

4·26 Perspective of supermarket and penthouses in the Central Area of Cumbernauld New Town

4·27 View of supermarket and penthouses in the Central Area of Cumbernauld New Town

4·26

Although much smaller than the Cumbernauld proposals, and thus much simpler in terms of its provision for traffic circulation, Ralph Erskine's Lulea Shopping Centre in northern Sweden makes an interesting comparison with it. The concept for the project was developed by the architects in an earlier scheme for the town of Kiruna in the mountains well north of the polar circle. Describing this they write:

'This "sub-arctic centre" included dwellings, shops, restaurants etc. and even a glazed nursery garden, grouped round a system of covered and heated streets and squares. The same principle was applied to the Lulea centre. As in the arcaded and mat-hung streets of tropical countries, climatic protection is extended outside the building, and includes the public streets and meeting places. Since, however, it is cold air, heat loss, and snow and ice which have to be met, and not sun radiation, the open structures of the hot climates must here be exchanged for compact heat economical buildings with a protective skin covering the whole structure and with moderate window areas where glass is not essential. These principles can of course be applied to all architecture in cold climates, and in larger

units of city-centre type can become a conception of a roofed unit covering several blocks, with covered connections to secondary units.

'The Lulea project consists of two interconnected buildings, the one with the majority of the shops, a cinema, restaurants, cafes, and it is intended, a hotel; the other with service functions—loading bays storage space, parking and garage space, and an amusement and exhibition area. The shop building is largely complete and is already in use, the service building is under construction (1954).

'The streets of the city are drawn into the buildings through a warm air curtain, and continue as a system of 'public spaces' with varying size and character. Selling takes place partly direct to the public through opened shopfronts, cafés and restaurants with tables on the public spaces, a cinema opening from the main hall, an upper terrace with service shops, beauty parlours and so on—all the life of a city centre. Dances and religious meetings, fashion parades, sales' drives and art exhibitions, follow one another in the central hall and there the people of Lulea meet one another, talk and drink coffee. There is no doubt that this has become the central square of Lulea, giving

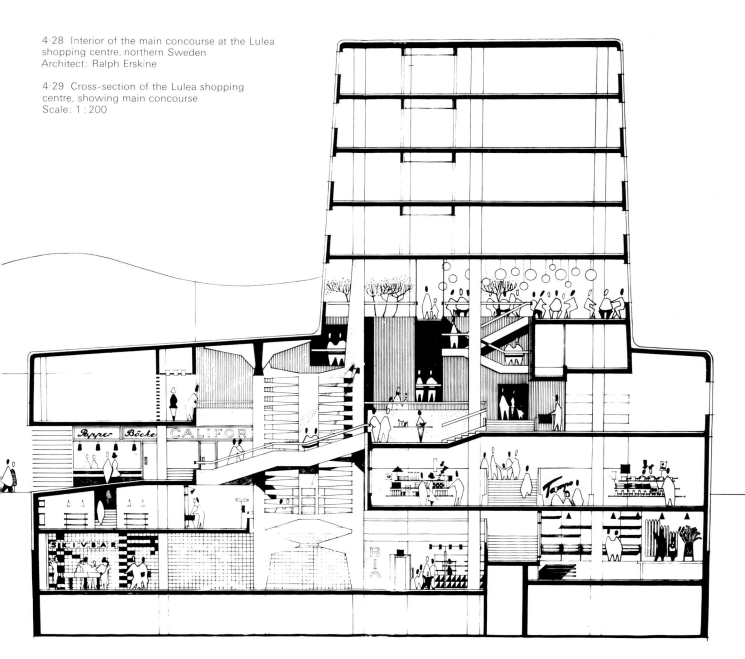

4·28 Interior of the main concourse at the Lulea shopping centre, northern Sweden
Architect: Ralph Erskine

4·29 Cross-section of the Lulea shopping centre, showing main concourse
Scale: 1 : 200

possibilities in its artificial climate for a social life which has hitherto been impossible during the long dark winter in the north, and hardly possible in its often chilly summer.'

Despite its small size, occupying a block some 80 × 25 m, the shopping building provides sales area on three main floors, with storage floors above and below. This is further complicated by half-levels, galleries and bridges which are formed within the building. The complex circulation system thus created is tied together in the central hall which rises through the middle of the block and to which each of the levels refer. This, 'the central square of Lulea', forms the heart of the building, from which malls extend outwards to tunnel and bridge their way across to the service building and establish a new centre circulation within the old. Like the old, the new building is subject to change, and, writing 6 years later, in 1960, the architects note:

'The structure of shops in the centre has changed, the multiple store and the effective small shops expanding in size at the expense of weak shops, and certain active shops who could not find sufficient extra space moving out.'
and then a postscript in 1972:

'Due to certain changes which have taken place in Lulea and its centre during these 18 years of the life of Lulea Shopping Centre, the question has recently been raised as to whether the building should be rebuilt and put to other uses.'

It would be sad if this should occur, for, in response to a severe climate, the Lulea centre was exceptional in its early intimation of one option for the urban core, as in its architectural vitality. In its concern with mixture of uses, climatic control and use of materials, it shared many of the intentions expressed at Cumbernauld, yet its solution was in a sense the opposite. Its organisation is dominated by the internal space, rather than the external form; in its exterior it is rather simple and unassertive, while it is the interior that becomes a playground of board-marked concrete structure.

The history of the Lulea Centre, whereby its brief was radically altered during the design and construction stages to quadruple its size, followed during its life by internal changes in the size and disposition of tenancies, and culminating within 18 years of its opening with plans to redevelop it, illustrates a problem which received considerable attention in the design of the 'Mark Three' New Town centres which followed Cumbernauld. For while shopping floorspace calculations might predict gross areas of accommodation which would be required at stages in the town's growth, the breakdown of that overall area could not be anticipated, and would be subject to change throughout the planning and letting periods, as well as during the building's life. Yet that breakdown into multiple stores, supermarkets, service units, specialised trades, and so on, would produce very specific requirements of both the general layout of the centre, and of its ability to service particular elements within it. While the principles of the circulation systems developed for Hook and Cumbernauld offered a basis for a solution to this problem, the highly specific forms imposed upon them appeared to limit their ability to respond to change, as had occurred at Lulea. In the next stage of development, of which the British centres at Runcorn and Irvine are examples, attempts were made to meet this difficulty with designs which owed much to contemporary studies of other buildings uses, such as Arup Associates' plan for Loughborough University, in which the ability of the design to accept change and growth was a priority. In each example a drastic simplification of the mix of uses in section was entailed, and the notion of using shopping as a 'filler' or linking element between non-retail uses in the centre, as in the early New Towns and at Hook and Cumbernauld, was abandoned. Instead the shopping centre, as a dense, highly serviced building capable of accommodating change, was proposed as the generator of systems of structure, services and circulation which would establish an urban megastructure for the central area as a whole.

The implications of this can be seen in the way in which the circulation systems proposed at Hook are developed in the Runcorn centre. Like Hook, a series of anti-clockwise rotational one-way road loops is established for the traffic circulation at ground level, with a pedestrian deck above feeding out to higher ground surrounding the basin in which the building is located. Again, cores of vertical circulation are provided within the loops to connect the two major levels. At Runcorn however these cores are not simply notional circulation points, but become the nodes for structural, services and circulation systems by which the building volume is supported. 18 ft (5·5 m) square on plan and spaced 108 ft (33 m) apart in both directions, they establish a 'supergrid' within which the building, and beyond it the whole central area, is developed. At main deck level they become the sole structural elements supporting wide span roof structures between them, and providing clear sales area which can be subdivided at will. Below deck level, the more heavily loaded shop storage areas and service roads are accommodated, and secondary structure, generally on an 18 ft (5·5 m) square grid, provided to support the sales deck above as well as mezzanine floors which can be introduced within the storage spaces. Car parking is not, as at Hook or Cumbernauld, provided below the main shopping deck, but in flanking multi-storey structures to east and west.

A similar basic disposition of elements was adopted for the centre of Irvine New Town in Scotland, which, with a first phase completion in 1975, followed some three years after Runcorn. Unlike Runcorn however it was to be built on to an existing town and on a more constrained site. Formerly an important port on the Firth of Clyde, the old town of Irvine had grown inland to become separated from the sea by a river, railway line and industrial strip. It was intended that the central area for the new town designated

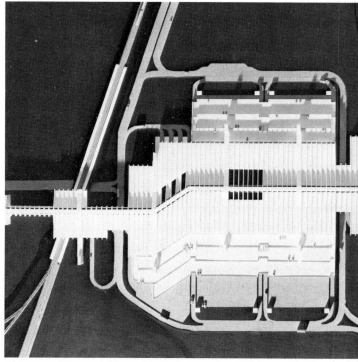

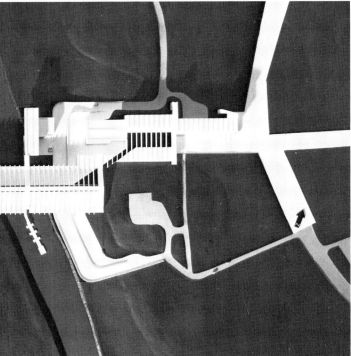

around the old, should reconnect it to the sea and develop its foreshore area as a major amenity for the region. The new shopping centre and commercial area was therefore to establish a bridgehead across the existing thresholds, to generate growth westwards towards the foreshore, and to shift the centre of gravity of existing development into itself as the core of a linear development extending back into the existing town and forward into new leisure, housing and education developments by the sea. Rather than an omni-directional supergrid as at Runcorn therefore, a linear form was adopted for the Irvine central area megastructure, in which major east-west spines of circulation were supplemented by secondary north-south feeders. The pedestrian deck level, growing directly out of the higher ground of the existing town centre, established a continuous route across river and principal roads, with servicing and storage areas below. Above this level the roof was designed as a services 'umbrella', with continuous plant room spine ducts coinciding with alternative positions of the main east-west malls running below, and carrying main air-handling plant and service distribution lines. At right angles to these was a secondary system of rib ducts for small plant items and secondary service distribution, and extending outwards from the building on the positions of north-south side malls.

The two schemes of Runcorn and Irvine are discussed in Chapter 6 as Case Studies, in which the background to their development is described in greater detail. In the present context, their importance lies in their attempt to develop the ideas proposed at Hook and Cumbernauld into an urban structure compatible with those changed circumstances which elsewhere have de-urbanised shopping or de-structured its urban context. The first proposes a system for incremental growth, potentially omni-directional; the second a system of linear growth, in which the primary and secondary circulations of pedestrians and services becoming the ordering elements of the urban megastructure. While developing solutions specifically for the shopping centre, they intended that these should be a part of an urban solution in which the street, now an all-weather pedestrian route, should be returned to the city, with the shopping, office and other uses occurring as specialisations along its lengths, rather than as private precincts separate from its public function.

4·3 European Main Centres

In his book *The Property Room*, Oliver Marriott describes the reaction of Fred Maynard, partner with Louis Freedman in the newly formed Ravenseft Properties Limited, on a chance visit to Plymouth in 1949; 'I was amazed. The whole of the town centre was flat. I rang up Louis at once and said "There are no shops here".'

The wholesale disappearance of city-centre shopping facilities during the war, to be followed by their wholesale replacement, produced new agencies of large-scale development whose activities continued beyond the reconstruction period to provide the framework for almost all post-war integrated centre developments. Following the

clearance of 60 ha of central Plymouth by bombing in
the spring of 1941, the city took compulsory purchase
powers to acquire the central area and a plan for its eventual
reconstruction was drawn up in 1943 by the city engineer,
J. Paton-Watson, and Sir Patrick Abercrombie. By 1949
the local authority had reached agreement with two insurance companies to finance an initial development of two
blocks of shops, and this was followed by an agreement
with Ravenseft to act as developers, applying the funds to
the site to produce the required buildings. This tripartite
arrangement, whereby local authorities assembled large
sites by the use of CPO's and provided a planning framework, and private development companies carried out the
work funded by financial institutions, proved irresistible.
For the new development companies it was reinforced
by the system of building licenses, which were only granted
for replacing bombed shops or shops for new housing
estates, so that cooperation with local authorities was
essential. On the strength of their early projects at Bristol,
Plymouth and Exeter, Ravenseft, the first company in the
field went on to conclude agreements with local authorities
in Hull, Swansea, Sheffield, Sunderland and Coventry.

The form of the first such schemes was a kind of 'rationa-
lised' version of the old pattern, with shops planned, block
by block, along straighter and broader high streets. Such a
plan was also prepared for the reconstruction of the
centre of Rotterdam, but was then abandoned and a new
scheme adopted and one which when opened in 1953,
marked the beginning of the evolution of the post-war
integrated centre. And with their Lijnbaan pedestrian
precinct, with its cruciform of wide, canopied pedestrian
shopping streets, Van der Broek and Bakema established
not only the new solution to the building problem, but
also the form of the new post-war architecture in Holland.

In England the equivalent development in terms of its
novelty and impact was the upper precinct at Coventry,
completed in 1955. That the form of the new European
precinct developments was rooted in the progressive
planning philosophies of the pre-war period, rather than
in an emergence of new post war shopping patterns as in the
case of the contemporary American out-of-town precincts,
is shown by the fact that the principles of the new Coventry
centre were established within 3 months of the destruction
of the old in the first raid of November 1940. In February
1941 the City Council adopted the plan prepared by Donald
Gibson, the City Architect, including proposals for a
pedestrian shopping core, with two levels of shops incorporating an upper pedestrian gallery and rear-access servicing and car planning. This plan, produced in response to
the exhortation of Lord Reith, Minister of Works and Buildings for 'bigness and boldness' in designs for the reconstruction,[6] was developed and confirmed by 1949, by
which time the legal and financial powers of the Town and
Country Planning Act, 1944 had provided a basis for its
implementation and for the acquisition by the City of 100
hectares of its central area. Following the completion of
the first stage in 1955, the development continued under
Arthur Ling, the Chief Architect and Planning Officer, into
the lower precinct, and the cruciform plan with covered
market and multi-storey car park facilities established.

Although acclaimed as a model development, the
Coventry precincts aroused controversy in their use of a
second, upper mall network, relatively weak in terms of
pedestrian flow. As with the similar, though more restricted,
experiments in the American open centres, it was held that
this made doubtful commercial sense. Yet it was precisely

4·32 Shopping precinct at Lijnbaan, Rotterdam, Holland
Architects: Van der Broek and Bakema

this element which formed the basis of the next stage of
development.

The Europa Centre in Berlin exemplifies the greater
density of site use and elaboration of the second mall
level which the integrated centres had begun to display by
the early '60s. Completed in 1965, this development forms
an appropriate example to follow that of Coventry, both in
its location in the blitzed centre of a city and in its similar
juxtaposition to a surviving ecclesiastical remnant, in this
case the Kaiser Wilhelm church on the Breitscheidplatz. In
contrast to Coventry however, the site area is only 2 ha,
upon which the architects, Helmut Hentrich and Hubert
Petschnigg, accommodated a 22-storey office building,
two cinemas, a hotel and numerous subsidiary uses in
addition to some 20,000 m² of retail and service trades
floor space. The shopping centre forms a densely packed,
three-layer podium for the other uses. Within the roughly
triangular site, the lowest shopping level, below ground,
provides storage areas for the shops above fed by a service
road entering at the base of the triangle, to the east, and
splitting to form two cul-de-sac routes along north and
south perimeters. At the same time a pedestrian underpass
from the Breitscheidplatz to the west enters the apex of the
triangle as a shopping mall running into an open square in
the heart of the development with circulation to the upper
levels. At ground-floor level the shops are grouped in
blocks between covered malls surrounding both the vertical
circulation court, and a second, larger square, used, like
that in the Rockefeller Centre on Manhattan, as an ice
skating rink in winter. Both this level and that above are

4·33 The Europa Center, Berlin, West Germany
Architects: H. Hentrich and H. Petschnigg
A) Upper-level plan
B) Lower-level plan

served directly from a multi-storey car park of 1,000 spaces lying on the adjacent site to the east along the base of the triangle. In addition the upper, first-floor shopping level is served by bridge links across the bounding roads to north and south, while its roof forms a roof-garden for the cinemas, restaurants, hotel and office tower above.

The high density of site use in this development therefore produced a multi-level shopping form in which each level was supported by a pedestrian circulation pattern into and through it. This was an important step, and equivalent to the similar discovery of the principles upon which a second shopping level could be supported in the third stage of the American out-of-town centre development. For the integrated centre it had the additional implication that, for a dense urban shopping centre on a restricted site, it was not only possible but highly desirable for the urban core around the centre to be as highly layered as the shopping element, in order that strong pedestrian movements could be sustained at all levels.

Open multi-level shopping centres of this type continued to be developed through the '60s, and in the UK the Croydon Whitgift Centre indicated the commercial success of the pattern where each shopping level was directly accessible from a pedestrian movement outside the site. By the time they began the construction of this centre, in 1965, Ravenseft had been joined by a large number of other development companies vieing to carry out central area developments throughout the UK, no longer to replace facilities lost during the war, but now to redevelop or expand existing centres. In that year R. B. Morgan of the Cooperative Wholesale Society drew up a list of new shopping projects in the UK either being built or else suffic-iently advanced for developers to have been nominated. This list, which he considered incomplete, comprised almost 500 schemes, in which over 100 development companies were involved. In only 18 cases were local authorities themselves acting as developers.[7]

Contemporaneously with the Cumbernauld experiment, designers of centres in existing towns were similarly attempting to combine the enclosure of new centres and their development on a number of levels—two advances which in the American case were taken singly. Through a combination of circumstances, the first examples of this, at the Bullring in Birmingham and the Elephant and Castle in London, were not immediately successful. Initiated in the same month, September 1959,[8] both schemes were seen as the first examples of a revolutionary new form of shopping centre in their planning of a large number of units under one roof and on many levels. The architects for each project— Sidney Greenwood with T. J. Hirst of John Laing, and Boissevain and Osmond, respectively—visited North America and both schemes claimed parentage from examples of one-stop shopping centres. Yet neither could have been built in the USA, where finance would not be available to a development lacking pre-lets to major magnet stores, and both schemes suffered from difficulties in their siting and in the complexity of their multi-level arrangements. At the Bullring five different levels of shops were created, and while these were supported by a 15 m fall across the site and by routes into the development at the lowest level from the central bus station, at a middle level from a 550-space car park and at the top level from a bridge-link to further shops and rail station, the complexity was such as to discourage potential tenants so that an initial letting campaign was abandoned until the project was completed in 1964 and could be inspected. Three shopping levels were formed in the Elephant and Castle scheme which opened in the following year. Of these only the lower ground floor was firmly connected to surrounding pedestrian flows, the others being dependant upon an external ramped approach and the small amount of shopping traffic generated by the adjacent main line rail station. The sites for both schemes were by-products of urban road proposals and, as it transpired, were not ideally placed to compete with nearby established centres. For these various reasons both projects experienced difficulties in letting their units, a total of 140 at the Bullring and 120 at the Elephant and Castle, in their early years. They were not therefore immediately followed by a rush of similarly ambitious projects. Instead the central area shopping developments which followed in the UK during the '60s tended to concentrate either on solving the problem of levels, as at Whitgift, or on more simple enclosed centres.

A more modest example of the enclosed centres which now began to be developed, and one which demonstrated well the possibilities of relating new schemes to strong existing pedestrian flows and magnet store locations within city centres, is the Grosvenor-Laing development at Chester in England, completed in 1965. The historic character of the walled city centre of Chester, within which the street pattern of the original Roman settlement had been preserved and embellished by its unique double level of pedestrian 'Rows' about the crossing of its main streets, presented a considerable problem for the introduction of a modern shopping facility, the justification for which lay in the strong draw of the city for durable sales over its surrounding region. The solution adopted was to develop within the core of one of the blocks of development adjacent to the cross and to link pedestrian malls through to the rows around its north and west edges, thus forming a new circuit of which the existing premium frontage around the perimeter would form an integral part. The Grosvenor Estate, a major land-owner in the city, acquired some 1·5 ha of this core area and then entered a partnership with John Laing and Sons Ltd., developers also of the Bullring project, to carry out the development which comprised a department store, supermarket and 72 standard units in addition to a restaurant, banqueting suite, motor showroom, 2,300 m² of offices and a 600-space, multi-storey car park.

By utilising a fall in ground level from north to south across the site, the architects, Sir Percy Thomas and Son, were able to form an enclosed pedestrian mall network which, from a square in the centre of the development, ran north to meet street level, west to the upper row level, and south to terminate in a ramped connection to grade. A service level could then be formed below, fed from the south-east corner of the site and comprising shop storage and service roads, while, from the same vehicular entry point to the site, cars could ramp up to parking decks located on top of the development. The resulting development thus introduced a major element of shopping floor space into the heart of the existing city, firmly linked to its existing major frontages, but unobtrusively, and necessarily so since 'Chester's face is her fortune, it is the character of the city: its rows and the charm of its architecture and environment generally which draws the visitor and which chiefly accounts for its high figure of retail trade per head of population.'[9] Apart from the southern frontage of the block, where the new development exposes itself, the implant could therefore claim that visually, if not in terms

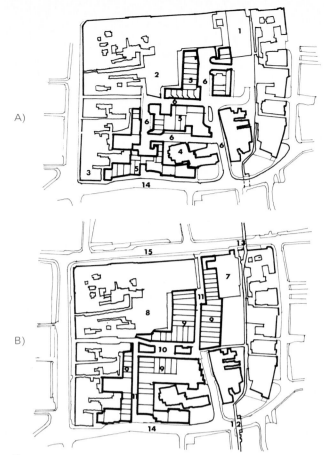

A)

B)

Key:
1 Grosvenor Hotel
2 Brown's department store
3 Church
4 Church
5 New shops (lower level) storage
6 Underdeck service road
7 Grosvenor Hotel (upper level)
8 Brown's department store (upper level)
9 New shops (upper level)
10 Central square
11 Shopping concourse
12 Footbridge across Pepper Street
13 Footbridge across Eastgate Street
14 Pepper Street
15 Eastgate Street

Scale: 1 : 4000

4·34 Chester re-development, England
Architects: Sir Percy Thomas and Partners
A) Ground-level plan at Pepper Street
B) Ground-level plan at Eastgate Street

4·35 View of the lower-level main concourse at the Middleton shopping centre, Lancashire, England
Architects: Turner, Lansdown and Holt and Partners with Percy Gray

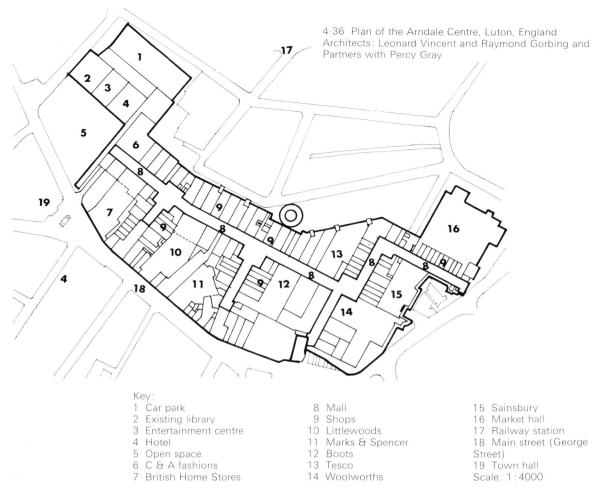

4·36 Plan of the Arndale Centre, Luton, England
Architects: Leonard Vincent and Raymond Gorbing and
Partners with Percy Gray

Key:
1 Car park
2 Existing library
3 Entertainment centre
4 Hotel
5 Open space
6 C & A fashions
7 British Home Stores

8 Mall
9 Shops
10 Littlewoods
11 Marks & Spencer
12 Boots
13 Tesco
14 Woolworths

15 Sainsbury
16 Market hall
17 Railway station
18 Main street (George Street)
19 Town hall
Scale: 1 : 4000

of traffic generation, it was a surreptitious and benificent growth.

The symbiotic relationship of new and old developments, whereby the latter provides established magnets and the former additional floorspace and car parking, was the basis of a number of successful covered shopping centre schemes carried out by Sam Chippendale of Arndale, latterly part of Town and City Properties Limited, during the '60s in the UK. Among so many developments in Europe claiming progressive North American parentage, the Arndale Centres were unique at this time in putting together a package based on the simple precepts of the American second stage centres, but applicable to the centres of provincial English towns. In the first Arndale Centre at Crossgates, Leeds some 8 ha of relatively low cost back-land were acquired on a block bounded on two sides by main streets. Within this site a simple dog-leg mall arrangement was formed, with magnet stores grouped about a square at its change of direction. The magnets for the open ends of the mall, which had a length of 120 m in each direction, were in effect the existing streets into which the malls connected and which now formed two sides of a square circuit, with the more comfortable, enclosed, heated and pedestrian-only malls of the new development forming the remainder. Car parking and servicing areas were formed around the 'L' of the new building, providing 400 parking spaces for about 15,000 m² GLA, a proportion of 2·7 spaces per 100 m² or about half of the American out-of-town standard.

The transformation of cheap back-land into prime shopping space; the adoption of a simple circulation, with well-disposed magnets and strong connections to car parking and existing shopping flows; and finally the enclosure and climatic control of the pedestrian street with all that that entailed in the way of open shop-fronts, mall features and functions in the square; all of these things combined to form a desirable package for the local authorities of industrial towns seeking to modernise their central area facilities during the '60s. Writing on the history of post-war development in Britain, the company later described how, at that time, 'Local Authorities began to adopt a more positive approach to the acquisition of key sites in order to provide the opportunity for comprehensive redevelopment.

'This new and enlightened attitude, facilitated by statute, resulted in the recognition by many local authorities, both big and small, of the value of partnership arrangements with reputable and experienced development organisations. Government departments, with an overall responsibility to ensure that Local Authority redevelopment proposals were commercially viable, also saw the advantage in the welding of the powers of Local Authorities and the commercial expertise of the property company. Over forty Local Authorities have now (1973) completed or are in the process of developing central area schemes in cooperation with Town & City Properties Limited.'[10]

It was found in successive developments that the form could also support a secondary upper mall level without benefit of direct pedestrian access or even escalator connections to the main ground floor, and that the introduction of this minor level had the merit of providing lower-rental positions for certain traders while increasing the density of site use. This feature arose perhaps from the typical mall section, very similar to that of the Yorkdale Toronto centre, in which a continuous run of deep clerestorey glazing was introduced between the shop fascia and the high mall ceiling. At the Crossgates centre this mall height permitted the introduction of a first floor cafe overlooking the the central square and connected to it by a free-standing staircase. Variations on this staircase were, along with the ebullient lighting, water and wall relief features, to become a part of the Arndale package, as the upper level was developed at Doncaster, Poole, Nelson and Stretford, generally as an arcade running down one side of the mall and often with two-storey shop units providing internal links between the two floors. In an unusual example, at Middleton near Manchester, the shopping was stretched to three levels by the aid of escalators and the major attraction of a Woolco Superstore on the top floor.

The form could also be extended to considerable size, and in one of the largest of the Arndale schemes, at Luton, some 70,000 m² GLA is encompassed by the development, together with 11,000 m² of office accommodation and 2,500 parking spaces. The mall now becomes not simply a loop off the main street, but a parallel alternative, some 430 m long. Cross malls connect the old and new high streets at approximately 100 m centres, and, as with the multiple stores in the Whitgift Centre and Brown's department store at Chester, major established units along the existing street are given new rear frontage onto the enclosed mall.

Few developments in the '60s were as firmly committed to the environmental control of mall areas as the Arndale Centres, but by the end of the decade the principle of providing at least a considerable degree of shelter, perhaps with a mixture of enclosed malls and open squares, was firmly established. As had happened with the first American centres, roofed areas were often added to open centres to modify the more exposed parts of their malls, while schemes under development during the transitional period were changed from open to enclosed mall solutions, as occurred at the large St James Centre development which Ravenseft was carrying out at the end of Princes Street in Edinburgh. In many of the new central area developments non-retail uses were incorporated, often 'civic and cultural facilities which are so necessary to keep central areas alive after the shops and offices are closed'. The dominance of the shopping element however, both in its relative bulk and in the organisational requirements which it imposed on the development, were generally such that the idea entertained by civic planners, of using shopping as a kind of background linking matrix to the monuments of social and civic life, was abruptly reversed. Instead these might form a rooftop element, a visual foil to enliven the silhouette of the shopping building below, and the edge of the new central core of the town was the perimeter of that building and its mall entrances, rather than, as before, some indefinable point along a street where housing gave way to commercial use.

While the Chester precinct or some of the Arndale Centres, modestly hidden behind existing frontage, might appear as adjuncts to the High Street, rather like the Victorian shopping arcades which were already present in many cities, the radically different organisation which the new enclosed, traffic-segregated centres actually imposed could not be misconstrued where the new development was to form a predominant part of the central area.

The redevelopment of the centre of Blackburn in Lancashire formed such a case, in which the major part of the centre of a town of 100,000 population was to be rebuilt in five phases covering more than 6 ha. While it could be expected that numerous brief changes would occur during the period of such a development, it could nevertheless

4·37

4·38

4·39   Scale: 1 : 2000

4·40

Scale: 1 : 2000

4·37 View of the Blackburn shopping centre, Lancashire,
England showing the office block above and the town hall in the
foreground
Architects: Building Design Partnership

4·38 Ground-level view of the Blackburn shopping centre
showing lift tower to night club

4·39 Main pedestrian-level plan of the Blackburn shopping
centre

4·40 Cross-section of the Blackburn shopping centre

4·41 Parking-level plan of the Blackburn shopping centre

Scale: 1 : 2000

4·41

be planned as a total complex, which would gradually exchange, phase by phase, the mall, service and parking roads of a new centre for the street pattern of the old. Starting in the centre of the overall area, on land already mostly owned by the local authority, the first phase of this scheme was completed in 1967, to be followed in 1971 by the second phase to the east. Each of these phases occupied approximately 2 ha, and together provided 32,000 m² of gross shopping floor space and 1600 car-parking spaces as well as a roof-top entertainments centre and a tower office block extension to the adjacent town hall. Using a site cross-fall from west to east the development could, as at Chester, provide a mall level corresponding to street level on the high side, and a service road and storage level below fed from the east. Given the existing pedestrian traffic along the lower street frontage, a lower mall was also incorporated along one flank of the service road circuit, connected by ramp to the main mall level. Car parking, again as at Chester, was provided at roof level and in multi-storey car parks above the shopping floors. With the same developer, Laing Development Company Ltd in partnership with Blackburn Corporation, the project therefore shared many of the features of the Grosvenor-Laing Chester centre, but without the benefit of a screen of existing frontage. Its distinction lay in the ability of its architects, Building Design Partnership, to make of it an urban architecture coherent both externally and within its network of malls and squares, avoiding the dichotomy of 'prison camp exterior and seedy nightclub interior'[11] with which the new urban shopping centre was to become associated.

The mature Stage 3 Sun Valley/Parly 2 centre form, first mooted at the Whitgift Centre, finally made its appearance as an integrated centre in the UK with the opening in 1972 of the Victoria Centre at Nottingham, developed by The Capital and Countries Property Co Ltd with architects Arthur Swift and Partners.

The influence of the American and French examples upon the form of this project is acknowledged by the development team which made two visits to the U.S.A. and Canada, as well as to Parly 2, and published the results of their research in 'two booklets, *Shopping for Pleasure* in 1969 and *Design for Shopping* in 1970. In their general arrangement and overall dimensions the shopping floors of the Victoria Centre do correspond quite closely to the French precedent. With a straight central main mall on two levels, 14 m wide and 200 m long, major magnets are located according to the same dumbell pattern at their ends, with a Scan superstore to the north, and Jessops department store and Boots multiple store to the south. Habitat and Miss Selfridge stores reinforce these end zones, with 83 units disposed between them providing in total some 60,000 m² GLA, in addition to which a market occupies a central position on both mall levels and provide another 11,000 m². Yet this correspondence is also accidental in the sense that the Victoria Centre was unusual in having a city centre site which, in terms of its overall dimensions and its form, suited it so well The major part of the site had formerly been a main line railway station which had been built at the end of the nineteenth century over some 4 ha of deep cutting to accommodate extensive tracks and sidings. With the closure of this station, and the addition of some adjoining sites, Capital and Counties were thus able to put together a 5·7 ha site in the centre of Nottingham, forming a rectangle 520 m long by 140 m wide at its maximum and an average

of 14 m deep. The two level shopping building then occupied almost the whole of that area at ground and first floor levels, while the cutting was filled with car parking and service areas below. While the shopping arrangements, within the conveniently rectangular site, resemble the out-of-town forms therefore, the surrounding land uses are here piled up within the same land area. Entries from the car parking to the shopping areas occur, not along side malls, but from groups of lifts discharging straight into the centre of the main mall, and continuing up to serve 500 flats which the local authority built above the development in a spine block up to 23 storeys high which runs the length of the centre, using part of its roof area as landscaped open space. In addition to this housing element and the market in the centre itself, cooperation between the developer and Nottingham Corporation also operated in the provision of a main bus station within the development. This lies at the north end of the upper mall and is an important generator of pedestrian traffic for that level, which is otherwise relatively weak in being unconnected to street levels outside the complex, and more remote from the basement car parking.

The resolution of circulation within the Victoria Centre is thus a more complex three-dimensional balancing act than in the out-of-town models, and the greater compression of the development within its site is reflected in its physical character. Its malls are made up of the same colonade, water curtain, and modelled ceiling features as Parly 2, but in the transposition to an urban situation they have become more massive, the shop fronts more cave-like, the decoration more serious and the exteriors more durable.

Although the manipulation of pedestrian flows in this centre occurs largely within its perimeter, the upper mall level does break out at its southern end to bridge Lower Parliament Street and connect with a Safeway store across the road. At its northern end it is also intended to extend it by an enclosed bridge across an urban motorway to connect at ground level to a new housing development area to the north-east.

This feature of the Victoria Centre becomes the major characteristic of those schemes of similar size which are accommodated to less regular sites. In a later Capital and Counties development, at Eldon Square in central Newcastle Upon Tyne, the 4·5 ha site falls into two irregularly shaped parts separated by a main thoroughfare. In such circumstances the self-contained arrangement of a main mall zone of fixed size, fed by side malls to a specific pattern, could not be appropriate. Instead the mall becomes a route through the centre of linked bands of shopping, or rather a number of routes, since it must divide and extend as the site form dictates. Picking up from pavement level in the north-east corner, the mall rises to the main block of shopping in the northern half of the scheme, with two major stores, in the centre of which it forms an enclosed square with escalator connections down to a bus concourse below. A side mall also connects this square northwards to a multi-storey car park with 300, and ultimately 1200, spaces. The main mall continues westward from the square, and then turns south through a further block of shopping, including one major unit, until it reaches Blackett Street, which divides the complex. Being now at first-floor level, the mall bridges Blackett Street to penetrate the southern half of the scheme, which forms an 'L' with a market hall against its southern arm. The mall now divides to run down each arm of the 'L', which has major stores disposed at its angle and at each end. The southward route leads to the market and to a second multi-storey car park of 700 spaces, while the eastward route gives onto another square with access down to a lower mall which discharges at its further end onto pavement level once more. The distance covered from the north east entrance to either of the mall ends in the southern block is about 550 m, and the mall becomes an alternative circulation route added to the city, with magnet stores and spatial incident incorporated along its lengths as appropriate. The building itself, which is served below mall level from independent service loops to each of its halves, must similarly be accommodated to the site constraints, grafting itself onto such existing facades and building fragments as may be required to be retained.

The necessarily more pragmatic layout which the architects, Chapman Taylor and Partners, produced at Eldon Square is paralleled in the design by Hugh Wilson and Lewis Womersley for the most ambitious Arndale Centre, off Market Street in the centre of Manchester. To be completed in three phases between 1975 and 1977, this project will provide over 100,000 m² GLA on its 6 ha site which occupies two large blocks of the city, each previously subdivided by numerous streets, lying astride Cannon Street. The approximately square site area is thus bisected, as at Eldon Square, by a main road. Since this road falls 8 m from east to west across the square, the solution which was adopted was to form two levels of mall circuit, the upper linking to ground levels on the east and linking over Cannon

Street on the west side, and the lower meeting ground levels to the west and connecting under Cannon Street on the east.

This basic organisation, served by a complete service road circuit at basement level, is then disturbed by a number of additional factors. As at Newcastle and Nottingham a bus station forms a major element in the scheme, and is located on the northern half at lower level, breaking the mall circuit at that point. The development includes 5 main space users and a Corporation market hall tactically disposed around its circuit, but in order to further extend its draw its upper mall throws out bridge connections across the surrounding streets to connect it to major multiple and department stores already established on adjacent blocks. Car parking in this project is provided in an 1800 space multi-storey structure at high level across the east side of the complex, and linking to ground at the north-east corner. In addition a direct link is planned with Manchester's new underground rail service.

While the above examples are by no means all of the significant integrated centres which could be discussed, and represent a very small part of the total development which has occurred in European town and city centres since the war, they do perhaps indicate that the stages of evolution of the type have been easier to define in terms of programme intentions than in plan forms. While almost all but the earliest substantiated their revolutionary features by reference to the advances made in out-of-town centre

4·42 The Victoria Centre, Nottingham, England: upper-level and lower-level plans
Architects: Arthur Swift and Partners

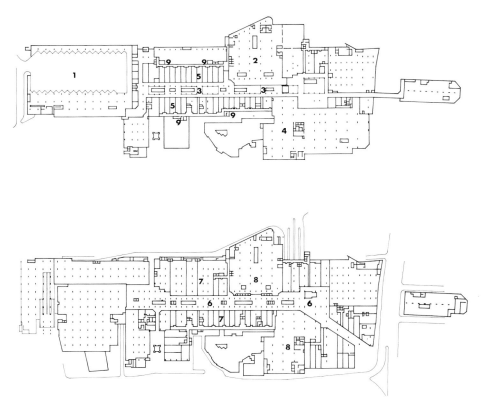

Key:
1 Bus station
2 Corporation market (upper level)
3 Upper-level concourse
4 Department store (upper level)

5 Upper-level shops
6 Lower-level concourse
7 Lower-level shops
8 Department store (lower level)

9 Access to apartment blocks
above centre

Scale: 1 : 4000

design, their debt lay generally in successfully applying the principles, rather than the forms, of that species. Thus the successful examples display the same careful regard for the establishment of balanced pedestrian flows and the timeous introduction of, first, segregation of pedestrian, service and parking traffic circulations, then provision of adequate car parking, and finally enclosure and climatic control of the malls. Yet, because of the fundamental difference in location, these aims had to be satisfied in different ways. In most cases their restricted urban sites were almost entirely filled by the shopping areas alone so that service and storage areas, car parking, and any additional office, leisure or residential accommodation included in the project, must be stacked vertically around that element. The conventional horizontal circulation patterns of the out-of-town centre were therefore replaced by vertical ones, and the creation of good pedestrian flows in the shopping malls depended at a much earlier stage upon the successful arrangement in three-dimensions of the possible contributors to it. The principal horizontal generator of mall traffic was an element not present in the out-of-town centres at all, namely the pedestrian flows established outside its boundaries, and whatever the provision of car parking, and bus and rail links within the complex, its successful relationship to this external context was vital. Thus in both of the schemes discussed which bear a close plan-form resemblance to the out-of-town Stage 3 centre type, the side mall entries lead in, not from surrounding car parking areas, but from adjacent shopping streets. The similarity in plan forms is therefore coincidental in that the application of common principles resulted in similar plan layouts within dissimilar circumstances. At the Victoria Centre, where the interiors most readily invite comparison with Parly 2, the upper mall is dependent on the vertical network of circulation, having no strong side mall connections. Similarly at the Whitgift Centre, which, despite its earlier open mall character had an organisation closer to Parly 2 with each mall level connecting directly to grade on one side of the development, the side malls have the function of tying it to a wider network of pedestrian movements of which its main malls then become a part.

The relationship between the new centres and their surroundings, while vital, was also uneasy, and one for which the out-of-town forms could offer little helpful precedent. Their abrupt introspection, in which the exterior form functions simply as an envelope with gesticulations to attract attention from the highway and indicate entry points, might be admired as non-architecture:

'On the commercial strip the supermarket windows contain no merchandise. There may be signs announcing the day's bargains, but they are to be read by pedestrians approaching from the parking lot. The building itself is set back from the highway and half hidden, as is most of the urban environment, by parked cars. The vast parking lot is in front, not at the rear, since it is a symbol as well as a convenience. The building is low because air-conditioning demands low spaces, and merchandising techniques discourage second floors; its architecture is neutral because it can hardly be seen from the road. Both merchandise and architecture are disconnected from the road. The big sign leaps to connect the driver to the store, and down the road the cake mixes and detergents are advertised by their national manufacturers on enormous billboards toward the highway. The graphic sign in space has become the architecture of this landscape.'[12]

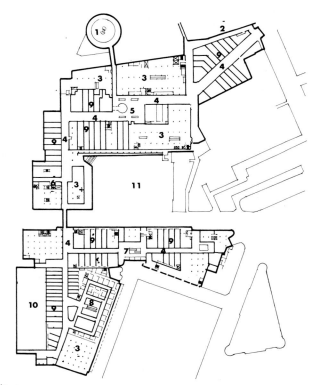

Key:
1 Northern car park
2 Marks & Spencer
3 Multiple stores
4 Malls
5 Northern Square
6 Office lobby
7 Southern Square
8 Greenmarket
9 Shops
10 National car park
11 Eldon Square
Scale: 1 : 4000

4·43 Eldon Square Centre, Newcastle, England: upper-level plan
Architects: Chapman Taylor and Partners

The same could not be true of a dense shopping complex on a tight urban site, and yet the integrated centre was also internally generated to a large degree, its perimeter similarly defined as the limits of a single building complex. In a critique of new shopping centres in The Architectural Review in 1973, Lance Wright emphasised the extent to which the relationship between the new creature and its context remained unresolved:

'Released from the discipline of the street, shopping is faced with the problem of acquiring an urban image of its own. Characteristically vast in extension, squat in height (unless mixed development can come to the rescue), requiring so much elbow room to let its traffic in and out that it must be virtually freestanding, shopping as we know it poses an insuperable problem in respect of urban continuum and coherence . . .

'. . . the building shows a great deal of back to the rest of the town centre, creating an unacceptable image of a "city within a city" . . .

'. . .commerce-plus-road transport have together replaced the social, human-scale city image with the vicious, impersonal image of the "city-of-the-future-which-nobody-wants..[13]

The dilemma is characterised by the uncertain nature of the shopping malls; the centre depends upon their integration with the external pedestrian networks, yet they read as private property; they are potentially the most comfortable, and therefore most social, parts of the city network, yet they may be closed down outside shopping hours; they may be used for any number of unrelated functions, but if a charge is made they become rateable;

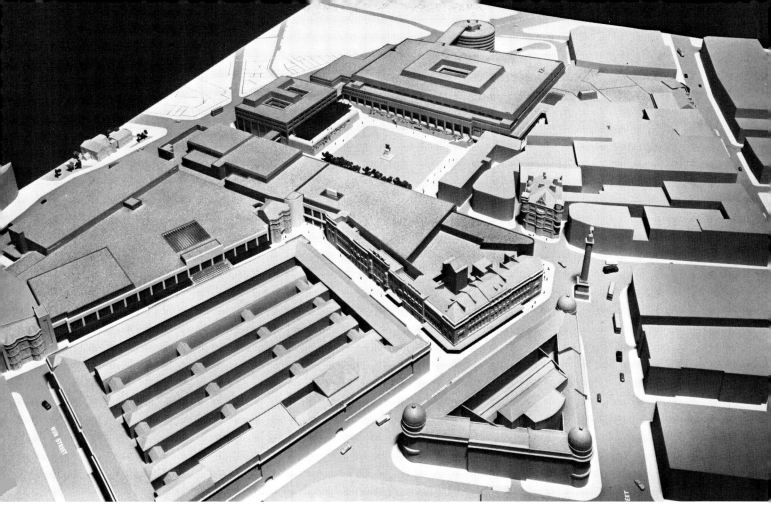

4·44 Air view of model of Eldon Square Centre, Newcastle

they are the natural means of escape in case of fire, yet they lie in the heart of the building, farthest from the open air. In a variety of symbolic and functional contexts the nature of the malls is ambiguous, and not least in terms of their relationship with the ground. Many of the centres discussed covered sufficient areas of their city centres for there to be appreciable differences in levels around their perimeters. Because of the three-dimensional nature of the problem of accommodating each of the articulated uses within the sites these differences were welcomed as providing opportunities for 'naturally' introducing low-level service access, or double mall levels, or car parking access, or whatever. A mall entered at ground level in one

part of the complex may thus emerge at another as an upper level bridge link.

The mall is therefore an 'artificial' thing, in its status, its environment and its relationship to grade. The impression of it as an alternative high-street system, rather than an extension of the existing one, is strong, and in the later examples it is seen how, as the centre becomes larger, it may grow beyond the building perimeter to link to any surrounding uses which may benefit its pedestrian flows. In these examples the shopping centre has become the instigator of a new megastructure within the urban core, and the discomfiture which it causes is a measure of the extent to which it differs from the old.

Key: A) 1 Bus station
2 Market
3 Cannon Street
4 Shopping concourse
5 Central Square
6 Department stores (upper level)
7 Ramp up to car park
8 Public houses (upper level)
9 Shops
10 Office lobby

B) 1 Cannon Street over
2 Market Street over
3 Market
4 Electricity transformer station
5 Plant room
6 Department stores (lower level)
7 Service road
8 Public houses
9 Shop storage
Scale: 1:4000

4·45 Arndale Centre, Manchester, England
Architects: Sir Hugh Wilson and Lewis Womersley
Consultant Architect: Percy Gray

A) Upper-level plan
B) Basement-level plan

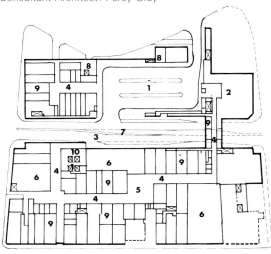

A)

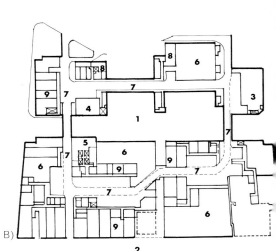

B)

4·4 European District and Local Centres

Although the most dramatic examples of post-war development in integrated centres have occurred in main centre locations, and the efforts to review, and in some cases restructure, the urban core have been most traumatic, significant changes have also occurred in the form of smaller shopping facilities serving district or local needs. This scale of provision was the most widespread area of shopping development between the wars, and particularly in the UK where they were built to meet the needs of the new suburbs and of the expanding chains of multiple and cooperative stores. The typical form was of a row of shops, generally with flats above, and sometimes with canopy protection to the pavement in front. This form continued in the post-war period as sections of older ribbon development were renewed, or new housing areas appeared. Sometimes they simply adopted the format of the ribbon, perhaps, as car ownership increased, being set back a little from the street to allow a parking layby in front; sometimes they recalled earlier urban forms describing crescents or squares around a traffic intersection.

At the upper end of the range, serving a district catchment area of 40 or 50,000 population, their post-war evolution merged with that of the main centres. Passing through examples of open and then enclosed precincts, they adopted such innovations as roof-top parking as might be appropriate for their site conditions and smaller scale, and suffered a similar isolation from their milieu, itself often in a fragmented state.

In the case of the smaller shop groups, providing between, say, 2,000 m² and 8,000 m² in GLA and serving local populations up to 20,000, this broad retailing context was often less important than the local physical context, dominated by housing, to which the small centre must relate. This produced a number of interesting post-war solutions, some of which are described here. In these situations the local shopping centre might be seen as defining a social space within the housing, or as a bridge linking two residential areas. Whatever the adopted role, these examples are less significant as technical solutions to the problem 'shopping' than as studies of the relationship between shopping and the community.

One of the first Danish examples of a planned suburban centre was the Døesvej Centre, the largest of a number of local facilities serving a new suburb in Holstebro in western Jutland. In this scheme the shopping centre, with a final trading area of 1,935 m², forms a discrete block in a grouping of community buildings, including a school, church and youth facilities, around a central car parking area of 104 spaces which they share. The first stage of the centre was completed in 1960, and was then expanded to match the growth of the residential areas. It adopts a simple arrangement of single-storey rows of shops around a central courtyard, forming an overall rectangle on plan. The spaces between rows, in effect side malls, are given a light roof enclosure, which continues round the central court as a canopy protection to the shop fronts, while deliveries are contained within a walled area behind one side of the building. The Døesvej Centre is representative of a number of small Danish centres developed for new suburbs during the '60s[14] which share the characteristics of small, single-level, precinct building groups.

In a similar example at Myllypuro, the district centre, designed by Erkki Karvinen and serving a population of 10,000 people in a suburb 15 km east of Helsinki, is almost completely enclosed and is treated as a single building structure. Two open courts are situated in the centre of the building, whose simple plan form and straightforward use of concrete and steel give it an unpretentious industrial quality.

A more sophisticated piece of hardware was built in 1968 for a privately-owned housing district on the north-west outskirts of Lucerne, Switzerland, on the lake shore. The Schöenbühl centre comprised a shopping building, for which the architect was Alfred Roth, linked to a 17-storey apartment tower designed by Alvar Aalto, which together form an independent and elegant building group within the community. The shopping centre is compact and completely enclosed, with three short malls leading in to a central top-lit 'Plazza' around which three large stores of 1,000 m² each, and a number of small units, are grouped. Servicing is at grade around the perimeter of the building, but pairs of ramps along the north side give car access up to roof-top parking for shoppers and basement parking for residents of the tower, which contains a total of 96 apartments, arranged in a variant of Aalto's Bremerhaus fan plan to face south-east over the lake and mountains. The roof deck parking area of the shopping building is connected by lifts to the square below, and provides 180 spaces, together with a further 100 spaces at ground level around the centre, giving it a catchment well beyond the 3,000 residents of its neighbourhood. The quality of the interiors of the Schöenbühl centre matches the refinement of its plan, with shop fronts formed in simple glazed panels which slide open for trading, and elegant planting around the base of the high clerestorey lights around its central space.

If the Schöenbühl centre provides a sophisticated local facility matching the quality of its users' apartments and motor cars, two new town district centres built immediately afterwards, at the end of the decade, developed forms even more ambitious in their organisation, but directed towards the integration of the local centre as a link in a network of higher density housing routes. Very similar in their intention and form, both the Castlefields district centre at Runcorn

4·46 General view of exterior of the Schöenbühl shopping centre, Lucerne, Switzerland
Architect: Professor Alfred Roth

4·47 View of lift lobby at the Schöenbühl shopping centre

in England and the Mannheim-Vogelstang centre in Germany use the local centre as a bridge deck, carrying pedestrian routes across the rapid transit way which both connects the district to a wider community, but also tends to divide it into two parts. The immediate models for these two buildings were the Swedish New Town centres which were similarly built across underground suburban rail routes, but at the scale of the district centre this bridging function had a more overriding effect upon the shopping use, which was otherwise hardly large enough to sustain two levels of activity. The ability to provide low-level servicing to the shopping was thus a beneficial by-product of the main priority of the bridge as a wider element of circulation.

At Mannheim-Vogelstang[15] the bridge was achieved on a relatively flat site by raising the deck and lowering the tram route, each by half a level. This had the effect of forming two complete levels for a centre of 8,100 m², with the lower fed from surface car parks, service roads and the tram stopping points, and the upper from the main north-south pedestrian route, and secondary east-west bridge links, to the pedestrian circulation systems of the housing areas. The central malls at each level were connected by stairs and a travellator to each side of the tram route, and enclosed by a concrete canopy structure.

The creation of a double level shopping centre was not appropriate in the Runcorn example,[16] where the rapid transit bus-only route ran along a contour line on a north-facing slope. The bridge deck could thus spring from ground level on the high side, and connect at its outer end with the access deck of a major spine of housing in the Castlefields development.

The precinct centre at Manchester similarly adopts an ambitious multi-level organisation. Serving the developing Manchester education precinct, this development of 11,500 m² of shopping and showrooms and 5,400 m² of offices was unusual as a commercial project promoted by a University. Its plan form and deck-level mall derive from its function as the hub of a system of pedestrian routes serving the precinct, a function which is reinforced by the inclusion of accommodation for 240 students in six floors of superstructure over the shops. With its underdeck service road and escalator connections to upper deck level, this centre, fulfilling a specialised local need, accepts as did the Runcorn and Mannheim centres, the relevance of main centre solutions to its specific problem. In this it is radically different from another English local centre of the same period, which specifically rejects any such precedent. Describing his intentions at New Ash Green, Eric Lyons, architect to Span (Kent) Ltd the initial developers of the village, wrote:

'I wanted the centre to be something other than the usual commercial ghetto and above all, I wanted it to be a part of the housing "texture". Any ideal day-to-day shopping environment is where the shops reflect the growth of a place and are in converted houses, not in special commercial buildings.

'Fortunately Span didn't go to any of those great firms of valuers with their commercial "experts", otherwise we would have finished up looking like—well, you name your own new shopping horror, they're all more or less the same. Not that one should blame the valuers entirely; they really are a product of our wonderful Planning Machine and they go together to create our palaces of commercial culture. (I can't remember the name of that new town with its great multi-level, all purpose, totalitarian commercial

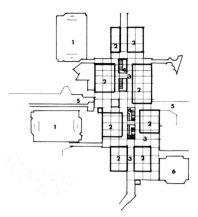

4·48 Mannheim-Vogelstang Centre, Germany
Architect: Prof. Helmut Striffler

Key:
1 Multi-Storey car park
2 Shops
3 Shopping concourse
4 Escalators down
5 Electric tramway under
6 Auditorium

Key:
1 Supermarket
2 Public house
3 Shops
4 Pharmacy
5 Pedestrian concourse
6 Community centre
7 Health centre
8 Busway under
9 Bus stops
10 Loading bay
11 Shop storage
12 Supermarket storage
13 Public house storage
14 Unloading platform

4·49 Castlefields Local Centre, Runcorn New Town, England
Architects: Runcorn Development Corporation: Chief Architect, F. Lloyd Roche, succeeded by Roger Harrison

Key:
1 Stage 1/stage 2
2 North square
3 Bus stop
4 Service court
5 Shopping street
6 Public house
7 Site for community centre
8 WCs
9 Car arrival
10 Car park

Scale: 1:4000

4·50 New Ash Green Local Centre, Kent, England
Architects: Eric Lyons, Cunningham and Partners

4·51 View of electric tramway beneath the Mannheim-Vogelstang shopping centre

4·52 Upper-level main concourse at the Mannheim-Vogelstang shopping centre

4·53 The Castlefields local centre, Runcorn New Town, England, spanning the busway

4·54 Main pedestrian way at New Ash Green Local Centre, Kent, England

4·55 Aerial view of model of New Ash Green Local Centre

4·56 Shopping centre at New Ash Green Local Centre

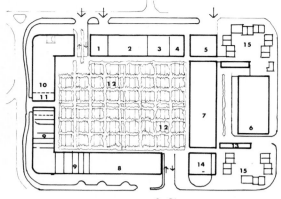

Key:
1 Pub
2 Health centre
3 Library
4 Roman Catholic church
5 Future pub site
6 Club
7 Future shops
8 Supermarket

9 Shops
10 Supermarket
11 Restaurant over super-
     market
12 Car parking
13 Garages
14 Future church site
15 Houses
Scale: 1 : 4000

4·57 Garden Square shopping centre, Southampton, England:
plan at street level
Architects: Farrell/Grimshaw Partnership

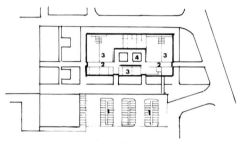

Key:
1 Car parking
2 Pedestrian concourse
3 Shops
4 Central square
Scale 1 : 4000

4·58 Myllypuro local centre, Finland: plan at street level
Architect: Erkki Karvinen

Key: A)
1 Computer building
2 Mathematics building
3 Sports centre
4 College of music
5 School of art
6 Business school
7 Church and chaplaincy
8 Student residences
9 Precinct centre
Scale: 1 : 20 000

Key: B)
1 Restaurant
2 Bank
3 Offices
4 Central square
5 Shopping concourse
6 Stairs to student apart-
    ments above
7 Escalators down to street-
    level
8 Public house
9 Shops
Scale: 1 : 4000

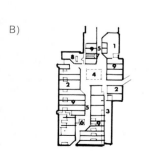

4·59 Manchester University Precinct Centre: site plan and plan
at first-floor circulation level
Architects: Sir Hugh Wilson and Lewis Womersley

temple to which the inhabitants trudge from their subsidised, minimum-standard houses.)'

The local centre to which the inhabitants of New Ash Green trudge had a similar programme to that of the Lucerne centre, serving as a local facility for a new middle-class housing development in the heart of Kent and within commuting range of London, but with the possibility of a wider local catchment. Rejecting also the cool technology of Schönbühl, the New Ash Green centre nevertheless provided an alternative product for a similar market. The shop units were contained in house structures, making the shopping street simply the most compact, interesting and social of the spaces between houses. Thus, with the exception of one double-bay unit, the shops were formed between brick cross walls at 5·4 m centres, having variety in depth for different unit sizes. The scheme, of which 4,800 m² of commercial space, comprising two-thirds of the planned total, was completed in 1969, incorporated a number of ingenious and idiosyncratic features into its simple plan form. Its shopping street, running east-west and little more than 100 m long in its eventual extent, was approached from a main car park to the south, and hence to the rear of the shops and beyond their servicing areas, and this entry was carefully controlled and screened, passing under a gallery serving first-floor studio/workshops and thence into a narrowing lane leading into the shopping street. At this point on the street a stair feature was incorporated, leading up to a first-floor gallery which ran the length of the northern side of the centre. Doubtful in its viability as an isolated run of poorly served small units, this gallery surely corresponded to an architectural, rather than a commercial, idea of what a local centre might be, as a place rich in spatial variety and promenades architecturales.

The desire to integrate the local centre into the community form, and to create a social place of its shopping street, is expressed also in the design for a local centre serving the Bourtreehill area of Irvine New Town in Scotland. Again the basis of the scheme is a short street of shops with service areas to the rear, and a main car park on one side beyond. A supermarket, café, public house and 12 shop units make up the shop rows, which are broken on plan to concentrate and form a focus for the pedestrian routes which lead in at either end.[18]

In both of the above examples the shopping element of the local centre is insufficiently large in itself to maintain the character of 'village street' sought for. The shopping is necessarily, and almost incidently, the means by which the housing street becomes rich and 'central' in its character, and it is perhaps a failing of the first that, in its uncompleted form at least, its lack of extension outwards into residential streets makes it too small to maintain the illusion; it becomes a fragment of a village set in a suburban estate. A demonstration of the cohesion of residential and other uses which is required by this view of the nature of a local centre is offered by Gordon Cullen's analytical sketch plan for the centre of Maryculter, a new community planned near Aberdeen in Scotland by David Gosling and Gordon Cullen with Dan Donohue of Christian Salvesen Ltd. The necessarily restricted physical content of a 6,000 m² centre servicing a local population of about 10,000 people is here disposed in a carefully considered sequence of elements along a 'causeway' link across a central bowl of green space and lakes defined by the terrain. The settlement is situated in a natural amphitheatre of land with the houses grouped around the enclosure and facing inwards to a central parkland. Urbanity builds up from the wild country

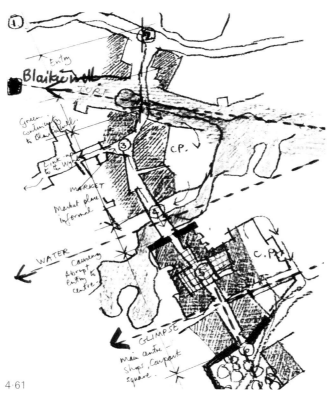

4·60

4·60 Maryculter New Town:
perspective of the local shopping
centre at Blakiewell utilising an
existing farmhouse

4·61 Gordon Cullen's town-
scape plan for the centre of
Maryculter New Town, near
Aberdeen, Scotland
Architects: David Gosling,
Gordon Cullen, Dan Donohue

4·62 Maryculter New Town.
Gordon Cullen's townscape
sequence showing progression
from outside to the town centre

4·63 Maryculter New Town.
Gordon Cullen's townscape
plan for the town
Urban Designer: Gordon Cullen

4·64 Perspective of the central
square at Maryculter New Town

4·61

4·62

4·63

4·64

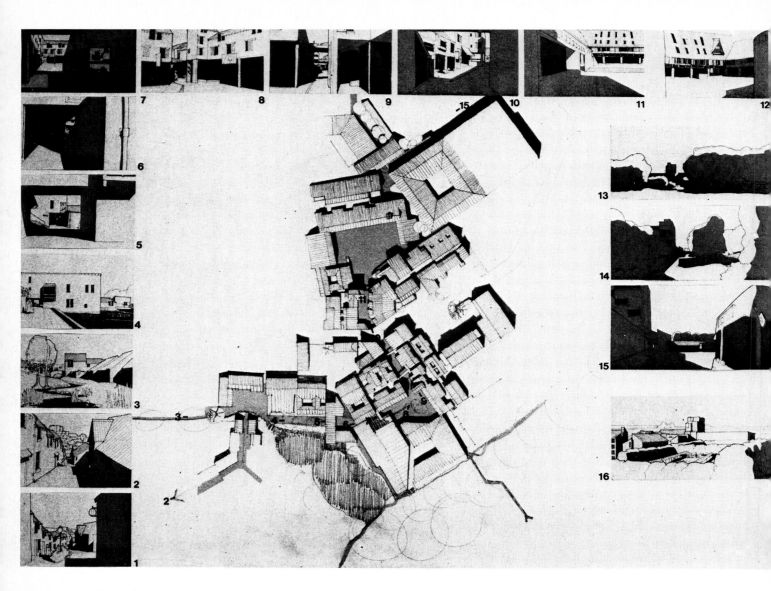

outside to the central street which links the north side of
the amphitheatre to the south. Each village or housing
cluster has, its own corner shop usually located as part of
the old farm steadings and associated with the local community centre. The centre itself as Cullen says 'although a
single continuous street is made up of a series of linked
spaces and events, the first being the small market place
with its shops. The road curves and crosses a humped bridge
over the loch into the main market place. This sudden but
short release of compression and the substitution of water
for brick and stone increases the stimulation, the incident
of the Centre. There is then the sudden release as the
water of the loch passes under the causeway—the real
centre is then presented over the water as a citadel.
Finally we arrive at the focal space. To the right and left are
views out to the parkland and lakes. This is the fix where the
two axes cross'.

A similar design philosophy is seen in a thesis project by
Bob Macdonald and Dave Lees at Sheffield University for a
district centre at Mosborough, near Sheffield. The initial
phase of shopping is about 7,500 m² and the designers
aimed to produce a town centre which was complete and
coherent at each phase of development. The plan links the
surrounding housing areas with the town centre in order
to achieve a continuous urban experience through the
town, intensifying towards the central public space. It
relies on the disposition of the built form to create a micro
climate compatible with English shopping habits and
establishes a hierarchy of routes with shopping located

4·65 Thesis design: Town Centre for Mosborough New Town,
Sheffield showing plan of centre with surrounding perspective
views
Architects: Bob Macdonald and Dave Lees (6th-year students,
Sheffield University, Department of Architecture)

along the primary pedestrian route and secondary routes
which traverse service areas for non-shopping uses. The
authors wanted to generate 'an idiosyncratic environment
by turning building complexes inside out' and stressed the
importance of human scale so that the urban form is so
structured as to become readable and memorable. An
alternative view of the means by which a small shopping
facility might, of itself, achieve a sense of place, is offered
in the project by the Farrell/Grimshaw Partnership for the
Garden Square shopping centre, serving a 14,000 population
in the Lord's Hill area of Southampton, England. This centre
for Stead Investments includes 7,000 m² of retail space and
2,700 m² of other community uses including a library,
health centre, public house and church, together with
400 parking spaces. In each of the local centre schemes
discussed, the site area occupied by car parking is at least
as great as that covered by the shopping buildings and their

4·66 Perspective view of development at the Garden Square
shopping centre, Southampton, England
Architects: Farrell/Grimshaw Partnership

4·67 The internal court at Myllypuro Local Centre, Finland
Architect: Erkki Karvinen

104

4·68 Myllypuro Local Centre, Finland: general view of exterior

4·69 Manchester University Precinct Centre, England: night view of exterior
Architects: Sir Hugh Wilson and Lewis Womersley

pedestrian streets, and is treated as an area without content, as a 'convenience' but not a 'symbol', to use Venturi's terms. In the Garden Square project this area is taken into the heart of the centre to form a landscaped court framed on three sides by single-storey shops and with the fourth reserved for future expansion. The case for this idea is argued by the architects as follows:

'The concept of the Centre is of a drive-in garden square. Major shopping and communal facilities are grouped about the square in the fashion of a market place—each benefiting from the proximity of the other. A sense of 'arrival at a place' is achieved by concentrating all pedestrian movements onto the square and by bringing private vehicles into the square. Vehicles parade close by the shops in a High Street manner before parking. At all times pedestrians will retain the right of way over vehicles.

'Landscaping at ground level and on an overhead network give the square the qualities of an internal space where car parking becomes an integral part of the shopping environment.

'Service movements are located in an outer perimeter zone, thus eliminating any conflict with shopping and communal activities.

'Whilst this is a simple concept it has been carefully selected as appropriate in scale and character for this project. It is important that this Centre is not based on the same design concepts as the more ambitious large scale Centres—it must have all the attractions of a village High Street or a continental place or square.

'The concept consciously rejects the idea that this Centre should attempt to 'hide' car parking spaces behind the service areas as in the now modern convention of shopping centre layouts. This solution is always a compromise as whilst a central pedestrian precinct can thus be created (a) it is essentially very introverted and becomes disproportionately more so the smaller the centre; (b) the car parking is then placed to the rear of the shops but not immediately so as servicing has to be immediately adjacent to the rear. So the cars are placed quite a distance from the shops themselves and access is inevitably confused with servicing both at pedestrian and motorist level. (c) Essentially this solution pushes away the cars, which are the main users on the site, does not attempt to integrate them into the scheme and exposes vast tarmacked areas of this forgotten land to the outside world.'

While the conventional reference to the village High Street would be as appropriate to the village centre forms discussed earlier, the solution is a quite novel and perhaps more honest attempt to reconcile those elements which disposed of the village high street in the first place.

The variety of small centre forms illustrated by these examples makes a refreshing complement to the variety of main centre forms, which could be seen as arising from a developing conception of how the internal requirements of the shopping centre could best be satisfied as it passed through the stages of its spiral evolution. In the case of the smaller centres the variety springs rather from alternative ideas as to the place of the centre within the community and its relationship to it. In this they perhaps offer some ideas for their main centre cousins which have not yet been taken up.

4·5 North American Main Centres

The city of Rochester, NY claims the first enclosed centre in a down-town area in the USA with Midtown Plaza, opened in 1962. The city's relatively early concern for its central area arose from the peculiarity of its history whereby, after a rapid expansion in the nineteenth century and an anticipated future population of over one million, its growth stopped at a level of around 300,000. This had occurred by 1930, and at that time also its downtown area began to decline, a process which accelerated during the '40s and '50s. In the latter period a series of programmes was begun to regenerate the centre of Rochester as a commercial area,

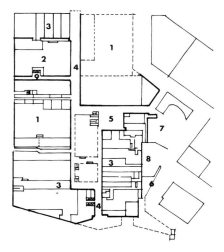

Key:
1 Department stores
2 Office building
3 Shops
4 Shopping mall
5 Central square with sidewalk café

6 Bus terminal
7 Post office service area
8 Service delivery
9 Elevator lobby

Scale: 1:4000

4·70 Midtown Plaza, Rochester, New York: mall-level plan
Architects: Victor Gruen and Associates

including a highways programme under which an inner motorway loop was constructed around it, a programme to provide parking facilities within it, and plans for a new shopping centre in its core. The last was initiated and carried out by two existing major stores, McCurdy's and Forman's, on the same city block, whose buildings were to be incorporated into the new centre. The acquisition of an additional 3 ha was negotiated privately and a rectangular site, 220 × 135 m, formed. Since almost half of this was to be occupied by the existing buildings or their extension into the complex, providing some 70,000 m² between them, the new centre was formed on two levels to accommodate a further 20,000 m² of smaller units. The design, by Victor Gruen, thus reflected the early use, as in Europe, of multi-level solutions within the confines of urban sites. The design was also unusual in its almost total elimination of malls for main frontage, with the great majority of units facing directly onto a large central space, 28 × 10 m, from the corners of which four short malls were arranged pinwheel fashion at ground level to lead out to the surrounding streets. At the upper shopping level mall circulation was confined, at least initially, to a gallery, 3·7 to 8·5 m wide, and cross bridge, around the full-height central space. In addition to this stacking of the retail provision, 2,000 parking spaces were provided in a three-storey basement,

107

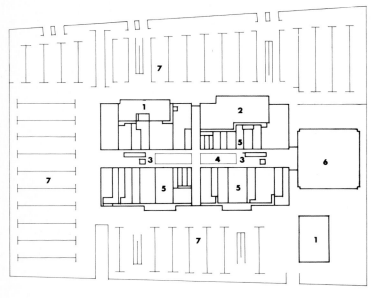

Key:
1 Office building
2 Hotel
3 Gallery
4 Ice rink below
5 Shops

6 Nieman-Marcus department
  store (4 levels)
7 Third-level parking

Scale: 1:4000

4·71 The Galleria, Post Oak Centre, Texas, USA: mid-level plan
Architects: Hellmuth, Obata and Kassabaum

4·72 Exterior of the Galleria, Post Oak, Texas

4·73 The Galleria, Post Oak, Texas: view of central mall and ice
rink

with shop service partly incorporated at this lower level, and partly at street level to the perimeter of the building. Finally an 18 storey office and hotel tower was located at one end of the complex.

During the '60s the effort to attract commercial uses back into the central area of Rochester took effect in the redevelopment of a series of city blocks around Midtown Plaza. To the south Xerox built a 30-storey office building over a complex called 'Xerox Square'; to the west 37,000 m² of offices were constructed in Lincoln First Tower, and on an adjacent block a further 1,800 parking spaces were built in a city parking garage. These developments were then linked together by a network of pedestrian and truck routes crossing over or under the intervening streets, and connecting with the circulation routes of Midtown Plaza, the former at upper mall level. This project is of interest therefore both in its early use of a multi-level enclosed organisation for a down-town centre and also in the way in which it subsequently generated an embryonic 'megastructure' circulation across four blocks of the city core.

The idea of developing a dense shopping centre form in levels around one large, full-height central space was taken a stage further in the Galleria at City Post Oak, a rapidly expanding area on the western edge of Houston. Here the shopping building is developed on three levels within a simple rectangular block, 190 × 105 m, with a single independent department store building located at one end of the major axis. The main mall circulation occupies a zone along the length of this axis, with a large space penetrating the full height of the building in its centre and knots of vertical circulation linking the shopping levels at its ends. Gallery malls of the upper levels cantilever into the central space, overlooking an ice rink at the lowest level and roofed by a glazed barrel vault, 168 m long by 12 m wide, in 'a 20th-century interpretation of the famed 19th century Galleria Vittorio Emanuele, Milan, circa 1865–67.'[19] External ground level corresponds to the middle of the three shopping levels, at which a single central cross mall, with bridge across the central space, provides a main access to the building, but in addition large multi-storey parking garages flanking both long sides of the centre provide direct access to the upper and lower malls. Servicing is accommodated in a continuous route at the lowest level, from which there is lift access to service corridors on upper floors.

Designed 'as a total environmental complex whose key elements contain all the vital ingredients of a planned city core', the simple and compact disposition of shopping and parking uses in the Galleria development is supplemented by two office towers and a hotel, providing within its 13 ha a total of 7,000 parking spaces, 56,00 m² GLA of shopping space, 63,000 m² NRA of office space and 404 bed spaces. The density of its site use, and the urban quality of its central shopping space thus give this development a place among the integrated centre forms, although its location is less truly urban than their down-town sites, arising from 'Houston's *laissez-faire* approach to planning' which 'can be as heartening as a barbecue'.

In terms of its tenant mix it is quite unlike any of the European examples discussed and is unusual even in North American terms. The 'compelling opulence' of the Neiman-Marcus department store is matched in the finishes of the malls and the list of its tenancies, which includes no less than five art galleries.

The Galleria mall, designed by Hellmuth, Obata and Kassabaum for Gerald D. Hines, was completed in 1970,

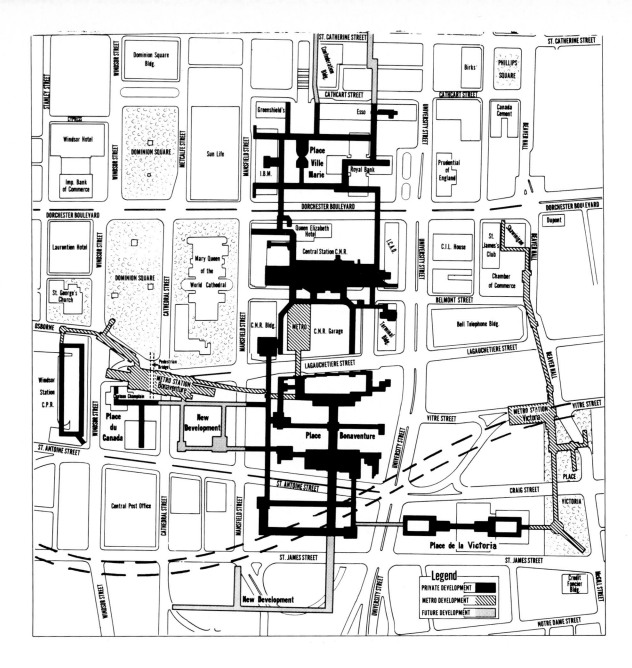

4·74 Ville Marie and Bonaventure, Montreal, Canada: plan of the pedestrian network linked to metro stations
Architects: Affleck, Desbarats, Dimakopolous, Lebensold and Sise

with development of adjacent office and parking buildings continuing until 1973. Another centre opened in the latter year serves as a further example of the development of downtown centres within similar overall design and accommodation criteria to the Rochester and City Post Oak projects. Broadway Plaza occupies a rectangular 1·8 ha city block in Los Angeles, bounded by Seventh, Eighth, Hope and Flower Streets, and again incorporated a mix of hotel, office tower, multistorey parking garage and shopping facilities. The last was made up of a single department store, the first to be built in downtown Los Angeles for 50 years, and a mall square arrangement again christened the 'Galleria', a term shared by a number of other developments and now almost synonymous with 'mall' for this type of central space in an urban development. In this instance a fall across the site generated two mall levels around the Galleria, with parking and service levels below and three floors of the Broadway Department Store over one half of the building, surmounted by a further six decks of car parking. Finishes in the Galleria space are generally brick and timber, with a top-lit space-frame roof, the intention being to create a 'lively meeting place with the atmosphere of an old world street with sidewalk cafés, boutiques, trees and flowers, flowing fountains, graphic

displays, benches, antique paving tiles',[20] a description which might stand for some of the English village centres, and illustrating both the pervasiveness of the sentiment and its ability to be applied to startlingly different concepts.

In these three projects the dense usage of relatively small sites produced the same kind of loosening of the relationship between internal mall levels and grade as occurred in the European centres, and a corresponding emphasis on vertical elements of circulation as other uses are piled above and below the shopping levels. In Mies van der Rohe's Toronto-Dominion Centre the comparatively small shopping element was simply sunk into the ground to act as a podium element to the 46- and 56-storey office towers which dominated the site. Access to the cruciform malls of the shopping centre was through its roof, which formed a landscaped square at the foot of these towers. In another Canadian city, Montreal, the similar, almost casual, introduction of a shopping basement level below a major office development at Place Ville Marie became the start of a whole network of alternative circulations extending outward from itself. And while the shopping developments had exploited site cross-falls to set up alternative levels of circulations within the street pattern and penetrating it to link up with adjoining blocks, the principle was extended here to cover the greater part of a city centre.

The unique scale of Montreal's 'superblock' experiments arose from the circumstances of its earlier development and a combination of ambitious projects which resulted in the 'ten golden years of Montreal's Downtown' between 1956 and 1966, culminating in EXPO 67. Lying between the high ground of Mount Royal to the north and the waterfront on the St. Lawrence Seaway to the south, the fall across the city centre was some 45 to 60 m from the McGill campus to the river. Two parallel linear settlements had been established across this slope, separated by a major escarpment. On the lower ground the old core of the original settlement had developed into the financial and trading centre of the inland seaport, while a new commercial core had grown above it with the main downtown shopping area extended along St Catherine Street. Penetrating into the heart of this arrangement with track, termini and marshalling yards, both the Canadian National (CN) and Canadian Pacific (CP) railroads were major landowners of a central zone which became increasingly strategic as office development began to transfer northwards from the old core between the wars. Schemes were prepared during the '30s to exploit this position occupied by the railroads, and in particular the 2·8 ha site of the CN marshalling yards cut into the ground immediately north of Central Station and only a block away from St Catherine Street. In the mid-'50s this, the Place Ville Marie project, was resurrected in an agreement between CN and William Zeckendorf, one of the most famous, and most bullish, of the North American post-war developers. He proposed to build 140,000 m² of office rental space on the site, a figure five times the annual amount then being constructed in the whole of Montreal, and commissioned I. M. Pei and Henry N. Cobb as architects and Vincent Ponte as planner to design not only this development but also to prepare a master plan for the whole 9 ha of CN property in the central area.

The major element in the Place Ville Marie project was the 45-storey cruciform office tower, christened the Royal Bank of Canada building when that institution decided to move from the old core into the new development. Beneath the piazza formed, as at Toronto-Dominion, at the foot of this tower, a single podium floor of shopping contained 15,000 m² of retail space, and below this again 2 floors of parking for 1200 cars were built above the CN tracks. The network of malls created at the shopping level, one floor below adjacent street level, was extended beyond the block occupied by Place Ville Marie to tie into adjacent buildings, so that, for example, a direct connection was formed with Central Station, and when the complex was opened in 1963 some 2·5 km of alternative routes had been created.

An appreciation of the possibility of creating multiple levels of circulation within the site cross-falls was shown in the pre-war schemes for Place Ville Marie, yet topographical features are not in themselves enough to explain the extraordinary expansion of the alternative all-weather networks which now took place across a central zone of the city, linking old and new cores, through the basements and podia of quite disparate redevelopment projects, and bridging and burrowing across the street grid. Rather this arose from the obvious success of the first section and a

planning intention to extend it; 'Planners are beginning to go beyond the 2-D of paper plans,' said Ponte, 'In this city we are concentrating the core functions into a tight, totally interrelated unit, doubling and tripling the use of the same parcels of precious Downtown land by inserting several levels above and below ground.'[21] This intention was reinforced by the construction during the '60s of an underground metro system for central Montreal, four stations of which—Peel, McGill, Victoria and Bonaventure—defined the corners of a 'superblock', approximately 700 x 1000 m, within which the new pedestrian networks of the core were to grow. With mezzanine pedestrian levels between the platforms and the street these stations themselves generated underground pedestrian malls which were to be connected through to the main north-south spine of routes springing from PVM in the centre.

From Place Ville Marie development proceeded southwards along the strip owned by CN, crossing Central Station to Place Bonaventure, probably the most remarkable single building element in the developing organism. Whereas most of the city block sites which now underwent reconstruction in downtown Montreal, with predominant office or hotel elements in their programmes, took the form of central core towers above multi-level podia, Place Bonaventure filled its 2·4 ha site with a single densely developed building cube providing a total of 186,000 m² rental area within its 17 floors. Half of this rental space was taken up by the Merchandise Mart, on five floors beginning 18 m above street level, carrying a roof top hotel and winter gardens and supported by the gargantuan structure of the 23,000 m² exhibition hall. Below that floor, and coming down now to street level, one layer of the cube was taken up by a main shopping concourse floor with a second retail level developed below it and connecting to the underground pedestrian malls of the metro. Below these two levels, which accommodated 14,000 m² of retail floor space, lay the CN tracks with a 1,000 space multistorey car park off-set beside them. The stack of building floors, each measuring about 145 x 130 m in an irregular square plan, was served by main cores of vertical circulation at its four corners, with secondary lift and stair positions in the centre of each side.

Place Bonaventure, developed by Concordia Estates and designed by Affleck Desbarats Dimakopoulos Lebensold Sise with Vincent Ponte again acting as planning consultant, was primarily a wholesaling, rather than a retailing building, and its retail areas, like those in the office projects, were its contribution to the horizontal networks of circulation developing within the city centre. Again as in those projects it penetrated the horizontal networks with vertical circulation cores from which the upper specialised floor areas were served, in this case in deep spaces filling in between cores. The special possibilities of this concept in developing the 'alternative' city circulation have been discussed in connection with the European centres, as have the special difficulties in relating the resulting megastructure to the former city within which it is growing. Describing the development of the project Ray Affleck, the partner in charge, noted 'The architecture of the internal streets and places became a major field for the direct application of our ideas, as did the creation of the special "fun-environment" for the Hotel. In retrospect, I would say that the environmental barrier (facade) was possibly the most difficult element to cope with—maybe because of the weight of historical baggage that we still carry with us

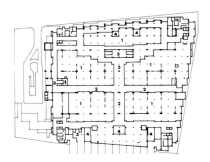

Key:
1 Shops
2 Shopping concourse
3 Elevators
4 Staircases
5 Escalators
Scale: 1:4000

4·75 Place Bonaventure, Montreal: plan at main shopping level

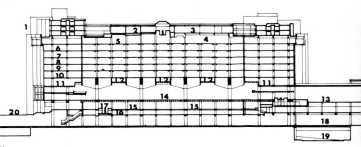

Key:
1 Hotel: 400 rooms
2 Hotel administration
3 Restaurants
4 Hotel function rooms
5 International show rooms
6 Merchandise mart: contract equipment
7 Merchandise mart: furniture and household
8 Merchandise mart: giftware and houseware
9 Merchandise mart: men's apparel floor
10 Merchandise mart: ladies' apparel floor
11 Merchandise floor
12 Services
13 Truck dock (connection to freight elevators)
14 Convention hall
15 Shopping concourse
16 Shopping at metro connection
17 Escalators
18 Canadian National Railway tracks
19 St Antoine Street
20 La Gauchetière Street
21 Metro tunnel
Scale: 1:2000

4·76 Place Bonaventure, Montreal: section

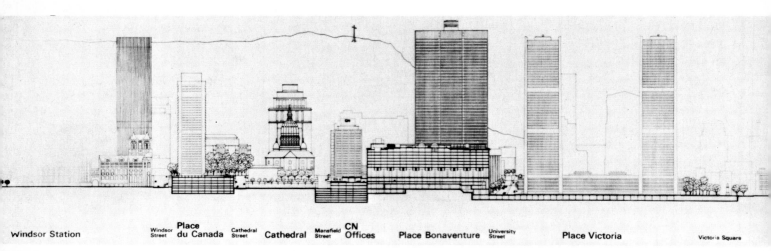

Windsor Station   Windsor Street   **Place du Canada**   Cathedral Street   **Cathedral**   Mansfield Street   **CN Offices**   **Place Bonaventure**   University Street   **Place Victoria**   Victoria Square

4·77 Place Bonaventure, Montreal: east-west section of the city

4·78 Place Bonaventure, Montreal: interior view of exhibition hall

4·79 Place Bonaventure, Montreal: exterior view from La Gachetière Street

4·80 Place Bonaventure, Montreal: interior view of upper concourse with jeweller's shop in foreground

in this area of expression.'[22]

This building was completed in 1967 in the same year as the Canadian Pacific completed their Place du Canada development at the head of their terminus. Two towers, one an hotel and the other offices, were here raised on a podium which incorporated shopping malls, a cinema and car parking on five basement levels and incorporated a pedestrian bridge connection to Dominion Square and link to the metro pedestrian level. Plans now proceeded for the extension of the network northwards in the McGill College Avenue Development with a procession of commercial buildings, each rooted in a large shopping promenade, and the connection of the extended network spine to the northern metro circulations and to the main department stores on St. Catherine Street. Montreal would thus be provided with about 10 km of new pedestrian routes, both above and below ground, and covering blocks in about 40 of the 75 ha of the city's core. This result is all the more remarkable for having been created through a series of independent developments, as visually diverse as in any other city, adopting a common planning idea, and also for the parallel initiative of the city government in creating a similarly articulated transportation net with the metro system and underground motorway.

The impression of spontaneity with which the alternative system of routes spread through downtown Montreal as it underwent redevelopment, contrasts with the conventional notion of a megastructure as being necessarily a highly controlled organism. This idea owes much to the seductive image of Kenzo Tanges' Tokyo Bay plan of 1960, in which the city megastructure left terra firma behind, to spread across the water of the bay and expose its rationally ordered systems and elements; 'we advocate a city structure composed of cycle transportation, civic axis, and three-dimensional lattice-like spaces unifying pilotis and service cores . . . it became possible to think in terms of unified handling of city, transportation, and architecture and of a hierarchy of space from private spaces to social.' The megastructure was developed by Tange in subsequent planning projects, notably those for Skopje and Bologna, and its architectural components implied in such building projects as the WHO Headquarters, the Dentsu Office building and the Yamanashi Press and Broadcasting Centre. At the EXPO 70 Space Frame and Theme Pavilions a further step was taken; '. . . we solved the problem of how to create a compound entirely by combining megastructure and capsules, which are dissimilar in scale. Here, public investment paid for the principal structural frame, and private investment paid for the minor details in the form of the capsules that gave variety to the whole.' This translation of the public/private, developer/tenant administrative separation of building roles into a powerful architectural language is relevant here in relation to the project by Kenzo Tange, in association with McCue Boone Tomsick, Lawrence Halprin and Associates and John Bolles and Associates for the Yerba Buena Center in San Francisco. As ambitious in scale as the Montreal experiment, the Yerba Buena Center Redevelopment Plan, approved in 1966, called for the planned redevelopment of 35 ha of the Market South district of the city. The area was to be divided into three superblocks, of which the nucleus was to be the YBC Central District, for which the architects produced a scheme in 1969.

In this a major element was the 5-storey deep lattice structured car park blocks, suspended $5\frac{1}{2}$ storeys above street level and served by tall drums of access ramps.

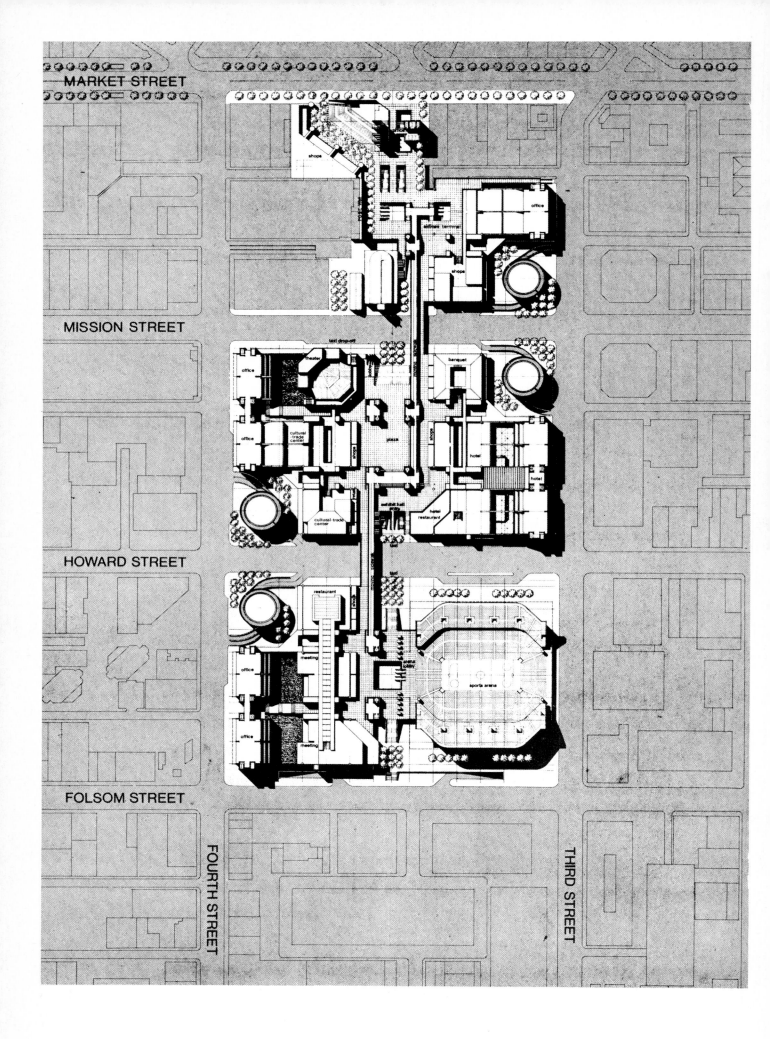

MARKET STREET

MISSION STREET

HOWARD STREET

FOLSOM STREET

FOURTH STREET

THIRD STREET

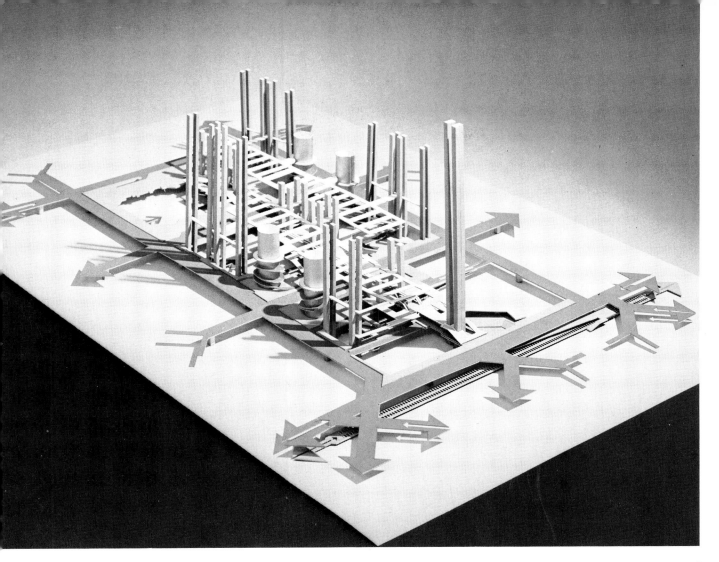

4·81 Yerba Buena Centre, San Francisco: concourse-level plan.
Scale: 1 : 3000
Architects: Kenzo Tange and Urtec

4·82 Yerba Buena Centre, San Francisco: design model showing
horizontal and vertical circulation systems

These parking structures spanned across the three city
blocks of the site and had bridge connections across to
flanking office and hotel slabs, with a discipline of vertical
service cores running through both. Space frame roofs
then covered the areas between and around these major
elements to provide enclosed spaces for sports arena,
exhibition hall and the other uses of the Central District.
Although in total area a relatively small element in the
complex, shopping was, as at Montreal, to play an important part in the definition and generation of its pedestrian
spaces and in particular the idea of shopping denoted by
the pervasive, and elastic, term 'Galleria'. This term was
intended to denote not so much a precise physical model as
a 'symbol in the life of the citizens', and as a measure for
understanding the relationship of private and public
enterprise; 'We had the experience of seeing that when we
met the men responsible for constructing and operating
individual buildings, architects and others, the word Galleria
had found its way into their thinking and provided a means
for reaching a consensus.' In subsequent development
the scheme lost some of its initial clarity, and the use of one
bank of parking buildings, its lattice structure abandoned,
was changed to an apparel mart. The function of the
Galleria however, as a large unifying space, lined with tiers
of shopping and other uses, remained. The YBC plan thus
represented an important development from the pedestrian

systems of Montreal, in which these became a controlled
sequence of urban spaces and in which the form of the
building elements of the megastructure began to indicate
the novelty of its implications.

4·6 Department Stores

Although the most dramatic area of new department store
construction since the war has been in the North American
out-of-town centres, a considerable number of new stores
have been built in urban locations, and particularly in
countries such as West Germany where the department
store has continued to be a competitive and expanding
trading form. In both locations the designers of the new
department store buildings have tended to adopt more
consciously monumental forms than in the case of the
shopping centres, in the out-of-town case often specifically
seeking by this means to distinguish the anchor store
from the abutting centre building. Yet, although more
compact than the shopping centre, the design problem in an
urban context was similar in its requirement for large
uninterrupted sales floor areas, with relatively blank
frontages, and closely related to adequate car parking.

An early and widely discussed example was Albini and
Helg's La Rinascente store in Rome, completed in 1961.
The first design for this building reinterpreted the 19th-
century department store programme in a Futurist structure,
with canted steel portal frames at roof level supporting
car park decks above the blank elevations of the sales

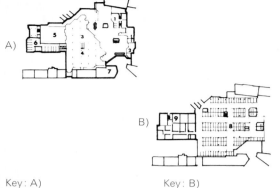

Key: A)
1 Boutique
2 Coffee shop
3 Sales area
4 Escalator to upper sales
  floors
5 Children and baby wear
6 Older children's wear
7 Teenage shop

Key: B)
8 Basement car parking
9 Plant room

4·83 Department store in Wolfenbuttel, Germany:
A) Sales-floor plan
B) Basement plan
Architects: Manfred Schluter and Klaus Orlich

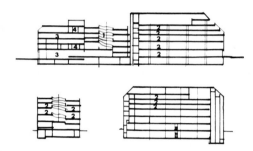

Key:
1 Car access ramp
2 Car parking floors
3 Sales floors
4 WCs

4·84 Department store in Basel, Switzerland:
sections
Architects: Suter and Suter

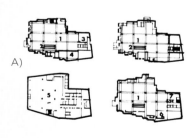

Key: A)
1 Sales area
2 Escalators
3 Restaurant
4 Administration
5 Storage area
6 Children's play area
7 Cafeteria

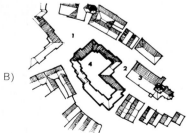

Key: B)
1 Market square
2 Church square
3 Church
4 Department store
Scale: 1 : 4000

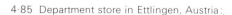

4·85 Department store in Ettlingen, Austria:
A) Floor plan
B) Block plan
Architect: Heinz Mohl

4·86 Department store, Basel, Switzerland: exterior view facing main shopping street

floors. Upon rejection of this solution a design more deferential to its classical neighbours was evolved with a projecting gantry superstructure and modulated wall panels incorporating perimeter vertical ductwork. The ingenuity with which these technical devices were employed to produce a 'classical' composition of pilasters, string courses and cornice, reflected the difficulties which the building type presented in an historical setting. A department store designed by Heinz Mohl at Ettlingen illustrated a similar attention to the treatment of the skin of the building volume when placed into a mediaeval street pattern and in juxtaposition with the town's Baroque church. In contrast to the simple clarity of its internal structural grid, the building's perimeter zone develops a complex and fragmented series of forms, irregular on plan and battered on section, parodying here not the classical orders but the domestic cross-wall scale and roof lines of its surroundings.

In another example, at Wolfenbüttel by Klaus Orlich, the department store is placed behind the mediaeval buildings of the street frontage, and the free form of the main sales floors is used to create an exterior space connected to the street and reflected within the store in an irregular polygonal central space which rises through its three storeys. The six storeys of the Ettlingen store were entirely devoted to the traditional component areas of the department store, from sales to restaurant, storage and staff accommodation, while at Wolfenbüttel a basement level provided car parking for 110 spaces, at a ratio of 1·1 space per 100 m² of gross shop area. Yet even this was comparatively low in comparison with a number of other contemporary store developments in which a substantial parking facility emerged as a major new factor of department store design in an urban situation. One solution to this new problem was to allocate, as at Wolfenbüttel, one or more floors of the building to parking, and in several examples these were placed at an upper level, leaving the basement free for sales and storage functions. In such cases a spiral ramp access to the upper parking levels became a major plan element as it passed through the lower floors, as for example in Suter and Suter's design for a store in Basle, in which sloping profile of the upper part of the building accommodates 4 parking floors above the basement, ground and first floors housing the retailing uses. Alternatively the division between parking and store might be a vertical one, with each part rising through the full height of the development and, typically, the car parking extending over both areas at roof level. Since three parking floors could be provided within the height required by two sales floors, a considerable parking capacity could thus be formed by allocating, say, one third of the site area to the parking building. In the department store on Ludwigsplatz in Darmstadt designed by Gartner and Stiens, for example, a ratio of 5·4 spaces/100 m² GLA was achieved in this way for a store of 11,900 m² gross. One of the largest of the new European department stores, for Innovation on the rue Neuve in Brussels, was planned on this basis by Polak and Stapels. The building fills its block, 140 × 95 m, with 6 shop floors paralleled by 8 parking levels and providing 850 parking spaces for 55,700 m² of gross shopping area. For smaller or more difficult sites the simple horizontal or vertical division of the building between its two uses might give way to a more intricate accommodation, as in a department store at Turku in Finland, by Ylihannu and Jalovaara, in which parts of the square floor plan at upper levels are given over to car parking reached by a ramp which climbs up one side of the square.

The novel, and sometimes uncomfortable, intrusion of the car parking structure into the department store brief for these buildings, all of which were completed between 1968 and 1971, is transformed in two final examples in which the traditional sales element becomes enveloped in its parking facility. Since the former requires no external wall openings at upper levels these two schemes contain a splendid logic which appears almost as a caricature of the out-of-town pattern transferred to an urban site in which the parking lot becomes coiled around the building that it serves. In Skidmore, Owings and Merrills' Rego Park branch of Macy's in Queens, New York, the combined elements are contained within a circular perimeter, 130 m in diameter within which the outer zone, 17 m wide, is occupied by a ring of parking on 5 levels fed from two independent helical access ramps. The three sales floors in the core of the doughnut are then accessible by half-flights of stairs, up or down, from customers' parking spaces, while at ground level, where no parking occurs, the sales area extends out to within 10 m of the building perimeter, forming a covered arcade all round the base of the ring. A similar solution was adopted by Antoine Dory for a Nouvelles Galeries store at Annecy, in which an annular parking loop of similar dimensions circumscribes a square store building, touching it at its corners and connected to it in the middle of its sides by bridge ramps up or down to sales levels. At ground level the undercroft of the parking ring is occupied by small independant shop units which form a screen around the central store, the routes to which pass through small open courts formed in the spaces between

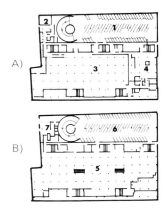

A)

B)

Key: A)
1 Multi-storey car park
2 Plant room
3 Central stock
4 Administration

B)
5 Sales area
6 Multi-storey car park
7 Staff rooms
Scale: 1:4000

4·87 Department store in Brussels: upper-floor plans
Architects: Polak and Stapels

4·88 Project for Kin Department Store, Tokyo: view of model showing flexible facade of interchangeable displays
Architect: Minoru Takeyama

117

the square and the circle.

An unbuilt departmental store design by Minoru Takeyama is the Kin Building, Tokyo. The design has a completely changeable kinetic facade using a vertical space frame for the overall structural support. It is 11 storeys high with 9 main sales floors.

4·7 Retail Markets

With their ancient origin in unsophisticated economies and their relative independence of permanent building structures, stall markets are often disregarded in reviews of shopping facilities or considered to be anachronistic, if picturesque, elements in the retailing hierarchy. Yet, while never establishing themselves to a significant degree in the New World they have remained a remarkably persistent and resilient trading form in Western Europe. It is estimated that there were about 86,000 market stalls operating in Great Britain in 1971, handling about 2% of the total retail turnover in the country, and 15% of total turnover in fruit and vegetables. In France and Italy the proportion is even more significant, and in Inner Paris approximately one third of all food selling points are located in its 121 retail markets, while three quarters of all outlets for fruit and vegetables are in the markets. Moreover it is now believed that the relative importance of markets has not been declining, either in parallel with the decline in other small traders, as had been suggested, or through the general shift in the proportion of consumer expenditure devoted to convenience and food items. Rather, stall traders have shown an ability to trade up where necessary and to diversify lines within the broad categories of small, low-cost items traditionally handled, from food, clothing and textiles to electrical goods, hardware, toilet goods, stationery, antiques and second-hand goods.

The traditional open-air markets, of which 2,800 were franchised in England and Wales by the Crown between 1199 and 1480 AD, remain a well established feature of European towns. In the UK there are 513 such markets,[23] 23 mostly administered by the local authority, but sometimes run by private individual or company, and including a number of street markets in the cities, which may be simply a collection of licensed street traders operating along designated streets. In rural situations and smaller towns the market is commonly held on only one day a week, so that the market trader may lead an itinerant existence, travelling from town to town to achieve a full days trading for six days a week if he wishes in contrast to fixed shop-keepers who will be busy for perhaps half of this time. He can also trade on fewer days if he wishes, having little capital tied up in equipment and premises, and a system of 'rights' exists to particular stall locations which can be occupied by casual traders if they are not taken up by 10 am on the market day. The open markets are thus a very flexible form of trading, attractive and with low overheads. They do suffer however from the disadvantages of susceptibility to the weather, which can be disastrous to a day's trading, the unstable life imposed on the traders, the labour involved in the erection and dismantling of stalls, a certain inconvenience to the local authority in terms of refuse disposal and traffic management, and finally difficulty for food stalls in complying in the UK with the hygiene requirements of the Food and Drugs Act 1955 which require washing and toilet facilities for traders and their assistants.

4·89 Stall at Chesterfield Market, a traditional open market in Derbyshire, England

Since the establishment of modern systems of local government, in France after the Revolution and in Britain with the Local Government Act of 1858, there has been a tendency to institutionalise the old markets and in particular to off-set the disadvantages of their open-air form by providing them with enclosed halls in which stalls could be permanent and facilities for refuse disposal and hygiene requirements could be provided. In Paris, Georges Haussmann's redevelopment programme under Napoleon III provided massive new market facilities, both open along the new boulevards and enclosed in new market halls. This work established the present distribution of retail markets in the city, in which the 53 street markets, operated from barrows by the 'Marchands des Quatre Saisons', occupy positions along the radial routes of entry into Paris and coinciding with concentrations of fixed trading, while the 16 covered and 52 open public retail markets are generally located away from the main shopping centre, in the middle of wide avenues and boulevards and in roughly concentric lines parallel to the fortifications. The strength of these retail markets has been a deliberate policy of the City of Paris as of other towns in France for 170 years, and as regards the distribution of food they are regarded as a form of public service entitled to subsidy where necessary. This sympathetic attitude has extended also to their growth, allowing traders to take up places in surrounding streets when the enclosed markets became full.

In the UK the development of covered markets, both in the latter part of the 19th century and again since the war, has occurred mainly in the north of England, in the Manchester/Liverpool and Leeds/Bradford conurbations, and to a lesser extent in the Midlands, South Wales and the South-West Peninsula. Whether their distribution was related to rainfall or to the inhopitable climates of industrial cities in the last century, there were 275 covered market

halls operating in 1971, some in their original Victorian structures, some in new purpose-built halls, and some forming parts of major shopping centre developments. A number of examples of the last category occur in the centres described in Chapter 4·3, as in the Victoria Centre at Nottingham where the Victoria Market occupies 11,000 m² in a central position on both mall levels, and in the St. Johns Precinct at Liverpool a city which had built one of the first covered markets with the St John's Market Hall in 1822.

The form of the original market halls had commonly been that of a solid perimeter of lock-up shops facing into a central space covered with a glazed roof supported on a wide-span cast iron structure.[24] Within this space goods were sold on simple trestle stalls, without individual roofs or canopies, and thus visible from an upper gallery of stalls and cafe running round the perimeter lock-ups, which originally had no frontage outwards to the surrounding streets. This organisation persisted in several modern structures built specifically to rehouse markets, but with detail modifications which produced unfortunate results. There was a tendency for the market stall to become more elaborate, with greater storage space and security, so that it gradually moved away from the trestle table form—literally the open-air market stall with canopy removed—towards a kind of mini-shop unit, with corner posts, fascia boards, security grilles, and even a roof. This progression effectively destroyed the character of the earlier halls, and in more recent developments the spacious glazed hall has been replaced by an organisation more strictly comparable to that of a shopping centre, in which the units are permanent booths, often integrated with the structure of the hall itself. A good example of this is the Castle Market at Sheffield,[25] completed in 1962 by the City Architects' department under J. L. Womersley, which accommodates a complex of market stalls together with conventional shops, storage, service and refuse facilities, market police office and restaurant and cafe within a 40 x 15 m city centre site adjacent to existing meat and fish market. Using both natural and artificial pedestrian levels generated around its site, the

4·90 Sheffield Castle Market, England: view of the new multi-level enclosed market with photomontage of the minitram system
Architects: Lewis Womersley, City Architect, succeeded by Bernard Warren
Project Architect: Andrew Derbyshire

4·91 Runcorn New Town Shopping City, England: view of Trader's Hall, showing a new enclosed market on the shopping deck
Architects: Town Centre Group, Runcorn Development Corporation

building provides two main shopping floors together with two intermediate mezzanines and an upper gallery. The shop units, rising through 2, 3 or 4 levels form an external frontage to the block on its south and west side and enclose the market hall, through the 4 levels of which voids penetrate from roof glazing above. Servicing is from a subway running around three sides of the block at the lowest level, and the sign of the market booths is fully integrated into that of the complex as a whole.

In such developments it could be argued that the market stall has undergone a far more dramatic transformation by spiral development than has the fixed shopping centre, considering the difference in capital investment between the timber or tubular steel framed open stall and the

4·92

4·93

multi-level, serviced, custom-built structure. Coexisting with that extreme is a whole range of intermediate forms of market structures, including new open air markets built as permanent structures, as at Bedworth in Warwickshire, and traditional open markets provided with an umbrella roof, as at Leicester, to provide weather protection without entirely losing an open character. Finally the street market, of which London has 88, continues to thrive with little more in the way of 'structure' than a barrow rented from a central base which can provide storage space close to the street 3,000 traders now operate in Petticoat Lane and there is a waiting period of many years for a pitch on the Portobello Road,[26] which nicely reflects adjacent land values in its trading range along its ¾ mile length, from the antique stalls on Notting Hill Gate, through fruit and vegetables in the middle area alongside the major multiple stores, and then north under the motorway to link up with Kensal Road. The success of these more famous examples is reflected in pressure on many local authorities throughout England and Wales for additional market spaces and in the recent appearance of private open markets at seaside towns, particularly in the South-East, and is an indication of the continued liveliness of this ancient method of trading in all its forms.

4·8 Rehabilitation

The construction within existing town centres of new shopping centres with pedestrian-only malls, together with new urban road-works, parking buildings and traffic management plans, has been matched in a number of cities with schemes to improve and rehabilitate the existing fabric. The most common instance of this has been in the pedestrianisation of shopping streets to form precincts served by whatever servicing and car parking facilities could best be accommodated to the existing pattern, to produce a result approximating in its organisation to that of the first post-War New Town and Stage 1 centres. Thus at Nottingham, for example, the enclosed malls of the new Victoria

4·92 Altringham Market, Cheshire, England: exterior view of the food market

4·93 Altringham Market, Cheshire, England: interior view of the original market hall (1879) with durable-goods sales area

4·94 Street market in Copacabana, Rio de Janeiro: food markets are held once or twice a week in Rio and have the village atmosphere of street fairs

4·94

and Arndale centres are related to a series of pedestrianised existing streets within the city core, devised as part of a comprehensive plan which includes car parking facilities around the perimeter of the core and free bus service within it.

One of the earliest and most ambitious pedestrianisation schemes was for the Strøget in Copenhagen, in which a series of five successive shopping streets, running from Rådhuspladsen by Tivoli to the Royal Theatre on Kongens Nytorv, were closed to traffic and planted and paved. Since this was done in the early '60s further roads running off the Strøget to the north have been pedestrianised and an extensive network of shopping streets created which contains a great variety of shop types, from department stores and expensive specialist traders to small toy shops and boutiques. An early example in England was the pedestrianisation of London Street in Norwich, by the early '60s a narrow and congested traffic route from the Market Place to the Cathedral area.[27] In 1965 this street was closed for a short period for emergency sewer repairs, an event which convinced shopkeepers that the elimination of traffic would not harm trading as had been feared. This was followed by an experimental pedestrianisation of the street for 6 months in 1967, during which the effects on trading and public reaction were gauged. Since there was no

provision in the Road Traffic legislation at that time to close a street to vehicles for reasons of environmental improvement, a provision of existing legislation allowing closure to 'avoid danger to persons using the road' was used, and following the success of the experiment the street was permanently closed to traffic, resurfaced and landscaped, in 1969. Since then the Town and Country Planning Act 1968 and the Transport Act 1968 have made it simpler for local authorities in the UK to carry out pedestrianisation projects. For small centres it has often been possible to build a bypass route through the rear areas of the high street allowing both its closure to traffic and rear access servicing and car parking fed from the new road. The rehabilitation of Old Harlow in 1970, by Frederick Gibberd and Partners in association with the Harlow Development Corporation, exemplifies this approach, in which the pedestrianisation was accompanied by the refurbishing of existing buildings along High Street and the insertion of new shops and flats into gaps in the street frontage.

While such examples of the rehabilitation of streets by their pedestrianisation and the refurbishing of adjoining frontages have become comparatively common in cities in the UK, there have been few cases of the rehabilitation of individual buildings and their conversion, rather than redevelopment, to shop use. This contrasts with the in-

4·95 The Strøget, Copenhagen: a section of five pedestrianised streets in the central shopping district of Copenhagen

4·96 The Lanes, Brighton, England: a nucleus of small pedestrianised shopping streets and alleyways in a south-coast resort town

4·97 London Street, Norwich: one of the first pedestrianised shopping streets in England
Planner: A. A. Wood

4·95

4·96

4·97

creasing concern over the past ten years with rehabilitation in housing, or, to take a parallel commercial case, the numerous and successful conversions of old buildings to office use. It is perhaps paradoxical that the most interesting examples of conversion and rehabilitation for shopping have occurred in North America. Of these, three of the best-known examples have been developed in old industrial buildings around Fisherman's Wharf in San Francisco. Ghirardelli Square was formed within a city block of low brick buildings which had formerly housed the Ghirardelli chocolate factory. Demolishing only one wooden structure, a four-storey underground car park was inserted into the complex of old buildings and a terraced square formed above. Around this the brick buildings were sand-blasted, gutted and internally arranged to accommodate 5,050 m² GLA of shops, cafes and offices. Nearby, the Del Monte Fruit Cannery, a building which had survived the 1906 earthquake and fire, was similarly converted. Within the old brick shell the new three storey structure of the Cannery was erected with a maze-like variety of horizontal and vertical, interior and exterior spaces. Across the street a four-storey warehouse was converted by the same architects, Esherick Homsey Dodge and Davis, but for different clients, into two office floors above two levels of fashion shops, restaurants and museum, and the latter again evolved into a network of meandering, intricate routes and spaces threaded through the old structural brick walls and timber columns.

These conversions share a refreshingly un-academic approach to the old structures upon which they are based. Writing on the Cannery, its architects state that,

'To us there is too much beady-eyed, dead-serious

4·98 Old Harlow, Essex, England, showing pedestrianisation of an old town core attached to new town development
Architect: John Graham of Sir Frederick Gibberd and Partners

restoration going on, much of which isn't all that good. Old buildings such as this center should be approached with a sense of humour—a common sense approach that acknowledges the building's anachronistic aspects.'

Interesting and useful fragments of the old are seized upon, as with the huge 'Ghirardelli' sign which advertised the chocolate factory, and which the architects for the conversion, Wurster, Bernardi and Emmons Inc, restored and illuminated. New work is done in materials sympathetic to the old but may contain strange elements, such as an escalator sliding up the exterior of a brick wall at the Cannery. And the tenants of these buildings, although subject to

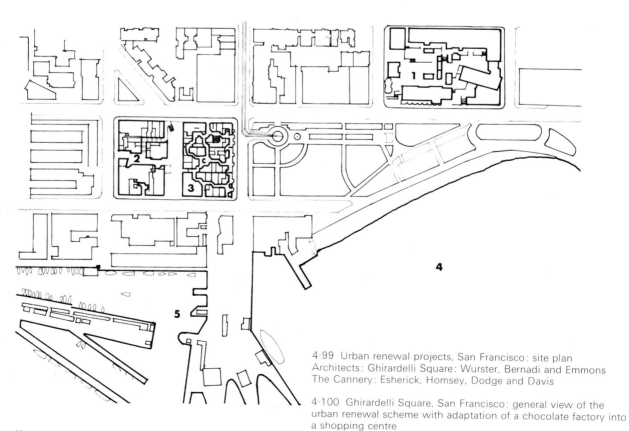

4·99 Urban renewal projects, San Francisco: site plan
Architects: Ghirardelli Square: Wurster, Bernadi and Emmons
The Cannery: Esherick, Homsey, Dodge and Davis

4·100 Ghirardelli Square, San Francisco: general view of the urban renewal scheme with adaptation of a chocolate factory into a shopping centre

4·101 The Cannery, San Francisco: two views of an urban renewal scheme with the adaptation of warehouse buildings into a shopping precinct

Key:
1 Ghirardelli Square
2 The Cannery
3 The Wharf
4 San Francisco Bay
5 Harbour
Scale: 1:4000

4·102 Faneuil Hall Market Place, Boston, USA: an urban renewal
scheme showing the adaptation of old market hall buildings into
a new shopping development
Architects: Benjamin Thompson Associates

124

careful control, may throw up anachronisms of their own which, to European eyes, might appear somewhat alarming. Thus, again at the Cannery, the 'English Restaurant' comprises the long Gallery of Albyn's Hall, 29 m long and made in 1620, a Jacobean staircase and two Elizabethan upper rooms, all authentic and obtained from the William Randolph Hearst estate where they had been in storage since the early '20s, and coexisting now with the Very Very Terry Jerry Shop across the mall.

In Boston, Ben Thompson, designer of the unique Design Research building in Cambridge Massachusetts (see Chapter 5·5) published a rehabilitation plan for the Faneuil Hall Quincy Market Area in 1971. The development is composed of three long parallel buildings, the centre one of which is the 1824 Quincy Market. The proposals retain the open street character around the block with pedestrian priority. Sheltered arcades contain outdoor traders and pavement cafés with continuous shopping and restaurant development along both pedestrianised streets; so that both day time and night time activity will be generated. The Quincy Market will become a food market at first floor level with specialist food trading along an internal street, the central dome of the building will become the focal space with balconies around the rotunda housing specialist shops overlooking the 'crossroads' of the market place. The north and south buildings on either side of Quincy Market will house restaurants, night clubs and boutiques, with an emphasis on local restaurants, clubs and cafés under owner-management.

References

1 Farsta Centrum, *Arkitektur* No. 3 1961
2 See *Architectural Design* 6/1973 and 8/1974 and MK booklets *Central Milton Keynes* and *Central Milton Keynes: Shopping*
3 Reyner Banham on CIAM, *Encyclopaedia of Modern Architecture* Thames & Hudson, London 1963
4 *The Planning of a New Town* London County Council 1961
5 *Architectural Design* 5/1963; see also *The Architectural Review* 12/1967 and Cumbernauld Development Corporation, *Town Centre Report; Technical Brochure* et al
6 See John Holliday (ed) *City Centre Redevelopment* Charles Knight & Co Ltd, London 1973 for descriptions of development in Birmingham, Coventry, Liverpool, Leicester and Newcastle-upon-Tyne
7 From *The Property Developer & Investor* cited by Oliver Marriott in *The Property Boom* Pan Books, London 1969
8 See description of background in *The Property Boom op cit*
9 From the Grenfell Baines report *Chester—a Plan for the Central Area* 1964
10 From *Town and City Properties Limited; Arndale Covered Centres* 1973
11 Derek Walker on shopping centres, see *Architectural Design* 8/74
12 From Robert Venturi, Denise Scott Brown and Steven Izenour *Learning from Las Vegas* MIT Press, Cambridge Mass. and London 1972
13 From Lance Wright, 'Shopping the Environment' *The Architectural Review* March 1973
14 *Shopping Centers; Planning for Changes and Flexibility; Seven Danish Examples* Institut for Center—Planlaegning 1968
15 See Ingesta Report 1/70
16 See the Building Study in *The Architects' Journal* 5 January 1972
17 *The Architects' Journal* 4 July 1973
18 *Bourtreehill Local Centre planning report 1973 by* Irvine Development Corporation Department of Architecture
19 The Urban Land Institute, *Project Reference File* Vol 1, Number 9; see also *Architectural Forum* April 1972
20 *Broadway Plaza brochure* by Odyer Development Corporation
21 *Architectural Forum* September 1966; see also *The Architectural Review* August 1967
22 *Architecture Canada* July 1967
23 Source: J. H. Kirk, P. G. Ellis and J. R. Medland, *Retail Stall Markets in Great Britain* Wye College Marketing Series: No 8 April 1972
24 See Barrie and Helen Shelton, 'Updating Market Halls' *Official Architecture and Planning* January 1972
25 See *The Architectural Review* August 1962 See Jim Burgess, 'Street Markets': An Extendible Resource' *Built Environment* August 1974
27 Road Traffic Regulation Act 1967; see *Norwich: the Creation of a Foot Street* by A. A. Wood, City Planning Officer, Norwich 1969

5 Special Forms

5·01 Furniture Showroom, Milan: new direction in shop design began to appear in Europe in the early 1970s. This Italian example shows a return to a more geometrical and architectural aesthetic than the ebullient designs of the 1960s; epitomised in Garnett, Cloughley, Blakemore and Associates' Chelsea Drugstore
Architect: Mario Bellini

5·1 Introduction

In the 1960s several completely new forms of mass retailing appeared. Extending from the evolution of boutiques in London's King's Road district to the development of specialist furniture, household goods and toy shops associated with new mail order systems, they were a part of a design and cultural explosion at the beginning of the 1960s which lasted through the decade. London became, during this time, a centre of new developments in fashion, popular music, art, films, television and theatre, while in the United States a parallel movement took place, visually expressing itself most vividly in the field of supergraphics.

A number of these developments, of interest for the novelty of new trading philosophies they encouraged and the quality of retail design they produced, are discussed in this section.

The most visible developments in this change manifested itself in the small fashion shops, but in some ways the specialist mini-stores such as Habitat or Galt Toys in Britain or Design Research in the United States are likely to have a more far-reaching effect in the long term. The Habitat display and merchandising methods both in its retail outlets and mail order service is without parallel with the possible exception of Ikea in Scandinavia on which a number of Habitat's methods are based.

The affluence of the mid-'60s may have had a lot to do with these phenomena. It appeared during that decade that most families in Western Europe and North America could look forward almost indefinitely to rising incomes and a consumer orientated society. The amount of money available to the young, and in particular to teenagers, probably did much to justify the explosive demand for high fashion as well as expenditure in other areas such as popular music and entertainment generally.

The decline in consumer spending in the decade that has followed has lead inevitably to the diminution in the growth and number of boutiques, but the growth of specialised mini-stores/mail-order outlets continues.

5·2 Habitat

Terence Conran, the founder of Habitat, was trained as a textile designer at the Central School of Arts and Crafts in London. He originally worked for an architect and interior designer but in 1952 at the age of 21 he set up as a freelance industrial designer and worked from a studio and workshop in Chelsea where he designed and made furniture. An exhibition of his furniture at Simpsons in Piccadilly was an instant success and a small showroom was established and a catalogue printed. Conran and Company was formed with a specially designed factory, warehouse and office complex built at Thetford in Norfolk. The Company expanded with the establishment of a Design Group in 1955 providing a consultancy service in interior, product, graphic, packaging, display and exhibition design. Conran Fabrics was set up in 1956 to design, import and market textiles.

In 1964, Terence Conran opened the first Habitat shop in the Fulham Road, South Kensington, as a prototype for a chain of retail stores selling modern furniture and furnishings for the home. The merchandise included, as well as furniture, fabrics, rugs, linens, lighting, kitchenware, china and glass, toys and home decorating equipment. Until that time most contemporary well-designed furniture was highly priced and beyond the majority of incomes. Habitat

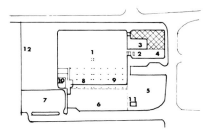

Key:
1 Main warehouse area
2 Coffee area
3 Children's play court
4 Showroom
5 Showroom car park
6 Truck compound
7 Staff car park
8 Goods in
9 Goods out
10 Staff
11 Sprinkler plant
12 Future expansion

Scale: 1 : 4000

5·02 Habitat Warehouse, Wallingford, England: plan
Architects: Ahrends, Burton and Koralek

5·03 Showroom interior at Habitat, Wallingford, England

5·04 Exterior view of Habitat, Wallingford, showing showroom and warehouse

5·05 Warehouse interior at Habitat, Wallingford

provided in furniture and household wares much the same sort of service which Marks and Spencer had been providing in clothing.

In 1968, the Conran Group merged with the Ryman organisation to form Ryman Conran Ltd and after this merger a large factory and warehouse was acquired at Wallingford to form the basis of Habitat by Post, providing a mail order system of self-build component furniture. In 1970, Habitat separated from Ryman and seven Habitat stores were established together with the Mail Order operation at Wallingford. By 1973 the number of shops had grown to 14 and by 1974 to 19 extending from Glasgow to the Home Counties. The first mail order catalogue, Habitat by Post, was published in 1969 and offered the same range of merchandise contained in the larger Habitat shops. The catalogue has been published annually with a new range ever since that time.

The latest development has been the establishment of Habitat shops in Europe, the first of which was opened by Habitat Designs France in Tour Montparnasse, Paris in 1973.[1]

Operating Philosophy

In commencing the Habitat Operation, Terence Conran felt that the marketing methods in the furniture industry were wrong for retailing because they were operated on a large mass-produced scale by a relatively small number of manufacturers. He felt that if the manufacturer could also operate the retail outlets then an assessment of market need would be far easier to obtain. He believed furthermore that shopping should be entertaining and as easy as possible.

Habitat shops were not necessarily established on prime sites and the great variation in their locations was not considered to be important. Ranging from the end of High Street development at Bromley Kent, the centre of redevelopment in Churchill Square, Brighton, the renovation of hotel buildings in Clifton Heights, Bristol, the conversion of a Georgian house at the end of a promenade in Cheltenham, the pedestrianised street in Watford with Sainsbury's food supermarket opposite and British Home Stores and John Lewis on either side, to the prime sites of the Victoria enclosed centre at Nottingham or the New Street rail centre at Birmingham, the choice of premises is claimed to be a function of price and space. A lot of space is the most important attribute. Terence Conran believes that the Habitat store was 'originally suitable for the intelligentsia but has now grown to be a reasonable alternative to the average high-street store.'

In the present stage of development in the 1970s, Habitat is considering the hypermarket approach. The one planned for Wallingford was finished towards the end of 1973 and one was planned for Milton Keynes for 1975. Because of the fuel crisis in 1974 and the possible decline in car ownership there has been some revision in this approach.

In France apart from the Central Paris location at Tour Montparnasse, a Habitat shop has been located at an out-of-town shopping centre, Les Ulis. This latter location is interesting in that it includes a vast Carrefour hypermarket. A third one is planned for Orgeval on the west side of Paris on Autoroute N30. This will be a hypermarket operation including warehouse distribution centre and out-of-town shop. The three Paris Habitats are in three quite dissimilar locations.

Terence Conran attributes some of the Habitat inspiration to the Scandinavian Ikea developments. British fire regulations prevented an exact copy of the Ikea furniture hypermarkets, where furniture is displayed on racks in exactly the same manner as a warehouse. Selection is made and furniture trucked through cash tills to the customer's car. The Wallingford operation does not follow the simplicity of this plan. The Scandinavian use of a balcony viewing area to inspect all furniture in the main area is not possible because fire regulations would demand four hours' fire resistance material between the two areas.[2]

Hypermarket Example: Wallingford

The development includes a 7,400 m² warehouse, showroom and head office complex. The original 3,700 m² complex at Wallingford was purchased in 1969 and since then the head office and warehousing functions for the shops and mail order have been centred there. A small showroom was also open to the public. Families from all over the country visited the small showroom, and whilst parents inspected the furniture, children would use the playground and a Habitat café was also provided.

In 1971, Ahrends, Burton and Koralek were appointed architects to design the new complex on a 1·75 ha site opposite the existing buildings. The brief required the provision of a 4,700 m² warehouse with loading facilities, 1,600 m² for packing and offices and 900 m² of showroom. The total area is 7,650 m².

The warehouse was to serve all the Habitat shops together with mail order packing and processing facilities. The car park accommodates 50 staff cars and 50 visitors cars and truck compound. There were special security requirements and the designers had to bear in mind that the use of the building was likely to change substantially. As Habitat's head office complex, the design had to reflect the Habitat corporate image. The building was completed in February 1974.

There are two buildings: one containing the warehouse etc. and one, the showroom, linked only by a conveyor for security reasons. The buildings are related in such a way that a children's courtyard is created between them. The construction consists of peripheral precast concrete columns with a group of four columns in the centre of the building supporting a cruciform of beams which in turn support areas of space frame roof covered with metal decking. The mezzanine is made of preformed permanent wood-wool shutters. The walls are an asbestos sandwich painted externally. Windows are aluminium with neoprene gaskets.

The site is an industrial estate on the western edge of a predominantly agricultural town. The solution for enclosing a considerable volume of blank space at high speed and low cost with every day industrial materials and yet achieving high visual standards epitomises the general excellence of design approach in the Habitat organisation itself. The use of giant graphics externally applied to cheap materials provides the scale and impact necessary. It has been pointed out elsewhere (Lance Wright, *The Architectural Review* August 1974) that the customers who would use the place do not want a building . . . they want "accommodation" only, out in the blue, outside the community. It is a giant mail order establishment linked with an edge-of-town shopping outlet'. As a new form it succeeds brilliantly.

5·3 Ikea

Ikea, which is a Swedish organisation operating throughout Scandinavia has parallels to Habitat, and preceded the Conran organisation. Ikea's policy was to sell a large

5·08

5·06 Ikea, Almhult, Sweden: exterior of the headquarters building
Architects: Ikea Architect's Department

5·07 Air view of the Ikea Super Store at Stockholm, Sweden

5·08 Interior view of the sales area at Ikea Sundsvall

131

variety of home furnishing articles of good design, function and quality at the lowest possible prices. It has five furniture hypermarkets in Sweden itself, the largest being at Almhult, one in Norway and one in Denmark. Apart from the hypermarkets it has Habitat-style shops in nine Scandinavian cities. Ikea was established in the early 1950s and, unlike Habitat, all its goods initially were sold through the mail-order catalogue. The firm was founded by Ingvar Kamprad who still controls the group as managing director. The open plan head office is located at Almhult in Southern Sweden and the central services of manufacturing, marketing and administration are also located there.

History

After establishment in 1950, the first showroom was opened in 1958 at Almhult. This covered an area, including warehousing at 7,000 m² and was rebuilt in 1970. The sales area was increased to 12,000 m². The first Ikea establishment outside Almhult was located in Norway at Nesbru near Oslo in 1963. The largest showroom and retail outlet was established in 1965 at Kungens Kurva south of Stockholm with an area of 32,000 m² (it is interesting to compare this with the relatively small size of the Habitat Wallingford complex of 7,600 m², or the proposed Milton Keynes complex of 5,500 m²). A 2-storey extension of Kungens Kurva was started in February 1972 and completed in 1974. Ikea is progressively introducing self service/quick service in all of its retail outlets. All central warehousing is however still concentrated on Almhult. In 1972 the Ikea building at Sundsvall in northern Sweden was changed from a specialised furniture hypermarket of 25,000 m² to a shopping centre. Ikea Stormarknad was established and included nine other companies. The companies work independently but have the same objectives of low price, good design and quality. The companies include Hemköp—foods; Lindex AB—women's clothes; Herr-City—men's and boys' clothes; Bamcenter AB—children's clothes (3–16 years old); Bokman AB—books, stationery, records, toys; Buketten—flowers; Rolf Nilsson AB—sports goods; Malungsbutlkema AB—leather clothes and goods.

In 1967 a new method of merchandising was introduced with the establishment of Malmo. This is one of the smallest hypermarkets of 5,000 m² and goods were supplied from the central warehouse at Almhult.

The largest Ikea hypermarket of all is at Almhult itself. The central warehouse serves all Ikea units and increases the delivery capacity considerably. The warehouse is very big (84,000 m²) and is continuously being enlarged. There is in addition an export warehouse being planned. Retail showrooms are planned on two levels, with display areas arranged in a series of viewing balconies, and incorporating coffee shop and childrens' play areas. Within the complex, apart from warehousing and administrative buildings, there is a motel and indoor swimming pool managed by Ikea.

Ikea employs 1,500 people of which 450 are employed at the Almhult centre. 1,000,000 Swedish households are registered in Ikea's customer card index with credit facilities. The catalogue has an annual edition of almost 2 million (1,950,000 in 1972). 500,000 copies of the Danish catalogue and 700,000 copies of the Norwegian catalogue are published. Ikea feel however that in Sweden in particular with the highest per capita car ownership in the world, and in Scandinavia in general, the mail order side will gradually diminish. Ikea is expanding into other areas of Europe with developments in Austria and Switzerland, as well as further developments in Norway and Denmark.[3]

Merchandising Policy

75% of the Ikea merchandise is the product of their own design team or freelance designers appointed by the Company. It has its own research and development group composed of architects, pattern shop technicians, construction engineers and textile laboratory scientists and technicians. The development work is based at Almhult. Ikea claim that the rational handling of goods and flexible internal supply of goods maintain lower costs than the more conventional construction and storage by an independent manufacturer. Long term budgeting and sales planning is carried out as well as internal co-ordinated product development. Extensive use is made of computer data processing. All Ikea outlets are located in edge-of-town locations with low site acquisition costs. Extensive car parking is free of charge and additional facilities at each Ikea centre include restaurants and children's playgrounds. Each showroom displays completely decorated 'homes' for comparison shopping as well as a free design advice service.

Market Philosophy

The founder/managing director, Ingvar Kamprad, had a reasonably simple philosophy, though for the mid-'50s it was quite unique. He felt that a low price was not useful to the consumers unless it combined with high quality. Furthermore, he questioned whether an article of beautiful design had to be expensive. It was apparent in those days in most countries that beautiful design was only intended for the high-income market and Kamprad pointed to Italy as a prime example of that time. The philosophy of Ikea was the combination of high design standards, high quality and low cost. It was in order to achieve this that he integrated various manufacturing firms into the Ikea organisation. Suppliers were provided with the raw materials by Ikea as well as technical advice. Ikea took over the responsibility for selling the manufactured articles. Instead of maintaining stocks throughout the country, one central stock of 100,000 m² was established. This integration with the manufacturers gave and maintained lower prices. From 1955 to 1970 the price of food in Sweden rose from Skr 100 to Skr 197; in the corresponding period the price of furniture rose from Skr 100 to Skr 135.

Hypermarket Example: Malmo

The Malmo establishment is the smallest of the Ikea outlets, but the plan serves to illustrate the general principles. The plan is E shaped wrapping round a central car park yard. On one side there is the single storey administrative wing and the link between this and the two storey warehouse building is the showroom. It basically operates on a cash-and-carry system. The customers enter through the showroom link building which is arranged on an exhibition system with complete rooms in sequential function (living room, dining room, bedroom etc) so that the customer as the opportunity for comparison shopping. On the upper floor of the warehouse wing is the textile section and floor covering section and a coffee shop. Below this is the do-it-yourself shop. All moveable items are then checked out through cash registers in much the same way as a food supermarket and loaded into the customer's car in the central yard. Normally the warehouse is sufficient to supply the entire range of knock-down furniture, though Malmo is at present too small and an additional warehouse a few blocks away is provided.[4]

5·4 Toy Retailing

One of the chief problems in the toy industry is that half the year's turnover is done in the six weeks preceding Christmas. Giving toys on a grand scale at Christmas is a fairly modern custom which has grown rapidly in the last fifty years though its origins stretch back over centuries and were religious. The main opportunity for buying toys was on Feast days when big fairs and markets took place.

In the 18th century most toys were sold by pedlars. The British toy industry, as a manufacturing industry, is virtually quite new. Originally, major manufacturers in Europe came over to England with their samples and showed them to the importers in the English trade. If sufficient orders had been obtained, the continental representative returned to Europe and production was commenced accordingly. From these beginnings grew the early toy trade fair. From about 1850 to 1940 this fair was held in Manchester; after the war with the Manchester hotels destroyed, it moved elsewhere and became well known as the Harrogate Toy Fair. It was originally a fair for imported toys.

The rapid growth of the British toy industry led to the formation of the British Toy Manufacturers' Association which started in 1944 and established a separate fair held at Brighton, also in the very early part of the year. This period of growth in the British toy trade coincided with a period of completely new thinking, outside the industry, about toys. Most of this new philosophy was due to the work of psychologists and teachers over the past fifty years. One of the earliest experiments of the idea that toys are more than trifles was the teacher, Froebel, born in Germany in 1782; he used play materials and practical occupations and invented the term Kindergarten. Maria Montessori, born in Italy in 1870, was another great teacher who enormously influenced methods of education; much of her work was with mentally defective children, for whom she developed sense-training apparatus. In 1904 a USA trade paper wrote 'The Kindergarten idea is taking strong hold of the manufacturers of domestic toys—any toy which combines a spate of education with a whole lot of pleasure and fun is likely to prove popular'.

The major work leading to modern ideas of toy and play was done by psychologists in the 1920s and 1930s, by Gesell in the United States, Charlotte Buhler in Vienna and Melanie Klein, Margaret Lowerfeld and Susan Isaacs in England. Out of this research came the knowledge which should have had an enormous and immediate impact on the toy trade but it had no such effect at all. This knowledge gave the toy industry a social responsibility which it has only just begun to understand. There are few reputable manufacturers now who will not try to ensure high safety standards, but the dubious social value of war toys or the potential educational value in toy design remains unchallenged. There is the problem of colour. Every toymaker knows that red is a top favourite, nearly every toymaker thinks that ten colours are better than one. On the other hand, it is well known that nursery school children play best with plain coloured bricks of unpainted wood. When children first start playing with bricks they do not use them for building (that is an adult idea), but for imaginative play, in rows on the ground or standing up as trees, or two on top of each other like a bus. A red brick will make a good bus, but it is not much use as a tree.

Toy design is of tremendous importance to the industry and designers who understand the needs of children. In Britain a production and demand for good toys exists in a specialized part of the toy trade from nursery schools and playgroups. These toys cater for the needs of the younger child up to 7 years old. For many years the supply of this type of toy was confined to schools but in the last few years the public demand for good toys has increased. In London by the mid '60s there were several retail shops specialising in this type of toy: Galt Toyshop in Carnaby Street, James France Toys (Bagatelle Toy Shop) in Kensington Square London. In New York there was only one shop and in Europe one in Amsterdam, one in Zurich and one in Vienna.

5·5 Galt

Galt, an old established company, achieved in toy retailing what Habitat achieved in furniture and household goods. James Galt commenced as a company with the opening of an educational bookshop in 1836 in Manchester and received a Royal Warrant from Queen Victoria in 1848. By 1857 the company had started to print school stationery. James Galt died in 1876 and the company passed to relatives whose family run the business today. In 1946, expansion started with the stationery and printing department which produces 20 million exercise books annually. In 1950 the 'Early Stages' division of Galt started to meet rapidly growing demand for toys, teaching aids and equipment for Kindergarten and nursery schools. The catalogue of over 200 pages is subdivided into four main sections—playing (outdoor play, water play, indoor play, jigsaws etc), teaching (wall charts, measure, number, money, time etc), creating (percussion, woodwork, art, paperwork) and storing (cupboards and shelves). A new factory and offices was established at Cheadle, Cheshire.

By the early 1960s continuous demand from parents resulted in a Galt Toys company being established in 1961. A Galt Toyshop was opened at Great Marlborough Street, London and mail-order service introduced with a Galt catalogue. A Galt Toyshop was opened in 1963 within the Cheadle factory.

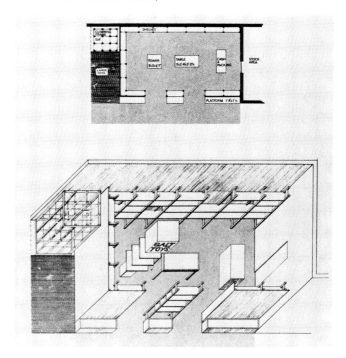

5·09 Galt display system A for a 'shop-within-a-shop'

A second Royal Warrant was granted in 1966 and demand from overseas markets created a substantial export industry. By the end of the 1960s there were 57 Galt Toyshops all over the country, many operating as shops-within-shops and opening from October to December. The mail order division expanded and by 1969, 150,000 catalogues were being printed.[5]

Operating Philosophy

Galt Toyshops differ from ordinary toyshops. They do not sell the normal range of commercial toys, and every toy sold has been specifically designed for the play purpose and age group it is intended for. Most of the toys are made by Galt at Cheadle or elsewhere to Galt's specifications.

Britain is considered one of the leading countries in infant school teaching. Children up to the age of 7 in these schools achieve all their learning through play. Their play has a purpose—it may be painting, or making things out of clay, or dressing up and acting, or playing with bricks and construction toys. The teaching has constant activity and participation of the children and is known as the Integrated Day. The materials and toys used by the teachers in Britain are almost universally provided by Galt. In addition to using the ideas of psychologists and others involved in child development Galt manufacture only toys which are found to be satisfactory by the infant teachers. Galt do not, however, consider them as 'educational toys'. The company feels that anything specifically intended to teach fails in its purpose; good toys encourage play, they stimulate curiosity and suggest ways of doing things. The toys are not luxury toys, but are strictly related to the limited budgets available in infant schools.[6]

The Display items are in the form of a centre tower display. This is about 2 metres high and displays mostly 3 dimensional toys on the tower, mainly smaller items in the up to 5 age group. Occasionally it is used for a self-service display. Small tables about 1½ metres long are used to display in piles or groups for customer self-service (jigsaws, boxed games etc.). Alternatively they are used to display one complete set (the range of bricks, wooden blocks and play bricks). Plastic trays are used for Christmas stocking filler items from 3 trays to 4 trays stacked close together.

Galt recommended that the Tower unit is used as a sign post and is placed where it is visible from a distance. Larger toys are shown in an area on their own. Display surfaces are in the form of tables and shelves in natural wood with one or two areas covered in coloured felt to provide contrast. The floors are generally in light natural wood, occasionally light brown or grey plain colour. Heavily

5·10 Galt Display System B for a 'shop-within-a-shop'

134

patterned or bright colour detracts from the toys. Charts are displayed on blank wall areas but lack of space generally precludes grouping. Display points for charts are sides of windows, staircase wall and walls where large toys are displayed. The Galt Toyshop operating in department stores should always look a shop-within-a-shop, in a self contained area clearly demarcated from surrounding departments.

The illustrations give an indication of typical layouts. The

5·11 Showroom display at James Galt & Co. Ltd., Cheadle, England

first alternative shows an open shop area partly enclosed by existing walls with access from several sides. The plan shows the Galt shop built into the shop window because the busy shopping area with shelves and tables full of toys is a great attraction to bring window shoppers inside. Large toys are displayed on the floor or platforms right at front of the window.[7]

The second alternative shows a self service shop. Self-service is suitable for small and medium size toys which can be displayed in groups for customers to serve themselves. The display is on tables and shelves in the enclosed area on the plan. Large toys, such as the Climbing Frame, are placed on the floor or platforms outside the self-service area. The layout works well if the storage area for stock is available adjacent to the cash counter; this enables it to run with minimum staff because even the larger toys can be supplied direct from storage area without the assistants having to leave the counter for more than a few minutes.

Store: Cheadle
The showroom is located in a link block between the administrative offices and the factory. It is planned on two floors with the entrance and exit to the shop through a floor to ceiling glass wall directly onto the customers' car park. Display on the ground floor at the front is confined to relatively small toys with a staircase leading to a similar display above. The upper floor overlooks by means of a balcony, an area for larger toys and play equipment (climbing frames etc) which is double height. Access into this is at the rear of the shop at ground level and children are allowed to play here. There is also smaller play equipment on the upper floor for younger children to use (rocking horse, small slide etc). At the rear of the upper floor showroom is a coffee shop and a small boutique selling childrens' clothing. The cash counter is downstairs close to the exit and it has direct access into the stockrooms at the rear.

5·6 Design Research

For a number of years, Benjamin Thompson, an American architect and chairman of the Department of Architecture at the Harvard graduate school of design from 1963–1967, had owned three shops called Design Research, similar in operation to Habitat. Design Research always traditionally picked congenial settings, in San Francisco it was a rambling chocolate factory on the harbour; in New York, an elegant fair house; in Cambridge, Massachusetts, it was a wooden three-storey house. In 1971, Design Research opened a mini-store designed by the group and Benjamin Thompson Associates to market its own particular type of merchandise. Unlike Habitat, (with the exception of Wallingford) Design Research was purpose-built.

Operating Philosophy
In the United States Design Research is the domestic equivalent of Knoll International. Their principle of merchandise selection is that used by people furnishing their house. Not, 'Will it sell?' but 'Is it for us?' The clientele appears to be composed of young families with little or no domestic help and the merchandise is such that can absorb the clutter of family life. Natural timber finishes, heavy simple pottery and glassware, vivid, heavy fabrics of cotton or wool and a preference for natural materials over synthetic materials.

Building Design

The building is planned on seven levels with a total of 2,500 m² of floor space. Four floors are above ground level and one sunken level visible and accessible from the street. The reception area is 1½ storeys high allowing views into display areas above and below. The upper two floors are office space reached by a lift and staircase core from the reception area or rear courtyard. The shape of the building is asymmetrical, with bays used to create room groupings (similar to the Ikea principle). Interior walls are unfinished concrete block; floors are brick, hexagonal ceramic tile, cork, sisal matting.

The displays were designed by the architects and offer ingenious solutions. Clothing is hung from stainless steel hoops suspended by simple brackets from the ceiling fins.

Building Construction

Sandblasted 203 mm reinforced concrete floorslabs and reinforced concrete spandrel beams are supported as a flat plate construction by round columns on a 6·1 × 6·1 m grid. The maximum cantilever is 3·7 m. The cantilevers form arcades at ground level. Throughout the interior the concrete is left unfinished. The central core contains lifts, stairwells, toilets and service ducts. Heating and cooling is by forced air in exposed perimeter ducts. Sheet metal ducts are located on the underside of floor slabs. The building is fully air conditioned with each floor zoned separately. The glazing system is composed of continuous ribbons of 10 mm tempered plate glass from floor to ceiling set between concrete slabs.

Visual Effect

The impact of the building is quite remarkable. It is, in one sense, a transparent non-building which utilises both reflection and the absorption of light. Because of its faceted plan, it creates an image of constantly changing volumes as one moves around the building inside or outside. In day time it reads as a shimmering opaque shape depending in colour upon the sky and surrounding landscape. At night all the colour and movement is inside, creating kaleidoscopic patterns. Inside the designs are brilliant, the customer being made aware more of the merchandise on sale than of the display techniques or architectural background.[8]

5·12 Design Research, Cambridge, Mass., USA: night view of the store exterior
Architects: Benjamin Thompson and Associates

5·7 Boutiques

The boutique is a shop unit conceived with a strong design image which is directed at drawing attention to new lines of merchandise sold on a quick turnover basis. Boutiques evolved at a time when older department store methods of selling were in decline and undergoing change. They resulted from demands for something unique by a more selective customer at a time when British design in film, music, fashion and the arts was receiving international recognition. Boutiques as a building type emerged in the early 1960s, starting as an amusing idea in Carnaby Street, a small Soho Street running parallel to Regent Street, and then developing in another part of London, in the King's Road area of Chelsea. New design concepts in the use of space were introduced and shops were created where the structural form, use of materials, colour and display were all related. The boutique achieved respectability as a legitimate form of shopping when the idea was accepted by Harrods department store with the creation of a fashion shop-within-a shop, called Way-In.

The British architects, Garnett Cloughley Blakemore and Associates led a real and important revolution in shopping design which was emulated throughout the country. Among the first shops designed by Garnett, Cloughley

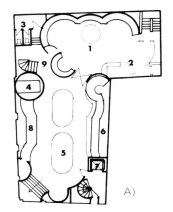
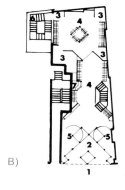
A)   B)

Key: A)
1 Bar area
2 Bar dispense area
3 WCs
4 Goods elevator
5 Tobacco/Book kiosk
6 Gift shop
7 Passenger elevator
8 Snack bar
9 Stairs to upper level (public)

B)
1 Brompton Road
2 Shop entrance
3 Changing areas
4 Display and sales areas
5 Display areas
6 Stairs to upper sales area
7 Cash
Scale: 1 : 2000

Architects: Garnett, Cloughley, Blakemore and Associates

5·13 A) Chelsea Drug Store, Kings Road, London: intermediate-level plan
B) Just Looking Boutique, Knightsbridge, London: street-level plan

5·14 Amber Fashions, Liverpool
Architects: Garnett, Cloughley, Blakemore and Associates

Blakemore and Associates were 'Just Looking' in King's Road, Chelsea (1968) and Amber Fashion Shop, Liverpool (1967). Amber Fashion Shop was built entirely of fibrous plaster and glass panels with a free plan relating walk-in display areas with the shop interior. It was a deliberate attempt to find a completely new pattern in shop design. 'Just Looking' was designed on geometric lines with the extensive use of aluminium sheet as cladding to vaulted circular shapes springing from the facade through the interior. Special importance was attached to finding suitable names for shops and giving each shop a new identity. The architects attach as much importance to the name and house-style as to the architectural design itself. The name of the first shop was arrived at by asking the client 'what is the first thing the customers say when they enter your shop?' 'Just looking' was the answer. In writing down the name, the two O's in 'Looking' gave the key to the elevational treatment.[9]

Chelsea Drugstore

The boutique idea was developed to an ultimate form with the Chelsea Drug Store in King's Road (1968) designed by Garnett, Cloughley Blakemore and Associates. The thinking behind this operation ran as follows:

'In recent years many of the traditional retailer/consumer relationships have undergone basic changes in the United Kingdom. For example, the growth of self-service and the supermarket and the new and exciting marketing and merchandising techniques being used by the traditionally conservative departmental stores.

All these developments and many more have one common objective and that is to increase the number and flow of potential purchasers within these outlets, increasing turnover and profitability.

The French drugstore operation is a sophisticated development of the original American premise of casual shopping, eating and drinking under one roof. Taken a stage further by the French and injected with their panache, the first two drugstores opened in Paris have been tremendously successful. The logical conclusion of this concept, allied to the English mentality and purchasing habit, convinces us that this theory will be as meaningful and as totally acceptable as the supermarket. This, plus the proposition of a complete 14-hour day, 7-day week trading complex (all units not necessarily operative the whole time) can offer a unique trading advantage and also minimise the high cost of premier multiple site rentals. With this objective in mind, it is intended that the Chelsea Drugstore should pioneer the development in this country of a totally new philosophy in retailing, combining drinking, eating and shopping. This, we believe, will be the blue print for the pub of the future.'[10]

The Chelsea Drugstore lasted six years and in its time was very successful commercially, representing a significant departure in both method and design.

The original building was a public house, 'The White Hart Pub', and was on two floors with two bars at street level and a concert room on the upper floor. The room heights were less than 3·35 m. In designing the new building, the architects had to create three levels within the same overall height. A new ground floor was formed 1·2 m above street level—the upper level was used for retail shopping kiosks and bar and the lower level as a general pub and snack bar area. The first floor was designed as a restaurant area with kitchens on the second floor and a new basement area forming a lower level.

The Drugstore became a restaurant—market—meeting place open from morning to night and sold newspapers, coffee, fashion, records and beer, wine and food.

Everything was designed to a reduced scale to achieve intimacy. Ceiling, bar and shop counter heights were all reduced from normal standards. Every surface was covered with fully reflective materials. Since the plan was based on a geometric design with all areas based on centres of circles axially arranged and all screen walls and counters formed segments of those circles, the combined use of reflective materials created an illusion of never-ending space. The reflective materials used were polished brass, polished aluminium, polished stainless steel and plate glass. In the shopping areas all floors were travertine marble, pub and restaurant areas were carpeted. Wall surfaces, bars and shop counter details had one single rectangular module with semi circular head and semi-circular base. Solid walls were covered with polished aluminium, bar counters with stainless steel, shop counters stainless steel and glass. The ceilings were polished aluminium. The exterior of the building was travertine marble, stainless steel and bronze tinted glass each on a different plane. The return of each plane was created by matt-black baffles. The entire building was air conditioned.

5·15 Exterior of the Chelsea Drugstore, London

5·16 Lower ground-floor pub area of the Chelsea Drugstore

5·17 The delicatessen/snack bar on the lower ground-floor of the Chelsea Drugstore, London

5·15

5·16

5·17

Just Looking

Garnett, Cloughley Blakemore and Associates completed a new Just Looking store in 1972. The first 'Just Looking' designed by them in King's Road (1968) was tiny by comparison. The original shop attempted a complex geometry of vaults which was not entirely successful. The new boutique replaced two shops and its wide frontage was made good use of by a double entrance set on the diagonal, so that one is drawn in almost without change of direction as one walks along the pavement. The ground floor is clearly divided into three zones—a deep entrance zone with an elaborate window display and a white marble floor; a narrower middle zone dominated by the mirror-lined staircase leading to the basement and by the cash desk; and a back zone which widens out again into a square shape and rotates around a central display stand. The interior is dominated by clusters of columns clad in polished steel. The glittering effect is enhanced by the use of floor-to-ceiling mirrors. In contrast to these hard surfaces, there is twill wall covering, carpeted floors and suede curtains in the changing rooms.[11]

5·18 Shop front of Just Looking, Kings Road, Chelsea, London

5·19 Upper sales area of the Just Looking Boutique

5·8 Supergraphics

In November 1967, *Progressive Architecture* included a significant article which described a new design phenomenon which the magazine entitled 'Supergraphics'. This phenomenon was to have a very considerable impact on shop design over the following six years, not only in North America but throughout the world. *Progressive Architecture* referred to it not as a decorative device but as a spatial experiment. Yet the idea of Supergraphics as a publicity device can be traced further back to Gordon Cullen's *Townscape*.[12] He noted 'one contribution to modern townscape, startlingly conspicuous everywhere you look, but almost ignored by the town planner is street publicity. This is the most characteristic, and, potentially the most valuable, contribution of the 20th century to urban scenery. At night it has created a new landscape of a kind never before seen in history'. He says, 'It is wrong to assume that large-scale advertisements are incongruous and therefore injurious to amenity. People still like to buy and sell, to proclaim and notice; it is part of our civilisation. Publicity is accepted as a normal element of city life. We are thus left with visual incongruity and surely that is something the townscaper should hasten to accept as a valuable aid. It is wrong to say that publicity degrades public taste. Public taste is already vulgar and also has the one merit of vulgarity i.e. vitality.' Gordon Cullen's drawings show how on the smallest street-corner scale the decoration of a building, by illustrative or written publicity, can have meaningful visual impact and create an effect of intricacy in colour and form which can be delightful; or an extension of the technique on a dramatic scale using the Cerne Abbas Giant translated into the fabric of the city.

5·20 Illustration by Gordon Cullen from *Townscape* showing the traditional folk-art publicity of the corner newsagent

5·21 Illustration by Gordon Cullen from *Townscape* showing the potential use of supergraphics in central city shopping and entertainment districts

Progressive Architecture's November issue praised the use of bold stripes, geometric forms and three dimensional images at a super scale. It was traced back in America to Charles Moore's interior designs in 1965 for the Sea Ranch condominium. The techniques use the painted application of giant forms as two-dimensional type-faces and signs on architectural surfaces.

'The aim in using such graphic devices is to produce optical effects that destroy architectural planes, distort corners and explode the rectangular boxes that we construct as rooms . . . Discordant scale is the fundamental force of this graphics technique.'

Progressive Architecture followed in October 1968 by devoting its entire issue to an examination of supergraphics, referring to this new design form as Mega-Decoration of Supermannerism.[13]

Media

Many of the early interior designs were carried out entirely with applied paint because it was the least expensive medium. The increasingly sophisticated use of materials from then on included mirror, polyethylene sheeting and silver mylar. Painted mirror images and painted shadows of real objects were also used to extend space and confuse experience. It was suggested that ultimately a feeling of weightlessness and the hallucination of infinity may be achieved. Synthetic materials such as epoxy resin coating were also used extensively. Electric lighting was developed to produce kinetic experiences in these environments, using neon and tungsten. A further development has been the use of lasers and holograms for projecting three dimensional images on walls or even in empty space. Jack Larson, a designer, suggests that 'interior design using an ever-changing array of projected colour and pattern can be as universally and inexpensively available as recorded music'. In combination with a series of mirrors, a laser and a single lamp might fill an entire building with light. At its simplest, automatic slide, film or video projection have been used. The present day use of such devices in discotheques was developed from these original ideas. Retail display included the use of sound controlled lighting in clothing boutiques which made extensive use of recorded music. There were kaleidoscopic silent projectors as well as liquid light projectors using multi coloured liquids sealed within a projector to create kinetic light shows.[14,15]

Shopping Development

The subsequent development of supergraphics into various forms of retailing was described in *Progressive Architecture* April 1969. It noted that 'Retailing is holding out a welcoming hand to the effects of supermannerism . . . In increasing numbers, shops are appearing with ambiguous environments and with a permissive attitude toward customer involvement. Some are kinetic boutiques that offer electrically changing devices to bring the customer closer to the merchandise. Other stores shout for attention with supergraphics. A third direction in store design evidences an interest in systems and construction kits.'

The shopfront of 'On 1st', a Manhattan store owned by a photographer moviemaker, made extensive use of supergraphics. Bert Stern and Sven Lunkin designed the shop window as a giant 'O' in which closed-circuit TV Screens showed changing views of the displays within. The letter 'N' formed the entrance and '1st' was painted on a very large scale on the wall.

Ulrich Franzen designed a group of shops in New York

called Paraphernalia. In the design published in 1969, he did not use painted or applied supergraphics but relied entirely on the use of projections. The two sections on the shop front comprised an opening which extended the full width of the shop and the shop sign which used white letters on a black background. The illuminated sign flashed a sequence of alternative red and white letters across the name 'Paraphernalia' going in the same direction as the traffic in the one-way street. Inside, a projection screen on the rear wall displayed coloured projections of clothing, girls and accessories from three overhead continuous projectors. Everything else was unobtrusive, the side walls clad in shiny black acrylic and the shop front glazed with minimal framing. The ceiling was black and carpet dark brown. The women's clothing on sale was not visible from the outside but concealed on low racks within circular or semi-circular island units clad in stainless steel. The projections and continuous music had all the atmosphere of a discotheque, Ulrich Franzen described his design thus: 'The work was an experiment in electrographic architecture. The basic notion was to create a magic box on the sidewalk with moving images illustrating the clothing for sale. Upon entering the store, each customer was handed a remote control for the various projectors to enable her to run through the entire line of products in the hope that this would be of enough interest and stimulus to then lead her to the racks of clothing contained in the stainless steel half cylinders.'[16]

A contrasting use of supergraphics was made in a downtown shopping development at York Square, Toronto, in 1969. The architects, Diamond and Myers, were appointed by the developer to design a scheme which would involve renovation and rehabilitation rather than re-development of

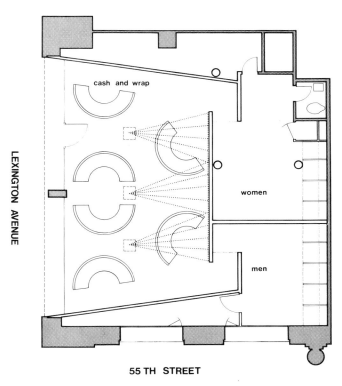

5·22 Paraphernalia Boutique, New York City: plan. Not to scale
Architect: Ulrich Franzen

the existing fabric which was composed of old two- and three-storey brick buildings, mostly painted white and which were overlaid with new shop fronts. Barrie Briscoe a Canadian supergraphics artist and architect, and perhaps one of the most outstanding of the new designers who developed expertise in this field, collaborated with the architects to develop a supergraphics image.

The new shop fronts were designed as a single storey perforated screen using huge circular openings for shop windows alternating with rectangular openings for doorways. The supergraphics were applied to the main external facades, one using a diagrammatic site plan of York Square set on the diagonal and painted in ochre inside a giant green circle, the entire design being superimposed over walls, windows and doors. The site plan is one eighth the size of the site itself, and provides a logo, identifying sign as well as a transitional view of the physical actuality. Barrie Briscoe has used the device of representational material in many of his supergraphic designs. A green circulation strip leads the eye around the corner to an arrowhead indicator towards a passageway at the centre of the facade. The passageway itself leads into a brick paved courtyard in the centre of which is an old maple tree. The ground floor houses shops and a restaurant and eating terrace at upper level. The square is extensively used by performing groups, ranging from Christmas carollers to summer dance theatre.

Finally supergraphics could be expanded beyond the original boutique-scale to that of the whole city block. In perhaps the most spectacular example, in Japan, they were applied to the exterior of two high rise developments, Omni-Rental Stores, in Shinjuku Ward Tokyo, which themselves represented an unusual departure in store design. In Japan, unlike North America and Western Europe where strict zoning and building regulations militate against multi-use commercial buildings, the tendency has been to encourage a complete mixture of residential, entertainment, shopping and other commercial use. The architect, Minoru Takeyama, thus proposed a development whereby each of the seven floors could serve as an independent building in its own right. Apart from shopping development at the lowest three levels, the upper floors include two clubs, a sauna, bar, restaurant and gaming rooms. The whole of the exterior is covered with supergraphic murals on an enormous scale, designed by Kiyoshi Awazu, using plastic spray-painted concrete. Huge numerals are applied to the top of both buildings, one of which has its blank walls painted with concentric circles and semi-circles, while the other is painted with straight lines in stripes or diagonals.[17]

Some of the most recent developments in American boutique shopping have been in Cambridge, Massachusetts. Two developments, the Brattle Truc and Cheap Thrills were designed by Cambridge Seven Associates and completed in 1971.

Centre around Harvard Square, Brattle Truc gradually evolved over four years as a varied collection of small shops centred on a pedestrian walk way spine connecting Brattle Street and Mount Auburn Street. Cheap Thrills is located on Massachusetts Avenue in Cambridge and started as the Orson Welles Cinema in 1969, catering for the student population with shopping facilities. At first it was a cinema with film workshop and inexpensive eating place and later expanded as a complex of two cinemas, film school and retail shops, including a record store opened in 1969 named Cheap Thrills.[18]

5·23 Cheap Thrills, Cambridge, Mass., USA: the application of supergraphics in infill development
Architects: Cambridge Seven Associates

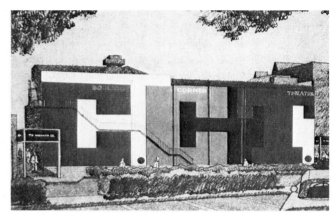

5·24 Coolridge Corner, Cambridge, Mass., USA: the application of supergraphics to a corner site
Architects: Cambridge Seven Associates

5·25 Hear-Hear, Ghirardelli Square, San Francisco: the application of supergraphics in a small record shop
Architect: James Burn

5·26 Paraphernalia Boutique, New York City: exterior at night

5·27 Omni Rental Stores, Tokyo, showing supergraphics employed on a total multi-storey (multi-purpose) structure
Architect: Minoru Takeyama

144

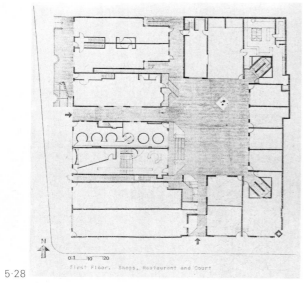

5·28 First Floor, Shops, Restaurant and Court

5·29

5·30

146

5·28 York Square, Toronto: ground-level plan
Architects: Diamond and Myers

5·29 York Square, Toronto: detail of the central square
Supergraphics Artist: Barrie Briscoe

5·30 York Square, Toronto: detail of central square showing the upper-level restaurant

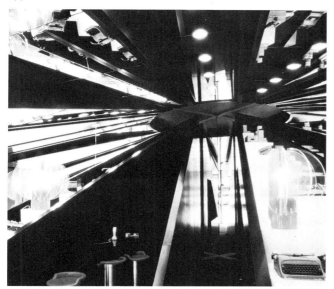

5·31 Olivetti Showrooms, Buenos Aires, Argentina: a sophisticated interior design involving supergraphic techniques. The use of reflective surfaces and exaggerated perspective creates a visual impact almost without parallel
Architect: Gae Aulenti, Milan

5·9 Sex Shops

One of the more curious forms of specialist shops to appear in the late 1960s were the Sex shops in Copenhagen. Because of the relaxation of laws restricting the sale of pornographic literature and films; a new lucrative trade established itself in the country.

An interesting feature of these shops is the highly organised way in which a relatively small floor area is used to display distinct catagories of merchandise. There are about a dozen or so shops in The Strøget in the Frederiksberggade area; all opening onto the pedestrian way at street level. The majority use normal shop fronts to display merchandise sold within. Inside the visual impact is much the same as a North American drug store or European chemist's shop. The organisation is on the same basis as a small supermarket with shelves displaying books and magazines in various catagories ranging from normal sexual intercourse to lesbianism and sado-masochism. Similarly in another section 8 mm films are displayed with equally meticulous care. The larger shops have additional sections selling sexual aids and equipment as well as contraceptive devices. The majority have a staircase to a basement room which provides continuous projection of films on sale in the upper shop on the basis of a simple entrance fee. Alternatively an arcade adjacent to the shop has batteries of slot viewing machines similar to the traditional fun-fair 'what-the-butler-saw'. The exit and cash register point of the shop is controlled by a turnstile at the combined entrance/exit doorway.

The great majority of the shops appear to be patronised by an extensive tourist trade and are largely ignored by local inhabitants.

5·32 Sex Shop, Copenhagen: a curious example of late 20th-century specialist trading

References

1 *Habitat Group History* March 1973
2 Habitat Showrooms, Wallingford *The Architectural Review* August 1974, Vol CLVI No 930, pp. 74–79
3 Conference paper by Ingvar Kamprad at Sverska Sparbanksföreningen in March 1972, pp. 1–10
4 1974 Ikea catalogue for Malmo. Those interested in developments at Almhult should consult the 1974 Ikea catalogue for Almhult
5 Paper by Edward A. Newmark to Royal Society of Arts, November 1967, pp. 1–7
6 Galt 1973 *Toy Catalogue*. See also the Galt 1972 *Early Stages Catalogue*
7 Manual for Galt Toyshops-in-Shops 1973. See also *Model Layouts for Shops in Shops* 1973
8 Benjamin Thompson 'Design Store' *Boston Sunday Globe* 4 July 1971. See also *Architectural Record* May 1970 Vol 147 No. 5 pp. 105–112; *Interiors* May 1970 pp. 108–117; *Contract* July 1970
9 Paper by Patrick B. Garnett 'Design of Boutique-style shops' on behalf of the Council of Industrial Design 1971
10 Paper by Patrick B. Garnett 'The Chelsea Drug Store—Case Study, March 1969
11 *The Architectural Review* Vol CLII No 907 'Just Looking' boutique p. 159–161
12 Gordon Cullen, *Townscape* The Architectural Press Ltd, London 1961, pp. 151–154
13 'Supergraphics', *Progressive Architecture* November 1967 Vol XLVIII No. 11, pp. 132–137
14 'Revolution in Interior Design' *Progressive Architecture* October 1968 Vol. XLIX No. 10, pp. 148–207
15 April 1969 Vol L No. 4 'Kinetic boutiques and Campopop Shops' *Progressive Architecture* April 1969 Vol. No. 4, pp. 106–221
16 'Urban Supertoy—York Square, Toronto' *Progressive Architecture* September 1969, pp. 144–153
17 'Omni-Rental Stores, Ni-ban-Kahn, Tokyo' *Japan Architect* August 1970
18 'Shopping-Truth in Truc and Cheap Thrills' *Progressive Architecture* September 1971 Vol. LII No. 9

6 Case Studies

6·01 Shopping City, Runcorn New Town: view of bus station interchange
Architects: Town Centre Group, Runcorn Development Corporation

6·1 Introduction

These new case studies are devoted to a full analysis of two recently completed major shopping centres (1971, 1975). This section examines the step-by-step development of each centre from initial planning and design to the final construction process. There is little formal documentation available on the complex subject of new building forms and the design teams in both cases initially found the existing information available inadequate to establish a realistic planning methodology. It would appear unreasonable to continue major building types on the basis of trial and error designs and the intention of this section is to provide some form of design guide or reference. Any new building form cannot immediately satisfy the complex planning, fire and building regulations and in the case of these centres new design solutions had to be found which would attempt to provide a secure and safe building.

The two studies are not intended to be comparative but rather to illustrate contemporary examples of major centres on two quite different sites within the framework of a New Town development. Both are totally enclosed centres with complete pedestrian segregation and maximum access to private car and public transport. The designs illustrate the application of a flexible megastructure solution to problems of services, structural design and shopping floor space requirements. Each has sub regional implications in terms of its catchment area. Runcorn, completed in 1971, is a new centre built on a green field site in the new town some distance away from the existing centre. Because of the urban expressway and motorway network it has a wide regional catchment area. Irvine, on the other hand, was completed in 1975 as a smaller development with a more limited sub-regional catchment area. It is located in the existing centre and forms part of an urban renewal scheme.

Both centres have been commercially successful and were extensively let to shop tenants before completion of construction. They both represent an attempt by the design team to satisfy the requirements of financial and commercial viability by the promoters within strict time and budgetary limits. The centres were the result of a financial and planning partnership between a public authority (New Town Development Corporation) and private developers. In both towns, ownership of the land was retained by the public authority and ownership of the building was retained by the private developer. In the case of Runcorn finance for construction was from insurance companies via the developer. In the case of Irvine the development company provided finance from its own capital funds. The New Town Development Corporation architects' department were appointed architects for the project by the developer at Runcorn and Irvine. At Runcorn, the development corporation's engineers and quantity surveyors were also appointed. At Irvine private consulting engineers and quantity surveyors were employed.

Both projects involved a multi-disciplinary team approach where the expertise of the development companies was combined with the expertise of the technical staff of the New Town development corporations.

6·2 Runcorn New Town Centre

Developer:	Runcorn Development Corporation General Manager: Derek Banwell
Developer:	Grosvenor Estate Commercial Developments Ltd Managing Director: Kenneth Eyles Project Manager: R. De Broekert
Contractor:	John Laing Construction Ltd
Design and Planning Team:	Town Centre Group: Department of Architecture Runcorn Development Corporation
Chief Architect:	F. Lloyd Roche succeeded by R. L. E. Harrison
Deputy Chief Architect:	David Gosling succeeded by Keith Smith
Original Design Team:	David Gosling, Keith Smith, Peter Edwards, John Lovibond, John Randle, Surya Pawar, Susan Thornley, Ronald Turton, Peter Thompson, Ewart James, Michael King

Implementation Team:

Deputy Chief Architect:	Keith Smith
Principal Architects:	Peter Edwards, John Randle
Senior Architects:	Ramesh Hadap, John Lovibond
Assistant Architects:	Brian Howard, R. A. Stunell
Quantity Surveyors:	J. Bramham (Edmund Kirby & Sons) C. Chambers (Runcorn Development Corporation)
Resident engineer:	C. Johnson
Heating and Ventilating Engineers:	H. Clayton, C. Trainor, J. D. Fitzsimon
Chief Engineer:	Jack Mercer
Structural Engineers:	Alan Bell, (deputy) Ewart James (principal) J. Brereton, K. Williams, D. Redhead
Roads Engineer:	K. Wight
Landscape Architect:	Neil Higson
Senior Clerk of Works:	R. Cheshire. R. Boyd

Planning Context

At the time of its designation in 1964, Runcorn, in the North West Region of England, was unique among British New Towns in including within the designated area an existing town of 27,000 people. . . . This was surrounded at a regional level by a ring of major service centres, including Liverpool, Chester, Warrington and Northwich. In preparing the draft master plan, Arthur Ling concluded that Runcorn was effectively part of the Merseyside conurbation, within which the flexibility of communications allowed people to shop around for goods and services, so that the boundaries of individual catchment areas were difficult to define.

The structure of the shopping hierarchy could, however, be determined. Although no regional plan at that time existed for the North West of England, a shopping study by Manchester University (Regional Shopping Centres—a planning report on North West England) had established a classification of centres. Within this context, the Census of Distribution 1961 showed that the existing town of Runcorn suffered a net outflow of trade amounting to 15% of its population's spending power. The comparative drawing

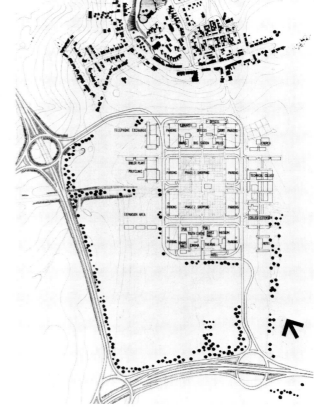

6·02 Shopping City, Runcorn New Town, Cheshire, England: existing site topography

6·03 Shopping City, Runcorn New Town: preliminary design showing deck level

6·04 Shopping City Runcorn New Town: preliminary design study

power of adjacent centres was established by dividing the sales per head of the towns by the regional average.

Changes to the existing pattern which would affect the trading position of the New Town were held to arise from four main sources; firstly, the planned growth of Runcorn itself, from a population of 30,000 in 1966 to 75,000 in the late '70s by immigration, and thereafter to 100,000 in 1991 by natural growth; secondly, changes in the pattern of regional communications, and in particular the construction of new regional motorways; thirdly, development elsewhere in the region, including a planned second New Town at Warrington a few miles to the north-east; fourthly, changes in the pattern of shopping habits arising from increased mobility and living standards. It was suggested that the external changes in the region might adversely effect the trading position of Runcorn, although in the event the great accessibility of the Runcorn Centre from the new motorway routes created a major inflow of trade after its opening in 1971.

Calculation of Shopping Floor Space

In their report of February 1966, Drivers Jones & Co, proposed future retail floor space requirements in the New Town by the assessment of probable figures of total retail turnover and average turnover per square foot. While the former might be assessed by direct comparison with other similar towns, the static character of this method and its reliance on incomplete data made it preferable to use it only as a check on the alternative method available, which entailed building up a total figure of retail turnover from an aggregation of individual expenditures and an assessment of the amount of such total expenditure likely

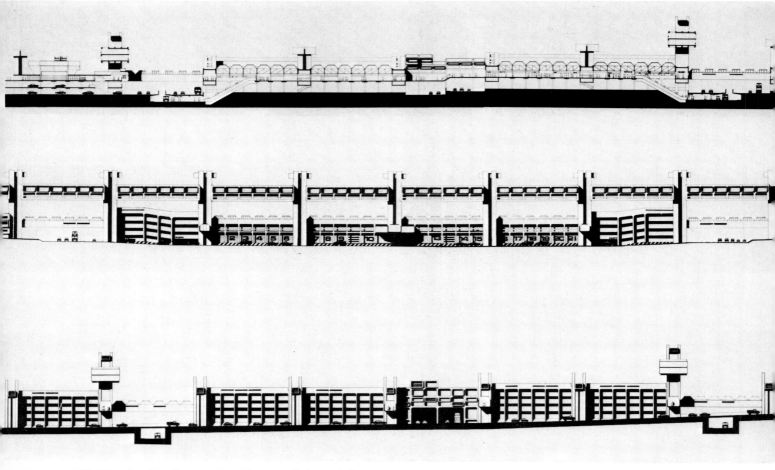

6·05 Shopping City, Runcorn New Town: preliminary design showing long section, cross elevation, side elevation

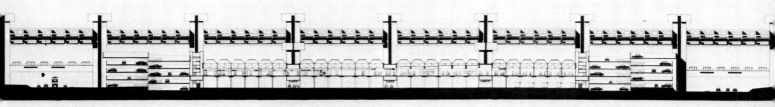

6·06 Shopping City, Runcorn New Town: preliminary design showing cross section

152

to be retained within the town.

From statistics on national and regional earnings and their growth in the preceding years, collected by the Ministry of Labour, patterns of expenditure were projected for the region, taking account of changes in those patterns which occur as incomes rise, and assuming alternative rates of growth in individual incomes. From this analysis, sales per head in the region were projected from 1961 to 1981 at 2·0% and 2·5% average annual rates of growth. With growth in expenditure, the percentage of total retail sales made in convenience goods had been declining by approximately 2·0% every five years, and stood at 56% in 1961 in the North West. The ratio of convenience to durable sales was thus anticipated to be 52:48 in 1971, and 48:52 in 1981, and the projected figures for total sales per head could thus be allocated to the two categories of traders. These per capita figures were then applied to the estimates of population growth for the New Town and the assumption made that it would retain 100% of expenditure generated on convenience goods and 65% rising to 75% of that on durables. To this result the figures achieved by the alternative method of direct comparison, used, for example, in the calculations for the New Towns of Cumbernauld and Skelmersdale, were compared and checked.

To convert these figures of turnover into a requirement for built area, it was necessary to apply a conversion factor of turnover per square foot. This represents in effect the efficiency with which retail sales are made, and tends to increase as old premises are replaced by new (structural efficiency), and as an increasing sales volume forces the adoption of more efficient techniques (managerial efficiency). Using current statistical information, Drivers Jones & Co, proposed conversion factors (1966) of £35/ft² (£377/m²) of gross retail floor space for food and convenience goods, and £25/ft² (£269/m²) for durable goods. It was also proposed that allowance should be made for increasing these figures by 1·5% for each year after 1971. The outcome of these calculations is given in Table 6 using the figures based on a 2·5% growth rate.

Table 6 *Forecast of Gross Efficient Retail Floor Space Required in the New Town (m²)*

Year	Convenience trades	Durable trades	Total m²
1966	8,000	6,100	14,100
1971	13,800	11,600	25,400
1976	21,200	22,300	43,500
1981	23,600	26,900	50,500
1991	29,100	37,200	66,300

These figures do not include retail market trading nor service trades. The latter are attracted to the higher regional centres, and include restaurants, cleaners, hairdressers, public houses, betting offices, gas and electricity showrooms, travel agents, estate agents, building societies and banks. Although the Census of Distribution, upon which the previous figures were based, does not give comprehensive statistics for service trades, Drivers Jones & Co, assumed that the area they would require would represent about 10% of that for retail trade, rising to 20% over the

plan period. The gross figures for both categories are given in Table 7.

Table 7 *Gross Retail and Service Trade Requirements (m²)*

Year	Retail	Service	Total m²
1966	14,100	1,400	15,500
1971	25,400	2,500	27,900
1976	43,500	6,500	50,000
1981	50,500	7,500	58,000
1991	66,300	13,200	79,500

Location of Shopping Floor Space

An important decision in a New Town lies in the allocation of floor space between main, district and local centres. In the first phase of post-war New Towns, neighbourhood centres were developed at the expense of the main centre, neglecting shoppers' desire for maximum choice of goods and services. The second phase New Town plans of Cumbernauld and Hook reacted against the neighbourhood concept and suppressed local shopping in favour of the town centre.

Arthur Ling's Master plan for Runcorn proposed an Urban expressway system and a public Rapid Transit System (or express busway), both of which would be immediately accessible from all parts of the New Town, bringing them within easy reach of a main centre located on a green-field site at the centre of the designated area, at Halton. Local facilities were also proposed at approximately ½ mile centres along the rapid transit route and each serving a local catchment of about 8,000 people. There was an additional dilemma, however, in the need to integrate, and establish the status of, the existing centre lying at the western end of the designated area. A number of interests in the existing community strongly advocated the redevelopment of the old Runcorn centre as the main centre of the New Town, as opposed to the development of a 'competing' new centre at Halton. Arthur Ling and Associates and the Development Corporation carried out a series of assessments to establish the implications of the two alternatives before the question was eventually settled in favour of the Halton site.

An important contribution to this decision was an economic assessment using a partial Cost-Benefit Analysis prepared by Drivers Jones & Co. This assumed that both the schedule of accommodation and the environmental standards of each town centre would be identical, and thus considered only single costs and benefits resulting from one or other location and differential costs and benefits arising to a greater degree or to different parties from the alternative sites. A schedule was prepared of the parties concerned and costs and benefits enumerated and ascribed to them. Although quantification of costs/benefits was difficult, the final balance sheet clearly showed that, as far as Public Sector interests were concerned, the Halton site was preferable, the only offsetting item being the discounted cost of Urban renewal in the old town. The existing centre site favoured Private Sector interests, but did so in part through a number of items of private benefits made at public expense. The conclusion of this partial analysis was thus that the development of the

153

Halton green field site was of greater public benefit, and this recommendation was accepted.

Regarding the allocation of shopping floor space between the main centre and the remainder of the town, the Consultant Surveyors recommended a split in the range between 60:40 and 75:25. Taking the first of these ratios, of the ultimate retail floor space requirement of 66,300 m², 39,600 m² was allocated to the main centre and 26,700 m² to the remainder of the town. Of the last figure, 12,000 m² was already committed to the existing built-up area, including the existing Runcorn centre which was to have the status of a single large district centre. 13,100 m² remained available for new local centres and corner shops, giving a ratio of 73:27 for new shopping floorspace allocated to the main centre as against the town as a whole.[19]

The technique of cost benefit analysis has been developed in the United States as an aid to reaching national decisions on questions of public investment. A complete cost benefit analysis would entail the following steps:

(a) Enumeration of all the parties affected by the decision
(b) The listing of the cost and benefits flowing from the alternative schemes
(c) Ascription of the costs and benefits to the various parties
(d) The quantification of the costs and benefits, so far as they can be measured in money terms, on a common capitalized basis
(e) The comparison of the total balance of costs and benefits generated by the alternative schemes, with an examination of the relative position of each of the parties under either scheme
(f) The decision

SIMPLIFIED BALANCE SHEET

Public	RUNCORN existing centre		HALTON green-field		Private	RUNCORN existing centre		HALTON green-field	
	benefit	cost	benefit	cost		benefit	cost	benefit	cost
1 Development Corporation	×	× × ×	×	×	2 Present Owners of On site Land and Buildings	×	×	×	×
	×	× × ×		× × ×		×			
	×	× ×	×	×					
BALANCE		×	×		BALANCE	×			
		×	×						
		×							
		×							
		×							
		×							
		×							
		×							
		×							
3 Urban District Council	×	×	×		4 Present Occupiers of On site Land and Buildings	×	×	×	
						×	×		×
BALANCE					BALANCE	×			×
5 Government		×		×	6 Owners of Off-site land and Buildings	×		×	
BALANCE					BALANCE	×			
7 Statutory Undertakers Bus Company etc.		×		×	8 Occupiers of Off-site land and Buildings	×			
BALANCE		×			BALANCE	×			
9 Persons and Companies of Town and National Community as a whole		×			10 Shopping Public. Town Centre Employees visitors. Other town centre users	×	×	×	×
						×	×		
BALANCE		×			BALANCE			×	×

List of Costs

Runcorn = old existing centre
Halton = green field site in DA

1 *Acquisition Costs*
C1   Acquisition of land   (differential cost)
C2   Acquisition of buildings   (single cost: Runcorn)
C3   Disturbance to existing businesses   (single cost: Runcorn)

2 *Constructional and Development Costs*
C4   Physical preparations of site for   (differential cost)
         building
C5   Provision of services   (differential cost)
         (sewers etc.)
C6   Overhead development costs   (differential cost)
         (approach to site, working
         space etc.)
C7   Overhead development costs   (differential cost)
         (differences in ease of
         providing same environment)
C8   Loss of rates during   (single cost Runcorn)
         period of redevelopment
C9   Overhead development costs   (single cost Runcorn)
         (slower phasing and rate of
         construction)

3 *Operational and traffic costs*
C10   Cost of operating   (single cost Runcorn)
         non-purpose built premises
C11   Costs of time and travel   (differential cost)
         to shoppers, employees and
         others
C12   Costs to operators of   (differential cost)
         rapid transit system
C13   Costs of delays to Regional   (single cost Runcorn)
         traffic
C14   Costs to local traffic   (single cost Runcorn)
         (other than rapid transit)

4 *Costs to Dispossessed on-site owners and occupiers*
C15   Costs to on-site owners   (differential cost)
         other than balanced by
         compensation
C16   Costs to on-site occupiers   (differential cost)
         other than balanced by
         compensation

5 *Grants and Subsidies*
C17   Housing grants payable by   (differential costs)
         Central Government

List of Benefits

6 *Benefits available chiefly to Public Authorities*
B1   Slum clearance and urban   (single benefit Runcorn)
         renewal in Runcorn
B2   Savings on construction cost (single benefit Runcorn)
         of buildings suitable for
         Town Centre purposes
B3   Rental income receivable by (single benefit Runcorn)
         Development Corporation as
         developer
B4   Savings on construction   (single benefit Halton)
         cost of buildings suitable
         for District Centre purposes
B5   Rates receivable by   (differential benefit)
         appropriate rating authorities

| B6 | Grants receivable from Central Government | (differential benefit) (differential benefit) |

7 *Benefits available to members of the public or to public authorities*

B7	Added value to owners of properties adjacent to Town Centre	(differential benefit)
B8	Added trading income (profits) to occupiers of commercial property adjacent.	(single benefit Runcorn)
B9	Capital payments to dispossessed site owners	(differential benefit)
B10	Capital payments to dispossessed site occupiers	(differential benefit)
B11	Added value to owners of suitable on site commercial building	(single benefit Runcorn)
B12	Added trading income (profits) to occupiers of suitable on site commercial building	(single benefit Runcorn)

8 *Social benefits*

B13	Retention of certain uses (e.g. cinema) to pay operational costs	(single benefit Runcorn)
B14	Exploitation of nodality in central site leading to maximum utilisation and growth of town centre services	(single benefit Halton)
B15	Freedom in planning for flexibility and room for expansion on virgin site	(single benefit Halton)
B16	Retention of social goodwill attached to an established central area	(single benefit Runcorn)

It was assumed by Drivers Jones that the schedule of accommodation derives from overall planning calculations and is the same for both locations and that the environmental standard of each design would be the same. Only costs and benefits that occur **(a)** in one location and not the other **(b)** in greater degree in one location than the other and **(c)** to different parties in different locations were assured. Costs and benefits under **(a)** are marked single cost and costs and benefits under **(b)** and **(c)** are marked differential costs or differential benefit.

Site

The Halton site lay geographically in the centre of the New Town area and to the south of the outcrop of Halton Rock with its surrounding village. From this high ground two ridges of land ran southwards, enclosing a shallow bowl. In their preliminary studies Arthur Ling and Associates investigated a number of sites in the area for the new centre, with upper levels relating to adjacent higher ground. This location was subsequently adopted, and was bounded to the south and west by urban expressway routes, to the east and west by adjacent housing areas and traversed by the rapid transit system serving those areas.

Design Objectives

An initial set of criteria was established by the Development Corporation for the Town Centre, governing its broad content and phasing in relation to the town as a whole and the financial requirement that it be viable, preferably within a 20 year period with a break-even point within 7 or 8 years of opening.

Following this a design brief was developed during 1966 to include the following principles for the shopping centre:

1 *Segregation of traffic:* pedestrian circulation to be vertically segregated from vehicular, and each form of the latter to be individually resolved. In addition to the normal circulations of private cars, service vehicles and conventional buses, the design also had to handle the independent rapid transit routes, the integration of which with the centre was particularly important

2 *Convenience:* this was held to include the complete enclosure of the malls and their approaches and a compact layout

3 *Integration with adjoining uses:* strong connections to adjoining areas of office development and high-density housing and the ability to accommodate commercial, entertainment, social and welfare buildings

4 *Adequate car parking:* calculated on the basis of an 85:15 modal split for shopping trips by car and other means. It was estimated that 4,500 parking spaces should ultimately be provided for shopping and 1000 for other town centre uses

5 *Flexibility:* the need for extension, expansion or change of use within the town centre elements should be recognised

Design Development 1: Alternatives

During the period of design development consultation took place with Drivers Jones and Company who were retained as shopping consultants by the Development Corporation, and also with the Multiple Shops Federation who assisted greatly in the refinement of the planning.

A series of alternative basic organisations was investigated, based upon the alternatives of horizontal and vertical segregation of pedestrians and vehicles. The latter designs resolved into two basic traffic circulations, based upon a central spine distributor or a loop or circular road system. Each of the alternative designs was tested against the following criteria:

1 Ability to satisfy the basic planning aims
2 Ability of the road systems to cope with projected traffic volumes
3 Extent of physical construction necessary
4 Implications of phased programme
5 Compatibility with topography

From these studies a preferred organisation was adopted on the basis of vertical segregation and loop traffic circulation. The main pedestrian level formed a deck across the site hollow, connecting to adjacent housing pedestrian routes. Below this deck level the basic road system comprised a series of loops arranged in a rectangular pattern running north-south, and containing within them those land-uses attracting major traffic movements. This pattern owed much to the Hook plan and to Kenzo Tange's Tokyo Bay project. Four loops were proposed, the northern one containing civic buildings, commercial offices and regional bus station, then two central loops for the shopping building, and finally entertainments buildings in the southern loop. As a one-way, anti-clockwise system, all turns would be left-hand, with exits from the slow inner lane.

Alternative arrangements of the structure within the loop system were also investigated. In the view of the Multiple Shops Federation a significant failure in the design of most modern shopping centres lay in their inability to cope with constantly changing briefs and subsequent tenants' requirements. From this the design team adopted as a major

6·07 Axonometric of the Shopping City, Runcorn New Town at the preliminary design stage

6·08 Shopping City, Runcorn New Town: model of 1st phase showing megastructure, service-tower system and rooflit space-frame

6·09 Shopping City, Runcorn New Town: model of 1st phase with roof removed showing flexibility of shopping arrangement within megastructure

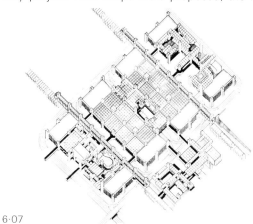

6·07

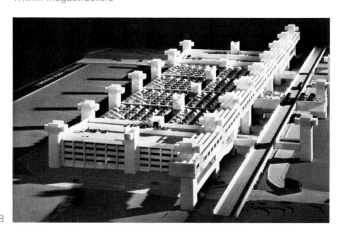

6·08

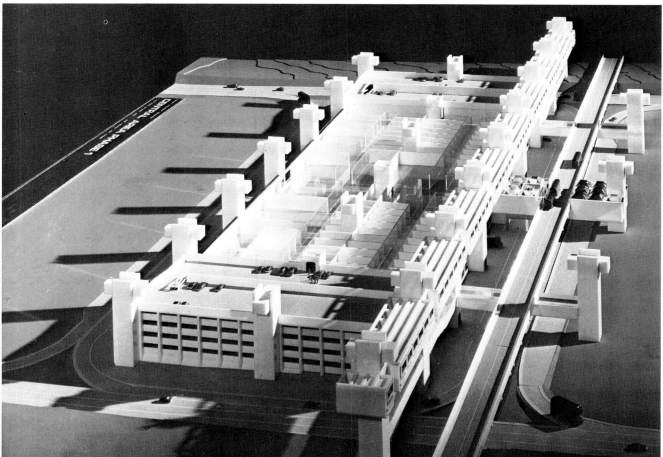

6·09

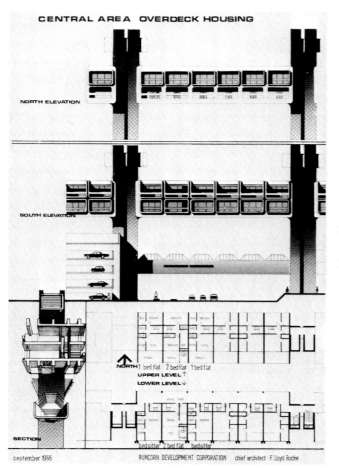

CENTRAL AREA OVERDECK HOUSING

NORTH ELEVATION

SOUTH ELEVATION

SECTION

NORTH
UPPER LEVEL ↑
LOWER LEVEL ↓

1 bed flat   2 bed flat   1 bed flat

bedsitter   2 bed flat   bedsitter

september 1966   RUNCORN DEVELOPMENT CORPORATION   chief architect: F. Lloyd Roche

6·10 Shopping City, Runcorn New Town: preliminary design for the overdeck housing project

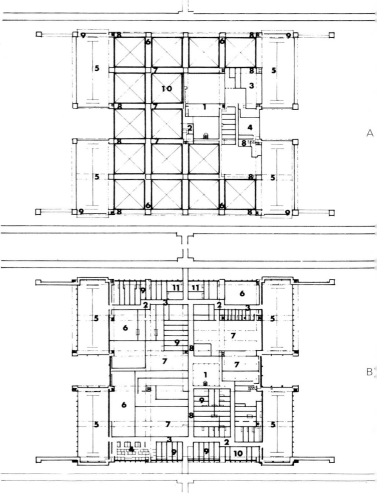

A

B

Key: A)
1 Restaurant
2 Pub
3 Upper-level department store
4 Upper-level sales area
5 Multi-storey car parks
6 Plant room
7 Plant room over void
8 Vertical access
9 WCs
10 Pyramidal roofs

B)
1 Central square
2 Small squares
3 Malls
4 Market
5 Multi-storey car parks
6 Supermarkets
7 Multiple stores
8 Main north-south mall
9 Shops
10 Post office
11 Banks
Scale: 1 : 4000

6·11 Shopping City, Runcorn New Town Centre
Architects: Runcorn Development Corporation Architect's Department
A) Second-floor and roof-level plan
B) First-floor (main shopping plan)

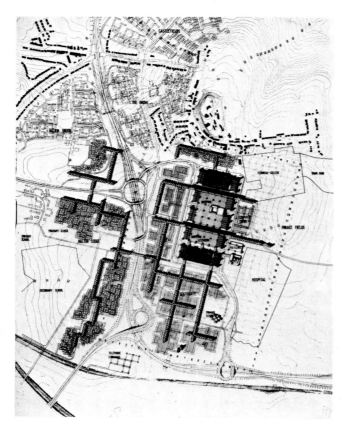

6·12 Shopping City, Runcorn New Town: district plan at the preliminary design stage

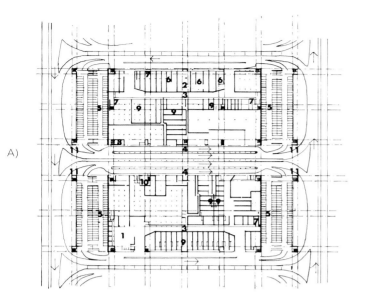

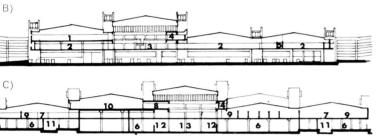

Key: A)
1 Market traders' service area
2 Pub
3 Service roads
4 Service lanes
5 Multi-storey car parks
6 Banks
7 Electricity sub-stations
8 Control room
9 Storage for shops above
10 Sprinkler plant room
11 Switch rooms

B)
1 Upper sales floor
2 Shop
3 Central square

4 Pub
5 Mall

C)
6 Storage
7 Mall
8 Restaurant
9 Shops
10 Dancing
11 Service road
12 Service lane
13 Through traffic
14 Kiosks

Scale: A) 1:4000
       B) 1:2000
       C) 1:2000

6·13 Shopping City, Runcorn New Town Centre, England
Architects: Runcorn Development Corporation Architect's Department
A) Underdeck (ground-level) plan
B) Section through central square looking south
C) Section through central square looking east

design aim the creation of a megastructure which would accommodate random packages of retailing into an overall hierarchy of traffic and land use. Various configurations of the basic uses were investigated including the location of car parking below both sales and storage areas at deck level. This option and its variants was rejected because of the incompatibility of the structural requirements of the two uses above one another, and because the areas of highest loading (storage) were at deck level. Thus, from arguments both of flexibility and structural economy the preferred solution was for car parking to be located in separate multi-storey structures flanking the shopping areas which would have storage at ground level and sales areas above at deck level. While columns at close centres would not limit the use of the lower level, the upper would be roofed by a wide-span structure offering maximum flexibility to the sales areas.

Design Development 2: Preliminary Design

From the foregoing, a preliminary design was prepared incorporating the following features:

1 *Vehicular circulation:* adopting the four-loop, one way system, service loading and unloading areas to the shopping centre were to be located along the cross-connectors of its two loops; this proposal was criticised by the Multiple Shops Federation as entailing excessive trucking into the depth of each block. Four multi-storey car park buildings accommodating 500 spaces each would be located on east and west sides of the central shopping area, and served from the north-south legs of the loop system. The car parks would be four-storey split-level structures entailing a maximum walking distance of 2 storeys to main mall level for shoppers

2 *Mall layout:* a main central mall was to run from north to south through the scheme, connecting the civic and commercial office buildings and regional bus station and rapid transit stop to the north with the second transit stop and entertainment area to the south. Cross malls from the car park would extend beyond those buildings on bridges to the housing on the adjoining ridges. It was proposed that these approach routes could be in the form of housing decks which would be tied across the centre by overdeck housing spanning the northern and southern edges of the shopping centre

3 *Rapid transit:* this would run in a viaduct around the centre at deck level, giving direct access into the centre from two stopping points, the northern one to interconnect with the regional bus station at ground level

4 *Structure:* a service and structural supergrid of 108 ft (32·93 m) square and a minor grid of 18 ft (5·49 m) bands was established. The 18 ft grid provided service and vertical access points and the 108 ft grid produced large spans which provided flexibility in the planning of large space users. The heavy loadings of storage areas were placed at ground level. An 18 ft² grid of columns and beams carried the deck, and the 18 ft² supergrid towers carried the tubular aluminium space frames which allowed natural daylighting throughout the centre. The 18 ft module had important implications. It coincided with the commercial designs for the split level car parks (two spans of 56 ft each supported on the periphery by an 18 ft column grid.). The 18 × 18 ft underdeck grid was the most economic for the heavy loading of the deck itself and where underdeck service roads were introduced it allowed a reasonably economic one-way

span of 36 ft to be introduced. 18 ft also coincided with the optimum shop frontage and mall width in the view of the Multiple Shops Federation. The 108 × 108 ft supergrid square coincided with the approximate maximum floor area for space users and for fire compartmentation. 108 ft was the maximum span for the vierendeel girders carrying the overdeck housing. For horizontal distribution of services 6 ft (1·83 m) deep ducts ran through the 18 ft-wide bands between service towers.

Selection of Developer

When the Ministry of Housing and Local Government was consulted in 1967 it became clear that Ministry approval to the project would be dependent on a considerable proportion of the capital being provided from private sources. Although Central Government had previously funded New Town Centres, and although the best return on development land was potentially available from commercial, rather than housing or industrial development, the change of policy required the Corporation to seek private investment. In March 1967 a formal application was made to the Minister under section 6 (1) of the New Town Act 1965 for approval to the project based on an estimate of total capital cost and projected return on capital by Year 22. Negotiations then took place with a development company which was already involved in office development in the New Town, with a view to securing the necessary finance for the project.

Agreement was reached between the developer and Corporation whereby the former was granted a 125 year site lease and undertook the construction of the complete shopping centre and car parking buildings, with the Corporation carrying out infrastructure and site works. The agreement also covered mutual control of such matters as the re-location of existing traders in the New Town, the administration and maintenance of the centre and car parking charges. A formula was agreed whereby ground rent was to rise from a base level in year one to an agreed level in years 14 to 21, and thereafter subject to 7 yearly reviews related to shopping rental levels prevailing. In this way the Corporation secured a minimum return from the project and a share in its increased value. The Corporation's Chief Architect and Chief Engineer were appointed to the project by the developer who was to pay professional scale fees to the Corporation.

While accepting the design already proposed, the developer caused a major change with regard to phasing. Recognising the accessibility of the new centre in relation to the regional motorway system, he proposed its completion in a single phase, which in the event became much larger than even the ultimate floor space requirements had predicted.

Design Development 3: Final Design

The final plan was evolved in 1967 as a product of a working party composed of the Corporation design team of architects and engineers, the developers management staff and consultant quantity surveyors. Similar to the subsequent method at Irvine, the evolution of the final proposals was conducted at two levels—a working party who met frequently, usually at weekly intervals, and a policy group composed of senior management from the Corporation and directors of the development company who met at

6·14 Shopping City, Runcorn New Town: view of south-east corner

monthly intervals. Construction started in 1968.

1 *Vehicular circulation:* the 4-loop pattern previously established was maintained, although the service road arrangements were modified to eliminate trucking to shop stores

2 *Pedestrian circulation:* the final mall plan resembled an H with a central square, the number of east-west side malls earlier proposed having been reduced to two on each side of the north-south route. Major stores were distributed carefully within this layout, with major supermarkets at the edges adjacent to the car parks, and major multiples at the centre around the central square. This square has an upper service trades floor around it and in addition a number of units have taken up sales space at mezzanine level below the main mall level

3 *Structure and services:* the principle of the structural form was maintained through the design development. The lightweight tubular space frame roof proposed earlier was, however, abandoned on cost grounds, and an alternative substituted using a square pyramidal roof form composed of intersecting steel trusses. The services distribution similarly follows the discipline adopted previously, running vertically through the service towers and horizontally in the bands between them. A district heating plant to the south of the centre heats the entire development, traders being able to take up individual metered supplies

4 *Phasing:* not only was the shopping centre project no longer to be phased, but in addition its content of gross rental area rose during the development stage to to reach 51,000 m², a figure considerably higher than than predicted, even on a phased basis. High density central area housing designed by James Stirling was also developed to the south of the shopping centre, and commercial offices to the north, to provide close support population in the early years of its opening until major housing areas to east and west were built

5 *Finishes:* externally white ceramic tiles to all vertical surfaces. Internally, mall floor in Terazza tiles, off-white, with brass joint strips at 9 ft (2·74 m) centres transversely. Division walls between shop units in concrete blockwork finished to mall with 150 mm-wide white marble strips. A continuous fascia 600 mm deep provided above all shop mall frontages, comprising 75 mm-deep ventilation grille and 525 mm-deep white marble. Mall ceiling fully illuminated suspended ceiling of 600 × 600 mm pvc profiled panel diffusers.

Runcorn: Design Feedback

One of the most useful exercises carried out by the Runcorn design team was a critical investigation of the design criteria after completion of the building. The results of this study are summarised below:

1 Structural grid

The 18 ft grid for the central area was chosen as being the most suitable for mixed uses (housing, car parking, storage and shopping). Taking advice from the Multiple Shops Federation, great emphasis was placed on the requirement for maximum clear spans. The 108 ft dimension was selected which accommodated maximum fire compartmentation dimensions. The 18 ft grid and 108 ft supergrid allowed for the location of circulation and service towers at regular intervals giving a flexible letting plan between. A 6 m (19 ft 8¼ in) grid might have been a better choice. The

plant rooms and staircases within the towers are cramped. The supergrid concept of servicing was worthwhile but even great flexibility is needed within the discipline to accommodate unforeseen service requirements

2 Roof form

Because surrounding areas overlooked the roofscape of the 108 ft major spans an 11° pyramidal pitched roof was chosen using diagonal lattice steel girders with purlins as the most economical wide span design. The decision to use long clear spans is still felt to be correct though heavier loading conditions in the valleys should have been foreseen. Precast concrete units, perhaps with an intermediate support would have been useful for the location of tenants' plant. The valleys should have been lower, in any case, to prevent this plant from being seen from below. The form of roof construction led to physical difficulties in constructing fire compartment walls. The choice was between locating compartment walls at the edge of the pitched roof supergrid or provide complete flexibility for tenants by allowing compartment walls to follow letting arrangements. This has the disadvantage of precluding complete flexibility in future letting arrangements

3 Shopping layout

The main aim was to produce a scheme with identical commercial values in all areas. A mall width of 18 ft (later changed to 16 ft and 20 ft) × 12 ft high was chosen and the hypothetical layout established the principle of supermarkets at the four corners and departmental stores around the town square. The layout of malls should be decided as

6·15

6·16

6·17

6·18

6·15 Shopping City, Runcorn New Town: air view of completed scheme showing megastructure and pyramid

6·16 Shopping City, Runcorn New Town: view of western side with Halton Rock and busway in background

6·17 Shopping City, Runcorn New Town: view of central square

6·18 Shopping City, Runcorn New Town: view of main mall

6·19 Shopping City, Runcorn New Town: model of final phase (southern loop) development showing the upper-level arcade from the south-east

Deputy Chief Architect: Keith Smith
Principal Architect: John Randle
Assistant Architects: Peter Garvin and Ian Risley

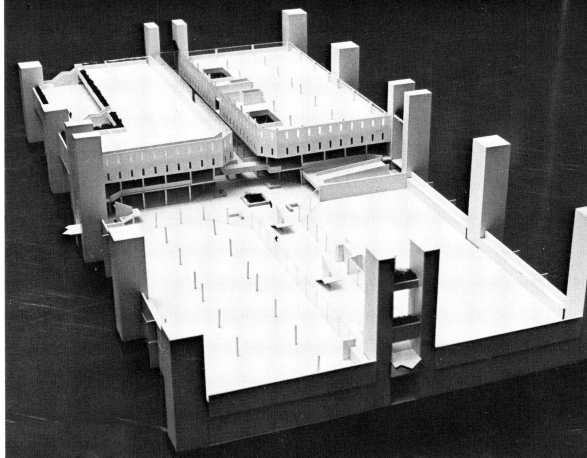

6·19

early as possible in order to finalise the services distribution scheme. Some major tenants had sufficient commercial appeal to alter mall layout after construction had commenced. This should be resisted. Public toilets and lifts should have been located in the centre of the scheme

4 Building regulations
In accepting the need for fire compartmentation waivers had to be sought to omit compartment doors in the malls. In allowing this waiver, sprinkler systems throughout the scheme were required as well as smoke control and detection equipment and adequate escape routes. Flank walls were required between fire compartments. The landlord's insurance company had even more stringent design requirements than the Ministry and should have been consulted much earlier in the design

5 General construction
Future expansion was either by means of first-floor additions or mezzanines beneath the shopping deck. The mezzanine floors were possible because of the 16 ft 6 in-high clearance required for service vehicles beneath the deck as well as a cross fall on the site itself. The structural frame supporting the slab was very economic. Ground beams between pile caps were eliminated by using the ground level slab as a restraining member. Shopping deck precast units related to the structural grid allowed staircase openings to be pre-planned and altered during construction without too much disruption. The design of the plate floor proved inflexible where used. The redesign of the service towers to specific user requirements was a mistake. The original decision to have a flexible, standardised design was correct, even if it appears to be uneconomic initially

6 Cost planning
A target cost plan was used. The target cost per ft² was satisfactory for a traditional precinct development but difficult to work within for a project as complex as this scheme. It meant that the specification offered to tenants was limited. The design team felt that if the tenants could be offered sprinklers, suspended ceilings and screeded floors throughout as well as the provision of standardised steel staircases this might have improved rental values

7 Final layout
Trolley runs beneath the deck for servicing was virtually eliminated by the introduction of underdeck service roads. These have the disadvantage of not providing facilities for tail-loading which affects supermarkets and pubs. On the other hand the space required for turning circles to accommodate articulated trucks would have been excessive if loop service roads had not been used

8 Services: general
The designers felt that wherever rental levels permit, tenants should be supplied with electricity, water and GPO services for use by the shopfitter. There should be sufficient ventilation into the malls to allow extraction only for small tenants. Service ducts in roadways would have been an advantage because of the great disruption caused during construction by the constant work on public utilities supply and destruction of road surfaces. Public utilities should be the responsibility of the main contractor. The positioning of sub-stations early in the design is critical. Services should, wherever possible, be routed through landlord's areas. There must be a strong accessible services spine relating to the line of the mall. The provision of the district heating plant obviated the necessity for flues which would have given immense problems in a project of this size

9 External finishes
The design provided simple maintenance-free finishes. The white ceramic tiles provided a self cleansing uniform finish to various construction materials and have proved highly satisfactory with no adhesion problems. The blue engineering brickwork used at the lower level in service areas was valuable in resisting wear and tear from sub-contractors during construction

10 Internal finishes
The original design continued the use of the external materials inside the centre with ceramic tiles to pilasters and floors. This was altered to include higher quality finishes of marble and terrazzo which gave a rather bland appearance. The introduction of more natural daylighting instead of the totally illuminated ceiling would have been more desirable. Steelwork in the roof was left unpainted and terrazzo unprotected: Though a cost saving, this has resulted in rust staining on ceilings and floors.

In the original design, the megastructure concept of service towers and wide span roof structures was intended to be expressed consistently with the use of ceramic tiles for external and internal cladding and continued on the horizontal floor surfaces. Within this strong framework, the random package of ever changing shop layouts was intended to be as free as possible and perhaps an over emphasis on the control of shop front design is not always desirable.

6·3 Irvine New Town Centre

Developer:	Irvine Developer Corporation: General Manager: Dennis Kirby succeeded by James Marquis
Developer:	Ravenseft Properties Ltd: Managing Director: Fred Maynard Director: W. Mathieson Project Manager: Donald Finlayson
Contractor:	Sir Robert McAlpine & Sons Ltd
Design Team:	Town Centre Group: Department of Architecture & Planning, Irvine Development Corporation
Chief Architect:	David Gosling, succeeded by J. K. Billingham
Principal Architect:	Barry Maitland
Original Design Team:	David Gosling, Barry Maitland, Brian Lowe, Mac Dunlop, Malcolm Hay, Peter Thompson, Roger Pead, Tony Scott
Implementation Team:	
Principal Architect:	Barry Maitland succeeded by Ron Bell
Senior Architects:	Ron Bell, John Russell, Bill Brown, Angus Kerr
Assistant Architects:	Vernon Monaghan, Maurice Rodger, Alan Willoughby, Sandy Wright, Hugh Cooper, Roy McGregor, Tom Donnan

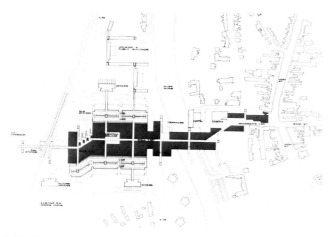

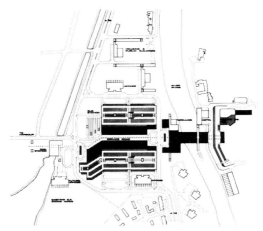

6·20 Town Centre, Irvine New Town, Scotland
Preliminary design showing plan level 40
Architects: Town Centre Group, Irvine Development Corporation
Scale: 1 : 10 000

6·21 Town Centre, Irvine New Town:
Preliminary design showing plan level 30

Quantity Surveyors:	Michael Coates, A. Nicol (Gardiner & Theobald) Peter Thompson (Irvine Development Corporation)
Structural & Civil Engineers:	Fraser Anderson, R. Nicol, J. Greenhough (Ove Arup & Partners)
Mechanical Engineers:	Alec Hamilton, M. Vincent, C. Pyle (Donald, Smith, Seymour and Rooley)
Site Engineers:	Irvine Development Corporation Chief Engineer: W. G. Conchie Deputy Engineer (Roads): Eric Prince Deputy Engineer (Services): H. McCall
Principal Clerk of Works:	P. Speakman

Planning Context

Located on the west coast of Scotland some 20 miles south west of Glasgow, the New Town of Irvine contained within its designated area the existing towns of Irvine and Kilwinning in addition to a number of smaller settlements. The pattern of retailing was dominated at a regional level by Glasgow, and at the level of the North Ayrshire sub-region by the two principal towns of Kilmarnock and Ayr. These centres provided for a high proportion of durable purchases in the sub-region and at the time of designation the New Town area experienced a considerable outflow of local durables trade. The planned growth of the New Town from 38,000 in 1965 to 120,000 in the late 1980s would place Irvine in a position comparable to Ayr and Kilmarnock in the sub-region and create a structure of three sub-regional centres with approximately equal catchment areas. While each of these towns was undertaking redevelopment of its shopping facilities, their plans were coordinated through the North Ayrshire Land Needs Working Party at which agreement on their relative sizes and catchments was reached. Of particular relevance to Irvine was Kilmarnock, since the distance between their two centres was just 7 miles and since a natural line of growth in the two communities lay between them.

Shopping Floorspace Provision

The New Town outline plan set out the following procedure:

Method

1.1   This method is applicable to the calculation of shopping floor space. It enables floor space to be related directly to population build up, rather than to specific points in time. This is necessary due to the variable nature of the speed and period of population build up. Estimates are based on Family Expenditure Surveys and The Census of Distribution (HMSO) together with information provided in the NBA New Towns Bulletins (nos 7 and 9) and by the County Assessor.

1.2   The demand for retail and service floorspace has been based on estimates of the probable future relationship between:
1   personal income and expenditure
2   population
3   turnover
Calculations of the extent to which local or central shopping centres retain the expenditure made by their surrounding population has been based on assumptions of each centre relative to:
4   accessibility and convenience in use
5   distance from competing centres and the relative attraction of those centres

1.3   In order to make sure, as far as possible, that initial floor space provision is made with regard to future needs, it is necessary to estimate a range of possibilities within which probable future needs lie. It is not possible to predict with great accuracy the exact demand for future floor space because:
1   expenditure will vary with: the economic structure of the town and growth in prosperity
2   population will vary with: family size and age groups and rate of growth
3   turnover will vary with: changes in the organisation of retailing technological developments
In addition
4   relative accessibility and convenience will depend on growth in car ownership,
provision of car parking

standard of public transport and roads
alternative growth in public transportation and decline in car ownership

5 relative attraction will depend on the growth and/or renewal of competing centres

Assumptions

1.4 In order to estimate the range within which future floor space demand will lie at both central and local level, the following assumptions have been made:

1 Income in the New Town is likely to be higher than the national average although this will probably be offset by the extra expenses incurred by young families

2 The predominance of large families in the early years of the town will mean that per capita expenditure will be lower than the national average

3 With increasing prosperity a higher proportion of income will be spent on 'durable' goods such as cars, labour saving devices, leisure equipment etc., and personal services such as holidays. A diminishing proportion will be spent on food and 'convenience' goods

4 With the growth and development of supermarkets brought about by the industrialisation of food production and improved methods of food processing, distribution and storage, daily food shopping will become less frequent

5 Most shopping will eventually be carried out at weekends, especially with the growth of car ownership. This situation will be reached when a majority of families have at least one car at their disposal. At present the ratio is approximately 1 to 3 in Ayrshire and it was predicted that it could have risen to 1 to 1 by the late 1980's when the New Town population will be in the region of 120,000. However with the change in the world fuel and energy situation in 1973 it is possible that the predicted rise in car ownership may not occur and that public transportation will take prior importance

6 Increasing prosperity will generally be offset by increased sales efficiency resulting in little change in the relationship between population and floor space

7 Increased prosperity will also result in higher expenditure on durable goods and a net loss in the proportion of floor space devoted to food sales will result both from this and an increase in the number of supermarkets

8 The most efficient size of supermarket at this time is between 1,400–1,900 m². Turnover can be expected to exceed £650/m² and such units will therefore require a considerable support population to function most effectively

9 In the long term, local shopping, which is dominated by food sales, is therefore likely to decline relative to the Central Area. However, growth in the field of personal services may offset any net loss in local floor space

10 The Central Area will become the location of most comparison shopping both in food and durable goods. It will be dominated on the food side by several large supermarkets and on the durable side by department stores, Multiple Stores, discount stores, and specialist independent retail or service

shops will also be represented in significant numbers

'Proposals

1.5 Despite the long term trend towards once a week centralised shopping there will be a need in Irvine for some considerable time for local shopping giving a reasonable range of choice and competition, together with a high degree of convenience. In consequence, it will be necessary to consider a minimal grouping which, whilst fulfilling the above requirements, will remain viable as and when central, weekly shopping predominates

1.6 This minimal local provision will comprise mini-markets selling a wide range of goods, situated within a few minutes walk of most housing areas. They will probably serve between 1,500 and 4,000 people and will as far as possible be associated with bus stops and primary schools

1.7 In addition, larger local centres associated with comprehensive schools, health centres, recreation and leisure facilities will be developed in due course to serve a population of between 10 and 15,000. They will comprise a relatively small supermarket and a limited range of food, durable and service shops. Provision will also be made for local industries associated with such centres

1.8 Consideration has been given to the development of a decentralised pattern of shopping with the Central Area becoming primarily a durable goods centre. In this case extensive parking could be provided locally at minimum land and capital cost, and it may be that in the short term such an arrangement would prove more profitable than a centralised pattern. However, this argument applies mostly to congested existing cities and has led to the rise of the 'out of town' shopping centre

1.9 In Irvine, where the Central Area will be congestion free, large supermarkets can be centrally located, attracting complementary specialist food outlets, and generating activity which could encourage the development of a wide range of shopping facilities. In this way, the Central Area will have the best chance of becoming a truly regional centre and supporting the recreational and entertainment facilities of the Harbour-Foreshore

1.10 Irvine New Town is similar to Runcorn in many ways. It was based upon an existing town of some 20,000 people and a total population in the designated area at the time (1965) of 38,000. The population had risen to 46,000 by 1971. Unlike Runcorn, however, it was decided that a new centre could not be built because of the existing competing centres in close proximity to one another—Kilmarnock, seven miles to the east, Ayr, twelve miles to the south and existing Irvine itself. Instead, it was decided to extend the existing centre across the river Irvine into derelict land on the west bank which could then act as a catalyst for further development. The three centres of Ayr, Kilmarnock and Irvine New Town could become sub-regional centres in their own right with approximately equal catchment areas and a turnover of approximately £10m each (1970)

1.11 Shopping floorspace was calculated on the basis of personal income and expenditure, population and turnover. Floorspace is related directly to population build up rather than specific points in time

Immediate floorspace provision for an incoming population of between 4,500–5,000 per annum rising to the target population of 120,000 has been calculated as follows:

1 1970 per capita retail expenditure in Scotland has been estimated as £220 p.a. (Family expenditure Survey 1961 = £167; 1966 = £204 2% growth rate assumed: 1966–70 = £220. This does not of course take into account the sudden rise in inflation rates in the post 1972 period)

2 1970 per capita service expenditure has been estimated as £20 p.a. (excludes Petrol Filling Stations)

3 A 10% reduction in total expenditure has been assumed due to larger than average families, leakage of expenditure via mail order, mobile shops, dairy produce etc

4 Once phase one of the Central Area is completed which will probably include departmental stores, it is assumed that regional gain in expenditure will probably equal regional loss

5 Total retail and service expenditure per 10,000 population increase would then be approximately

6·22 Town Centre, Irvine New Town: working model of roof structure and services system at the preliminary design stage

6·23 Town Centre, Irvine New Town: view of preliminary design model looking east

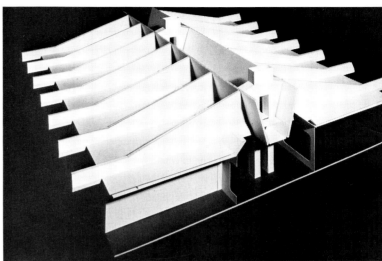

6·22

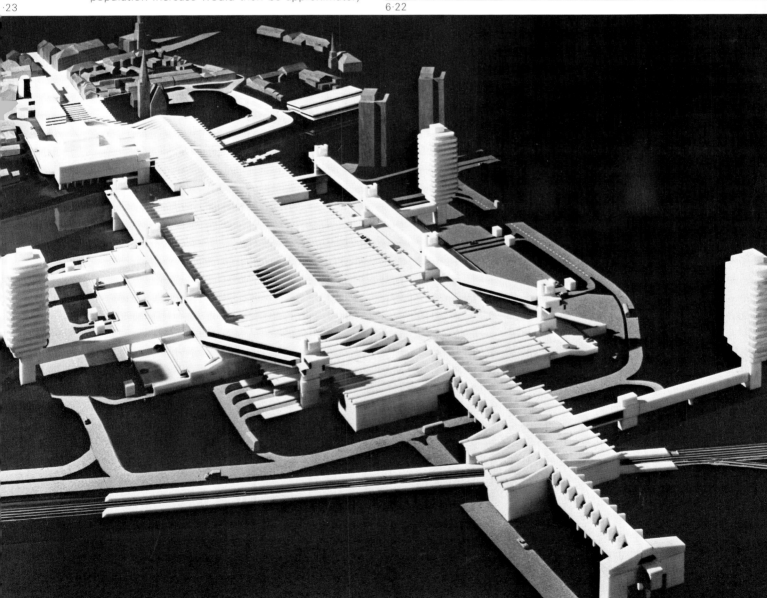

·23

167

£2·2 million per annum.

6 Minimum and maximum initial distribution of expenditure has been assumed to be:

Central shopping 50–65%
Local shopping 50–35%

With an eventual distribution when the target population is achieved of:

Central shopping 70%
Local shopping 30%

7 Minimum and maximum initial distribution of expenditure between the main categories of floorspace has been assumed to be:

	Convenience	Durable	Service
Centrally	10–15%	35–40%	5–10%
Locally	25–30%	5–10%	5–10%

and Eventually

Centrally	15%	45%	10%
Locally	20%	5%	5%

8 £¹000 expenditure per 10,000 population would then be:

	Convenience	Durable	Service
Centrally			
Minimum	220	770	110
Maximum	330	880	220
Eventual	330	990	220
Locally			
Minimum	550	110	110
Maximum	660	220	220
Eventual	440	110	110

9 Average turnover figures (£ per square metre gross) for conversion of expenditure to floor space has been assumed to be:

	Convenience	Durable	Service
Centrally and			
Locally	375–430	270–320	270–320

10 Resulting floor-space provision assuming the lower conversion factors:

	Convenience m²	Durable m²	Service m²	Total m²
Central				
Minimum	585	2,865	410	3,860
Maximum	875	3,275	820	4,965
Eventual	875	3,680	820	5,375
Local	m²	m²	m²	m²
Minimum	1,460	410	410	2,280
Maximum	1,750	820	820	3,385
Eventual	1,170	410	410	1,990

11 Resulting floor-space provision assuming the higher average conversion factors would be:

	Convenience m²	Durable m²	Service m²	Total m²
Central				
Minimum	510	2,380	345	3,235
Maximum	770	2,725	680	4,175
Eventual	770	3,070	680	4,520
Local	m²	m²	m²	m²
Minimum	1,285	345	345	1,970
Maximum	1,535	680	680	2,890
Eventual	1,025	345	345	1,710

12 Assuming higher average conversiob factors are used with maximum central, minimum local initial provision, then floor space per person would be 42 m² centrally and 20 m² locally for retail and service expenditure. Ultimate provision would be 46 m² per person centrally 17 m² per person locally

'Local Shopping

1 Local Provision might then be:

	Convenience m²	Durable m²	Service m²
Initially			
7 mini markets	465	185	
1 supermarket	280	95	
10/12 shops	465	95	370
Eventually			
7 mini markets	465	185	
1 supermarket	280	95	
6/8 shops	185	95	370

2 Local shopping turnover might then be:

	m²		£m²	£
Initially				
7 mini markets	650	at	320	208,000
1 supermarket	370	at	645	238,650
10/12 shops	465	at	430	199,950
	95	at	320	30,400
	370	at	320	118,400
Total				795,400
Eventually	m²		£m²	£
7 mini markets	650	at	320	208,000
1 supermarket	370	at	320	238,650
6/8 shops	185	at	430	79,550
	95	at	320	30,400
	370	at	320	118,400
Total				675,000

3 Local shops might include any of the following:
Convenience: Grocer, Greengrocer, Confectioner-Newsagent, Tobacconist-Sub Post Office, Butcher, Baker, Fishmonger.
Durable: Clothing, Footwear, Hardware, Chemist.
Service: Launderette, Dry Cleaners, Hairdresser, Cafe, Electricity-Gas, Betting Shop, Bank

4 Associated Service industries might include any of the following:
Carpenter-Joiner, Plumber, Electrician, Plasterer, Jobbing Builder, Decorator, Garden Centre, Tyre-Battery Depot, Taxi Depot, Bus-Car Hire Depot, Service Station, Local Authority Depot, Public Utility Depot, Bakery, Laundry

Central Area Shopping

Final Calculations

1 Existing floor-space in Irvine for a population of 22,000 (updated from the County Assessor's figures. Gross Areas include Internal Circulation and Storage, but excluding Petrol Filling Stations, Public Houses and Banks):

	Convenience	Durable	Service	Total
Central	4,595 m²	9,450 m²	1,100 m²	15,145 m²
Local	1,875	2,310	1,325	5,510
Total	6,470	11,760	2,425	20,655

Theoretical floor space needed in Irvine Burgh for a total population of 26,000:

Central	2,005	7,980	1,765	11,750
Local	2,650	895	895	4,440
Total	4,655	8,875	2,660	16,190

2 Assuming the following net floor space is retained in the Central Area (reduction due to redevelopment of 2310 m² in Bridgegate)

Convenience	Durable	Service	Total
4,650 m²	7,440 m²	745 m²	12,835 m²

3 Then the estimated total central area floor space required for a population of 120,000 would be:

	Convenience	Durable	Service	Total
Initially	9,265 m²	32,700 m²	8,145 m²	50,110 m²
Eventually	9,265	36,830	8,145	54,240

4 The required additional total central area floor space would then be:

	Convenience	Durable	Service	Total
Initially	4,615 m²	25,260 m²	7,405 m²	37,280 m²
Eventually	4,615	29,390	7,405	41,410

5 Additional Central Area floor space might be made up as follows:

	Convenience	Durable	Service
	2–3 Supermarkets (1,400–1,850 m²)	2–3 Dept. stores (5,580–7,440 m²)	
	10–12 shops (185–465 m²)	15–20 shops (465–2,325 m²)	20–30 shops (185–465 m²)
Totals	4,185–5,515 m²)	25,110–29,760 m²	6,975–7,905

6 Central Area turnover might then be:

Existing Centre

Convenience	Durable	Service	
4,650 m² at £430 £2·0m	7,440 m² at £320 £2·4m	745 m² at £320 £0·24m	
			Total 1 £4·64m

Total

Initially

3,255 m² at £645 £2·1m	11,160 m² at £320 £3·6m	7,440 m² at £320 £2·4m	
1,395 m² at £320 £0·45m	14,135 m² at £320 £4·6m		
Totals £2·55m	£8·2m	£2·4m	Total 2 £13·15m

Eventually

3,255 m² at £645 £2·1m	16,740 m² at £320 £5·4m	7,440 m² at £320 £2·4m	
1,395 m² at £320 £0·45m	13,020 m² at £320 £4·2m		
Totals £2·55m	£9·6m	£2·4m	Total 3 £14·55m

7 Total Central Area Expenditure for a population of 120,000

Initially	Total 1 + 2 = £17·8m
Eventually	Total 1 + 3 = £19·2m

12 × 10,000 population estimated expenditure would be

Initially	£17·2m
Eventually	£18·5m

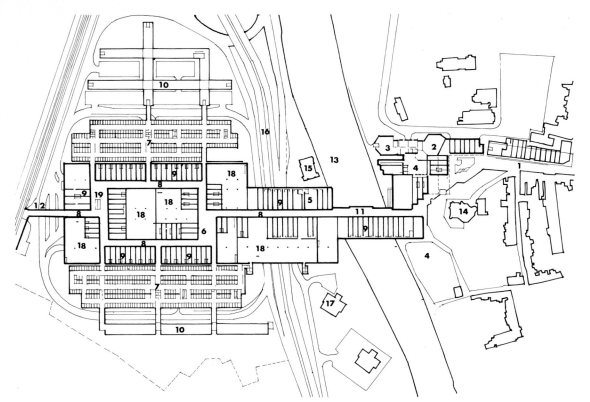

Key:
 1 Bridgegate (pedestrianised)
 2 Cinema
 3 Hotel
 4 Covered square
 5 Restaurant
 6 Central square
 7 Multi-storey car parks
 8 Shopping concourse
 9 Shops
10 Office buildings
11 River bridge

12 Railway station
13 River Irvine
14 Trinity church
15 Wilson Fullerton church
16 North-south principal
   road
17 Multi-storey apartments
18 Multiple shops
19 Escalators down to regional
   bus stations
Scale: 1 : 4000

6·24 Irvine New Town Shopping Centre, Ayrshire, Scotland:
plan at shopping-deck level
Architects: Irvine Development Corporation Architect's Depart-
ment
Chief Architect: David Gosling
Principal Architect: Barry Maitland

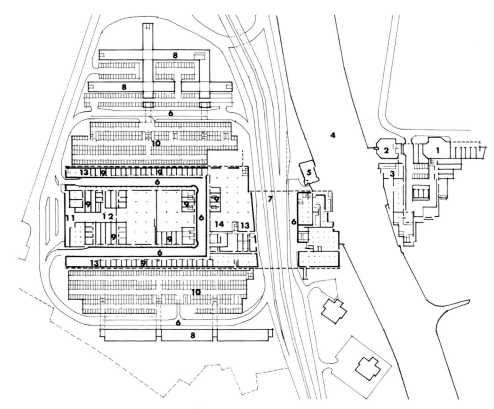

Key:
 1 Cinema
 2 Function suite
 3 Public bar
 4 River Irvine
 5 Wilson Fullarton church
 6 Service roads
 7 North-south principal
   road
 8 Office buildings
 9 Shop storage
10 Multi-storey car parks
11 Regional bus station
12 Shopping square
13 Plant room
14 Management
Scale: 1 : 4000

6·25 Irvine New Town Shopping Centre, Ayrshire, Scotland:
underdeck plan (ground level)

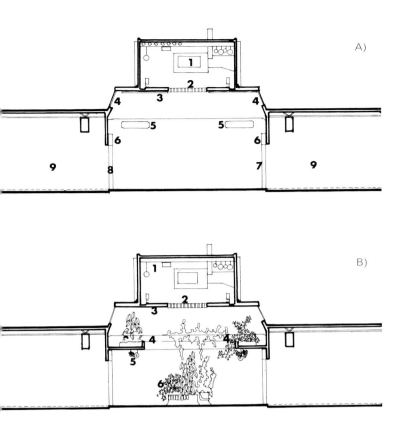

Key: A)
1 Spine duct
2 Smoke exhaust grilles
3 Main lighting
4 Roof lights
5 Suspended illuminated
  signs
6 Shopfront sign by tenant
7 Line of shopfront
8 Shopfront smoke curtain
9 Shop

B)
1 Spine duct
2 Smoke exhaust grilles
3 Mainlighting
4 Suspended planting
5 Display lighting
6 Planting/seating
Scale: 1:200

6·26 Irvine New Town Shopping Centre
A) Typical cross-section
B) Cross-section with landscaping

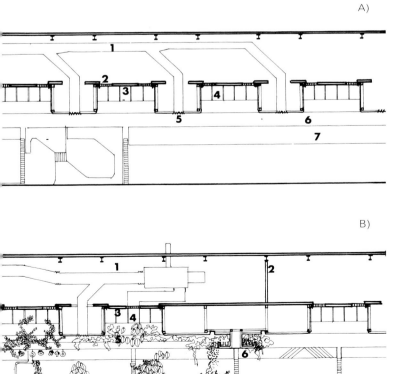

Key: A)
1 Spine duct
2 Smoke exhaust grilles
3 Main lighting
4 Roof lights
5 Air supply diffusers
6 Shopfront
7 Shopfront smoke curtain

B)
1 Spine duct
2 Smoke reservoir partition
3 Main lighting
4 Roof lights
5 Suspended planting
6 Mall smoke curtain
7 Display/planting/seating
  area
Scale: 1:200

6·27 Irvine New Town Shopping Centre
A) Typical long section
B) Long section with landscaping

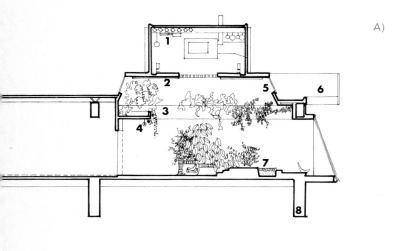

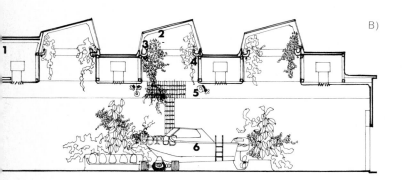

Key: A)
1 Longitudinal spine duct
2 Main lighting
3 Suspended planting
4 Display lighting
5 Roof lighting
6 Cross duct
7 Seating/children's play area
8 Bridge beam

B)
1 Inter spine duct walkway
2 Roof light
3 Plant trough
4 Main lighting
5 Display lighting
6 Display area
Scale: 1 : 200

6.28 Irvine New Town Shopping Centre
A) River bridge cross-section
B) Cross-section at main square

A) **'Location of Shopping Floor Space**
As at Runcorn, the question of location of the main centre gave rise to considerable study. Again an existing centre serving a population of over 20,000 was situated to one side of the designated area, and the first Master Plan proposals suggested the location of a new green-field centre geographically in the middle of that area. This option was eventually rejected and the decision made to locate the main centre adjacent to and integrated with the existing Irvine Burgh Centre. A major factor in this decision was the proximity of Kilmarnock centre to the east and the multiplicity of centres in close competition which would result from a location independent of the existing Burgh centre. Instead it was envisaged that the growth of the New Town and of Kilmarnock would give rise to a linear urban area best served by two balanced main centres at its east and west ends. Whereas at Runcorn the development of a major new centre would have entailed massive disruption of the old, the Burgh of Irvine contained derelict sites which would allow the retention of the old centre along with the new. This arose from the historical situation of Irvine whose original function as an important port on the Firth of Clyde had diminished. The town had thus grown inland away from the foreshore and separated from it by a river, rail line and belt of older industries. A large area of land trapped between these thresholds had declined and was available for redevelopment. A new centre in this location could thus relate closely to the old centre without seriously disrupting it and also, with its infrastructure, re-open the foreshore to the New Town as a major area of leisure and recreation.

B) In addition to Irvine Burgh Centre and the new main centre of which it would become part, the existing centre at Kilwinning was proposed as a district centre for the northern part of the New Town. New local shopping provisions were also planned on the basis of mini-markets servicing catchments of 1500 to 4000 people on a corner shop basis, and larger local centres serving a population of 10 to 15,000. The overall division between central and local shopping facilities was calculated over a likely range of distribution, and is given in Table 8.'

Table 8 *Range of Proposed Provision (m²)*

Population	Central	Local m²
40,000	15,145	15,180
60,000	22,785–27,435	9,300–13,950
80,000	31,155–35,805	13,485–18,135
100,000	42,780–47,430	14,880–19,530
120,000	52,080–56,730	18,135–22,785

The old Irvine centre would continue to act as district centre for its immediate catchment area and would provide a complementary facility to the new centre which would be carefully phased in relation to it. Where appropriate, the Development Corporation would buy the shops of traders in the old centre who wished to move to the new, and renovate them for reletting. In order to preserve the core of the old town, and concentrate commercial expansion in the new development, expansion of existing premises was limited to 10%. This was to be monitored through a data bank of land use, employing the computer facility shared by the five Scottish New Towns. The data bank involved the creation of an automatic mapping system so that information would be available in both graphic and statistical form, and is used for the creation and maintenance of 5-year physical and financial plan information.

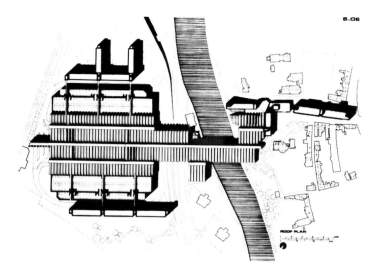

Site
A linear central area was envisaged, comprising five main zones running from east to west as follows:

Area 1 The existing Burgh centre lying on high ground at the landward end of the new central area, and based around the cross of its shopping streets, the westward arm of which would develop onto the lower land across the River Irvine, into—

Area 2 The Friars' Croft site, already substantially in public ownership and lying between the River Irvine and the rail line on its embankment, could readily be developed as the commercial core of the new central area

Area 3 The 'gateway' area to the Harbour—Foreshore beyond the rail line, with river frontage and ready access to the rail station. Envisaged as an area for mixed civic and commercial development

Area 4 The quayside area with potential for residential and recreational use

Area 5 The Harbour area, to contain a major Leisure Centre acting as a stimulus for the development of a Beach Park and related recreational facilities

This basic disposition was proposed as a framework for development to be undertaken by a variety of public and private agencies whose specific needs were uncertain in both the short and long term.

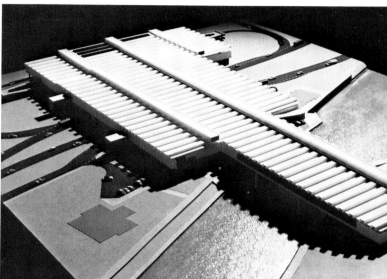

Design Objectives
A series of design objectives was established for the new shopping centre, a number of which corresponded to those proposed at Runcorn regarding its viability, enclosure, pedestrian segregation and flexibility. In addition the central area context imposed requirements on the commercial zone to create a new east-west circulation across the existing barriers to development, while those barriers themselves formed a much more restricted and constrained site in the Friars' Croft area than had been available at Runcorn.

Design Development 1: Alternatives
A design team of architects, engineers and surveyors was established within the Corporation to investigate alternative solutions prior to seeking funding for the new centre. A variety of alternative sites for the shopping and commercial areas in the vicinity of Irvine Burgh centre and the harbour/foreshore areas were investigated before the Friars' Croft site was selected. On that site a variety of basic organisations was then studied for the commercial centre comprising three approximately equal phases, each of 14,000 m² GLA shopping, 14,000 m² GLA offices and 800 car-parking spaces. It was concluded that a similar organisation to that of the Runcorn centre would be effective in establishing the required strong pedestrian connection to the existing Burgh centre by the creation of a deck level springing from the higher ground level of the cross, and extending across the Friars' Croft site with traffic circulation at grade below. The more restricted site form would not, however, allow as regular a traffic circulation system, and the site irregularities and features such as the

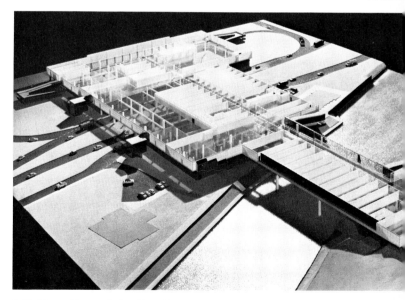

6·29 Town Centre, Irvine New Town: roof plan showing services system at the final design stage. Scale: 1 : 6000

6·30 Town Centre, Irvine New Town: model of roof structure and service system at the final design stage

6·31 Town Centre, Irvine New Town: model with roof removed showing internal arrangement at the final design stage

173

River Irvine and the existing buildings on its banks would produce a more specific building form, necessarily responding to and exploiting the opportunities created. In addition, the very strong differentiation between the main east-west line of growth and its secondary north-south development led the design team to consider a directional grid and structure for the Irvine centre, in contrast to that adopted at Runcorn.

Design Development 2: Preliminary Design

From the above considerations a preliminary design was completed in December 1969 as follows:

1 *Pedestrian circulation:* the scheme was based on a single major east-west pedestrian route, extending the existing western shopping street of Irvine cross onto a shopping deck as an enclosed mall crossing the River Irvine on a shopping bridge and continuing through as the spine of a new enclosed shopping centre to meet the rail station on the west side of the site at platform level. From this main artery cross malls extended north and south at 75 m intervals to give access to multi-storey car parking lying beyond the shopping centre, and office developments beyond that

2 *Vehicular circulation:* a main one-way circulatory system was proposed in the Friars' Croft area, giving access to car parking banks to north and south of the shopping centre and to an east-west service road running below its axis. The river bank areas were to be served by independent branches of this system, and service access to the river shopping bridge was to be by a trucking way below it

3 *Structure and services:* the structure was based on a 5 × 8 m grid which attempted to reconcile the requirements of shopping and car parking on a directional basis. Below the mall level, ground and mezzanine floors could accommodate either shop storage areas served from the centre of the section, or car parking from the edges. The main sales floor above was a simple single-storey area, covered by an 'umbrella' roof which effected the distribution of services over the area. Plant rooms and main service runs were to be located in a 'spine duct' over the main 8 m-wide east-west mall, with hollow roof beams distributing services out to north and south, and spanning from the spine duct out to the edges of the sales floor.

This design attempted to provide a coherent system of structure, services and circulation for the linear development, which could adapt itself to the varying site conditions. It was then extended to propose a continuous system of pedestrian all-weather routes serving the whole area

Selection of Developer

As at Runcorn, central government (in this case the Scottish Development Department) encouraged the Development Corporation to seek private finance for its town centre development. While infrastructure and land acquisition would be carried out by the Corporation, a partner was to be sought among property development companies who would lease the site on a long term lease and carry out the

6·32 Town Centre, Irvine New Town: perspective of the river bridge mall

6·33 Town Centre, Irvine New Town: perspective of the main mall

6·34 Town Centre, Irvine New Town: perspective of the central square

174

construction of the new development. In early 1970 the corporation circulated over 100 development companies in Britain with the preliminary designs for the town centre. Following a good initial response, interested developers were then asked to indicate the form of their financial offer in respect of ground rent, the rental levels which they anticipated from the development, their view of the Corporation's preliminary design and whether, if successful, they would appoint the Corporation's architects to the scheme.

The financial terms offered by most of the development Companies did not significantly vary, being based on a fixed ground rental to the Corporation until such time as the developer had achieved an agreed percentage return on his investment; thereafter an increase in revenue beyond that point would be shared to an agreed formula between the two parties. Reactions to the preliminary design did, however, vary considerably, some developers regarding it as basically sound, some expressing reservations and others proposing alternative arrangements. The design team was surprised by the variety of this reaction, and of the dramatically different alternatives proposed by some of the largest and most experienced developers in the UK. In view of the similarity of financial offers from the companies shortlisted and interviewed, their size, experience and availability of funds were major considerations to the Corporation, as well as their attitude towards the preliminary scheme, which unlike the alternatives offered, reflected the Corporation's broader planning concern with the central area as a whole as well as with the viability of its commercial component.

By September 1970 agreement in principal had been reached with the preferred developer, who proposed to adopt the Corporation's design and appoint the Chief Architect as architect on a normal scale fee basis, those fees being paid direct to the Development Corporation as at Runcorn. The company wished to appoint its own engineering and quantity surveying consultants, however, and a new team was therefore established to develop the design. Two levels of regular meetings were established to resolve (as originally: i.e.) difficulties as they arose, being:

1 *Policy group:* attended by Directors of the development company, chief officers of the Corporation and chaired by the Corporation's General Manager, this body was concerned with general policy, meeting initially each month and later at two or three-monthly intervals

2 *Working party* attended by members of consultant firms and chaired either by the developer's Project Manager or by the Architect, this group was responsible for technical questions and was joined by officers of the Corporation and later the contractor, at appropriate stages, meeting at two or four week intervals

Design Development 3: Final Design

In the ensuing months of 1971 a close working method was developed among the members of the new design team and the developer, three major viability exercises being undertaken and numerous modifications made to improve the functioning, attractiveness or commercial viability of the project. The major effects upon the preliminary design were as follows:

1 *Pedestrian circulation:* as the preliminary scheme was developed, the girth of the shopping floor gradually increased, with the effect that a considerable amount of frontage was created on side malls distant from the

175

main mall and with low rental potential. This was overcome by substituting two parallel main malls over the widest part of the centre, and connecting them at squares at each end to form a complete circuit, with very short side mall connections out to the car parks. A lower mall was also formed at the west end of the centre, leading from a bus station to escalator connections up to the main mall level

2 *Vehicular circulation:* engineering studies suggested that it was essential to have a north-south through-route in the Friars' Croft area, and that this should be separate from any circulating town centre system. In the confined site area the addition of a dual-carriageway principal road gave rise to considerable problems and formed an additional obstacle to be crossed by the westward growth of development. A service road loop under the main shopping floor on Friars' Croft was substituted for the earlier central service road, and car parking was withdrawn from the shopping structure to form independent terraced structures to north and south

3 *Structure and services:* a 5·4 × 5·4 m planning grid was adopted for the final design, corresponding to the traditional 18 ft module for shopping frontage. The structural principle remained as before, with a reinforced concrete frame supporting a wide-span roof. At service road level the structure must accommodate itself to a variety of conditions, from columns at 5·4 m centres supporting flat slabs, to the autofab beams of the river bridge section. At mall level the variety of lower structure could be simplified to a concrete column and beam system running with the main malls in an east-west direction, and supporting steel roof trusses running north-south across the main sales floors. These trusses, 1·5 m deep, were braced together in pairs, with one pair, 2·2 m apart, running down the centre of each 5·4 m bay and forming in effect continuous plant or services voids, referred to as rib ducts, across the building. The earlier notion of a simple central services roof-space running in a spine duct in the other direction, from east to west, above the main mall, was also developed. Since the main mall now occupied three possible locations on plan, three parallel spine ducts were formed above the roof trusses, 5·4 m wide and 2·7 m high, and occurring either over a main mall or else over a space user. In the former location this continuous plant room was to house landlord's air- and smoke-handling plant for the malls as well as service mains distribution to tenants on either side via the north-south rib ducts; where a spine duct alternatively ran over a space-user, it was then available as a housing for major roof-top plant items for that tenant

4 *Fire precautions:* it was apparent from an early stage that a major determinant of the building design would be the Building Regulations, and in particular those sections dealing with fire precautions. Since the regulations were devised around notions of safety applying to individual buildings, rather than large inter-related complexes, they were in conflict with many of the requirements of the latter and much time was therefore spent between 1970 and 1973 in consultation with local fire officers, government experts, and the national Fire Research Station in attempts to resolve the difficulties this raised. A major

6·35 Town Centre, Irvine New Town: air view of centre under construction at the principal road crossing

source of these lay in the nature of the shopping mall, which in a traditional high street would have been open to the air and at ground level, and hence a 'place of safety' for people to escape to from the shops or for fire-fighting vehicles to approach by. These characteristics no longer applied to the enclosed, deck-level mall, and it became necessary to devise elaborate compensating measures to maintain levels of safety in a building complex quite different from that envisaged by the existing regulations. In other words, just as the mall was supported by mechanical systems to maintain an artificial level of comfort, so also it must artificially maintain the required levels of safety.

At Irvine a major element in the fire precaution systems was concerned with the control of smoke in a mall which might be fronted by open or closed shop fronts in random pattern. This was done by treating the main spine ducts as emergency smoke ducts running along the top of the malls, and clearing them of smoke by the action of large extract fans mounted at 60 m centres along the spine ducts. Backing up this system, which was intended to perform the primary task of keeping escape routes clear, was a range of further systems designed either to attack the fire or assist the fire brigade. These included sprinklers, alarm systems, smoke extract from service roads, a converted Land Rover fire fighting vehicle for use in the malls, direction indicator screens to guide approaching fire-tenders to the affected zone of the building, public address system for emergency use, smoke detector operated door closers, and many other similar devices. These systems, coupled with the planning requirements of mall exit widths and locations, constituted a body of precautionary steps which the authorities could accept as compensating for a number of statutory requirements which could not be achieved in a building complex of this kind, and which were consequently relaxed

5 *Mall:* the design of the centre placed even more emphasis than normal on the section of the building in the area of the mall. Services, structure and circulation coincided at this point, which was the subject of a series of studies during the design period. These were concerned with

mall uses, and the relationship of zones of specialist trading along the length of the mall (eg food shops, luxury goods) with the character of the mall at those points, the activities which it might support (eg mall cafe, exhibition area, childrens' play) and its finishes and fittings. The variety of conditions which the mall met on its journey westward from the old town could thus be reflected in changes in its section, form and use

6 *Phasing:* during the design period the extent of the first phase was increased to about half of the projected final area. Running from the old town centre, it included the shopping bridge over the River Irvine, ramps and mezzanine levels down to pedestrian riverside walks, a second shopping bridge over the new principal road, and the first mall square on the Friars' Croft area with connections to first stage car parking and office buildings in that area

7 *Contract:* a two-stage tendering procedure was adopted in order that the contractor could become fully involved in the design and production drawing programme. Tenders were sought in mid 1972 from a short-list of 3 national contractors on the basis of provisional bills of quantities. Letters of intent were then exchanged with the preferred contractor who became a full member of the design team, contributing to the development of the detailed design and evolving a construction programme during a 9-month pre-construction period. A contract price was then negotiated with the contractor on the basis of final bills of quantities and the original tender rates, and the 92 week contract began in mid-1973

8 *Finishes:* externally, dark brown brickwork at road and river-bank level, with band of horizontal protected steel louvres at first floor soffit; white stove enamelled steel panels at mall level, with dark brown glazed areas; dark brown corrugated steel sheet finish to roof and plantroom housings, with louvre ends to rib ducts.

Internally, mall floors in buff clay tile, used also as finish to concrete block cross wall ends between tenancies. Mall ceiling in sprayed acoustic plaster to follow profile of rib ducts, accommodating clerestorey natural and artificial lighting, services outlets and high-level plant troughs

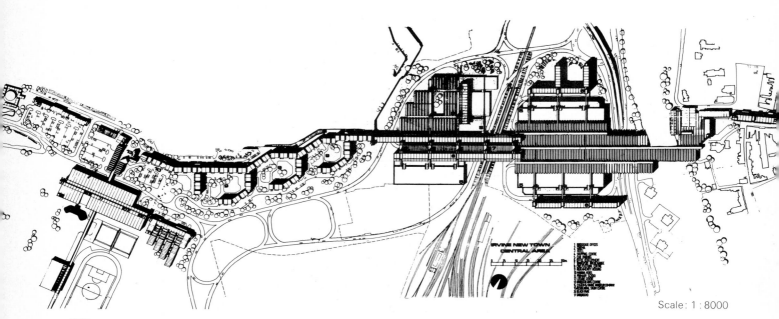

Scale: 1 : 8000

6·36 Town Centre, Irvine New Town: district plan showing the relationship of shopping centre to harbour and leisure development and the extension of megastructure and walkway systems

6·37 Town Centre, Irvine New Town: air view of centre under construction at the river crossing

6·38 Town Centre, Irvine New Town: centre under construction at the river crossing, looking west

6·39 Town Centre, Irvine New Town: centre under construction at the river crossing looking towards Trinity Church

7 Conclusions

For any study of the development of the new retailing structures, Henry Ford's remark early in 1975 that, in thirty years as a businessman, he had 'never before felt so uncertain and so troubled about the future of both my country and my company', must indicate that a significant point of review had been reached. The post-war growth of new shopping building types was so directly related to the effects of the automobile and the expectation of ever-rising living standards, that any significant change in those two basic parameters must mean an interruption in what had been a remarkably rich evolution of new forms. Yet even before the energy and economic crises which caused Henry Ford's comment, it seemed that at least some of the lines in that evolution had by the early 70s reached a stage of completion at which new directions were being sought. Thus, at the point that the North American out-of-town centre, for twenty years a vital source of retailing development, reached a peak of sophisticated organisation, attention began to shift back to the problems of development on down-town sites. Similarly, in the UK, there was a feeling that the major effort of redeveloping shopping centre facilities in urban cores on a widespread scale across the country may have passed, while at the same time the designation of new New Towns, the source of earlier pioneering work in town centre design, virtually ceased. This is not to say that significant new forms of American out-of-town, or British down-town, centres would not still emerge, but that, in the twenty years since the opening of Roosevelt Fields and the Lijnbaan, major strands in the evolution of the new shopping forms had worked themselves through to a point where it was meaningful to assess them comprehensively. The disruptive effects upon whatever line of development might then have occurred of the unexpected combination of inflation, depression and expensive energy upon the western economies, could only reinforce the impression in the early '70s that a stage of fulfilment and transition had already been reached.

The broad pattern of post-war development had been built around the question of location, a consideration which had been given a completely new meaning by the motor car and which divided that development into two streams, out-of-town and integrated. Whether or not these terms can be precisely separated, as has been challenged by some authorities, the distinction between them underlies the greater part of the post-war literature on shopping forms and remains a major source of contention in many areas of current debate.

In North America the out-of-town forms achieved their most vigorous growth as, from the early '50s onwards, centres were rapidly developed along the highway systems serving centres of population. The form of these centres became increasingly sophisticated as competition between them produced a spiral development towards ever more service- and variety-oriented types. At the same time out-of-town forms appeared in which the price parameter was of overriding importance, so that a complete range of out-of-town facilities was gradually built up over the whole market spectrum, from the most aggressively cut-price discount store to the most luxuriously appointed fashion mall.

In parallel with this progression in North America, the development of new integrated centres in European towns and cities also produced novel solutions which were equally affected, in terms of their forms if not their locations, by the car. Arising first from the need to rebuild the city centres destroyed by the war, then through the

New Towns programmes, and finally as a result of the redevelopment of older central areas, these down-town centres followed a similar line of development towards greater complexity and comfort to that pursued by the out-of-town forms, and did so often with one eye firmly fixed on their example.

Within this broad pattern, the differences in historical, economic and planning conditions between North America and Europe and between the countries and regions within Europe, gave rise to many interesting variants. Thus when circumstances in Europe in the mid '60s began to resemble American conditions sufficiently for out-of-town forms to emerge, they did so in their own way, which could neither repeat the American development nor ignore it. In the European context the out-of-town furniture store became particularly associated with its development in Scandinavia, the hypermarket with France and its variant the superstore with England. In some places lines of development seemed only partially explored, as for example with the European out-of-town regional centre which had not yet been taken to the levels of elaborate specialisation seen in North America. Again, other forms seemed to have come full circle, as in the tendency of some North American out-of-town centres to become the foci of new CBD's, and to be planned on the basis of more restricted sites with more intensive land usage, while at the same time one branch of European New Town experiment seemed to have arrived at a similar position from the opposite direction.

By the early '70s, twenty years of development had thus produced a wide range of shopping centre types operating at different market levels and in differing relationship to their catchment populations. Aspects of this development had been so dramatic and unexpected that few would be willing to predict what the next twenty years would produce. It was however possible to make intelligent guesses about the likely tendencies within any one area in the short term, and in 1972/73 the authors sought the views of a number of developers, retailers and planners on such tendencies within the UK. While by no means comprehensive, the results were useful as a general indication of the trends which seemed most significant in Britain at that time, and which ran as follows:

1 *Shopping habits:* it was generally agreed that the tendency of families to carry out the bulk of weekly shopping on a one-stop basis would increase considerably. The consequences of this would be a decline in the number of daily shopping trips and a concentration of shopping by car on Thursday and Friday evenings. This would be assisted by the increase in home-freezer ownership and would create a demand in the one-stop centres for increased services, such as crèches, and for longer trading hours

2 *Technical innovations:* it was felt that packaging techniques would increasingly be adopted to suit bulk purchasing. There would be an increased use of computers for stock control and management information

3 *The retailing industry:* the increased tendency to fewer shopping trips would be matched by the increased diversification of lines carried by the multiple stores. A continued decline in the overall number of shops was anticipated, as was the increasing habit of large food chains to retail goods under their own label

4 *Shopping forms:* the correspondents found it most difficult to agree on the future of out-of-town shopping in Britain. Most felt it likely that a few (ranging from 4 to 12) large regional out-of-town centres would be allowed

7·02 Cartoon by Steinberg of the Galleria, Milan

of France had encouraged her hypermarket and regional shopping centre developers to argue that the new forms were absorbing a growing demand and not detracting from existing outlets, a comforting thesis which could not be maintained in a period of economic stagnation. If it was difficult to guess the future directions of retailing when the components of the spiral path seemed set to continue, it becomes even more so in a situation where they may be abruptly set aside, far less to predict the longer term implications of scarcer and more expensive fuels. The retailing industry and the built forms it produces are so closely tied to the general economy that a clear picture of that in the future would first be necessary.

In the short term it is by no means apparent that the effects of economic and energy crises would simply reverse the most recent trends or act selectively against all forms depending upon the automobile. When questioned about the effects of recent sharp rises in petrol prices, one developer of superstore operations in the UK, observed that, by the time new out-of-town projects currently at planning stage began trading, Britain would be self-sufficient in oil and a new generation of cars would be on the roads. If this somewhat wry comment could be argued to represent a special case, it is nevertheless possible that, far from diminishing present trends, a reduction in car usage, as against car ownership, could reinforce and exaggerate certain aspects of them. The tendency of each family to buy the 100 lb of goods which it consumes each week in one single bulk purchase could well be encouraged, as might also the local facility within walking distance, while shopping forms operating between these two extremes might be those most affected. In this connection it should be remembered that the trading form which perhaps best symbolises the post-war years of growth—the supermarket —was in fact an invention of the depressed conditions of the '30s.

In the light of this situation, and by way of a conclusion to this study, we offer some final illustrations of the themes which have been discussed and of a few examples of possible new directions which they may offer.

1 Megastructures and Malls

A significant aspect of the later out-of-town regional centres was the increasing awareness of their ability to draw other uses around them and to become the hubs of infant CBD's. Thus their developers bought up surrounding land whose value would be increased by the new shopping centre, and planned adjacent offices, housing and entertainment buildings on a scale far removed from the incidental TBA and drive-in bank buildings accommodated on the earlier centre sites. This development had the effect of opening out the centre to its surroundings, at least in a planning and functional sense, although the tendency of the Stage 3 centre plans was to ever more complete and self-contained geometric models. An unusual solution in this respect, and one which reflected the greater indeterminancy of the shopping centre form as part of a wider development, was the design by Cesar Pelli of Gruen Associates for Santa Anita Fashion Park in Arcadia, near Los Angeles. Intended as a prototype multi-use urban centre, it comprises a triple department store centre, with all units disposed along an open-ended extendable spine mall, 330 m long, described by the architect as 'a modern main street—multi-levelled and air conditioned'. Two office buildings are also plugged into this spine, which is fed from upper or lower sides of parking in the classic

to follow Brent Cross at strategic points, either throughout the country or in the South-East only. These would be complemented by an increased number of superstores on the edges of towns. There would be a tendency for greater specialisation and conservation in a number of 'exclusive' town centres and for the growth of new suburban district centres, which would leave the main centres to concentrate on durable comparison trading. Some felt that a growth of second generation supermarkets was likely, and that these would be larger and better provided with car parking. Regarding leasing agreements it was felt that inflation would favour reduced periods of rent reviews, from 7 to 5 years, and a greater use of turnover rentals

These opinions were expressed at a time when it was generally assumed that living standards in the industrialised western countries, together with levels of car ownership and usage would continue to rise as steadily as they had done over the previous twenty years. The pattern of spiral development suggested by Agergard and Olsen was similarly based upon this assumption, being formed by two vectors, a circular movement in trading patterns and a linear growth in the standard of living. Should the latter not occur it would seem unlikely that a stable pattern would result; rather, the changes which would take place would do so according to a different and unfamiliar pattern, and one which would upset many of the earlier premises. Thus the dynamic growth

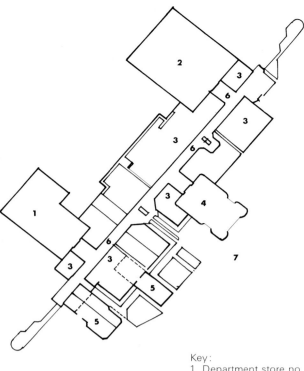

Key:
1 Department store no 1
2 Department store no 2
3 tenants
4 Department store no 3
5 Offices
6 Main mall
7 Lower-level parking
Scale: 1:4000

7·03 Project for the Santa Anita Fashion Park, Arcadia, California:
lower-level plan
Architect: Cesar Pelli of Gruen Associates

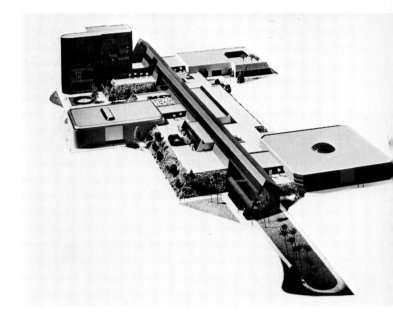

7·04 Santa Anita Fashion Park, Arcadia, California: view of the
preliminary design model

two-level mall arrangement. The concern which this
design shows to return some of the essential characteristics
of the street to the mall, is a mirror of the opposite tendency
among integrated urban shopping centres in Europe to
model their streets increasingly upon the malls of the
out-of-town examples. The ambiguous results of that tendency, whereby an apparently essential part of the public
circulation of the city becomes a private zone, were
remarked at the end of Chapter 4·3. At the same time the
size of these networks of private/public space has increased to embrace considerable sections of cities with
new pedestrian circulation systems extending out from the
shopping malls to connect them to any beneficial sources
of traffic generation in the surrounding areas. In effect, and
whether by conscious planned intent, or simply through
expediency, a number of urban shopping centre projects
have generated new megastructures in their city cores.

Even before the escalation in fuel costs in 1973–74, some
developers were questioning the levels of complexity,
particularly of servicing systems and hence of maintenance
charges on tenants, of the more advanced projects. In
the UK this was aggravated by much stricter Building
Regulations than applied elsewhere, and requirements for
increasingly more onerous safety provisions as project
followed project, so that, it was argued, a point would
shortly be reached where it was no longer viable to form
a 'safe' building of this type.

In the light of these difficulties it might be argued that
the highest standards of malls achieved in the isolated
North American centres are inappropriate as models for
the somewhat different problems of a mall as part of a
wider city network. It is interesting then to see that in the
North American examples of down-town centres, the
persistent image is not that of the luxurious department
store-like interiors of the out-of-town centres, but instead
that of an older European model, the Galleria in Milan.
This seems to exist less as a specific physical organisation
as of an idea of a commercial space which is also grand,
urban and social.

The arcades of the 19th century, themselves precursors
of both megastructure and mall, perhaps remain the
simplest and best starting points for their solution. In
one of the most elegant essays on this theme, James
Stirling and Partner's (Michael Wilford; Assistant, Leo
Krier) 1970 entry for the competition for Market Place,
Derby, illustrates its capacity to act as a basic organisational
idea for the variety of uses and scales of space produced in
a town-centre complex. It is described by James Stirling
thus: 'A major element which we have included in the
design is the arrangement of shops and other functions
along an internal shopping arcade (the same width as the
Burlington Arcade, London at walking level, increasing
in width higher up) and from this glass-roofed arcade,
covered access can be made to the principal accommodation, banquet halls auditorium halls, bars, art gallery,
offices etc. The intention is to increase the significance of
the market place square and achieve an entirely pedestrianised and protected area which will be the focal and
most important part of the town . . . which is of the
significance that the Piazza San Marco is to Venice . . .'

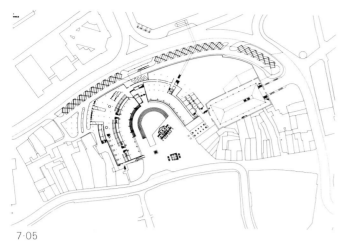
7·05

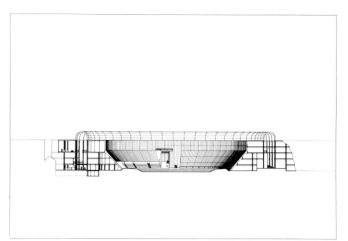
7·06

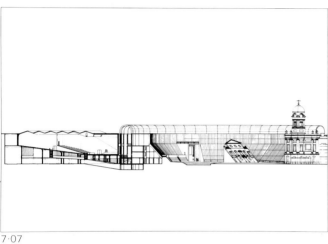
7·07

7·05 Competition entry for Derby redevelopment, England: plan showing proposed shopping arcade
Architects: James Stirling and Partner

7·06 Competition entry for Derby redevelopment showing cross-section of the arcade

7·07 Competition entry for Derby redevelopment: cross-section showing auditorium and preserved facade

7·08 Brunel Centre, Swindon: view of shopping arcade
Architect: Douglas Stephen

7·09 Competition entry for Derby redevelopment: perspective of arcade interior

7·08

7·09

7·10

7·11

7·10 Esplanade, Unicom Building, Toronto: an outstanding example (now demolished) of contemporary small arcade design integrated into speculative multi-storey office development
Architect: Barrie Briscoe

7·11 Esplanade, Unicom Building: interior of arcade

7·12 Knowsley Pavilion, Lancashire: external perspective looking along the main external mall
Architects: Foster Associates

2 Mixed Uses

The accommodation of office buildings on a shopping mall at Santa Anita, or a bus station at Derby, are examples of the kind of mixed use which commonly occurrs in all shopping developments. Other, less usual, examples of mixed use have occurred in this study, in which the success of the development depends upon the mutual benefit derived from the balance of two, roughly equal, components. Such a case occurs at the CAP 3000 shopping centre at Nice, where the body of small units complements a single large department store; again, at the Wertkauf out-of-town development at Wiesbaden, the two large elements of the Wertkauf hypermarket and the Mann Mobilia furniture store form a balanced binuclear relationship. An even more interesting situation occurs where the two elements are of quite dissimilar use, as in the two Foster hypermarket projects at Knowsley and Badhoeve-dorp. In these cases the notions that a shopping centre might benefit from a crêche or some leisure element, or that a leisure centre might benefit from a shop stall or two, become transformed by the combination of both elements at full scale in a 'hyper-centre' or 'leisure-market', which not only suggests novel possibilities for the shoppers' lifestyle, but is also offered in mitigation of the less acceptable features of the shopping element in isolation. Another example of this kind of dual use centre, this time in a downtown location, is provided by the design by Archigram Architects for Aquatels Ltd and Land Improvements Ltd for 'Bournemouth Steps' on the south coast of England. This project comprises a new shopping mode, as an expansion of the existing town centre shopping of Bournemouth at its southern end, coupled with a Convention and Recreation Centre connecting it to the beach and pierhead. Again the designers emphasize the social benefits to be gained from this approach, in contrast to 'the American outlook, (which) is strongly geared to profit and has been described as primarily a private money making proposition with incidental gestures towards amenity and cultural values'.

The architects intend that the resources of private enterprise can be used in order that creative planning might lead to promotion and profitable management. The proposals show a balance between revenue earning development and greater public amenity. The proposals identify the importance of conserving the existing public garden and emphasise the relationship between a regional shopping centre and sea front by way of the gardens area. It augments the existing system of arcades and covered ways and extends the present mix of entertainment centres with high-quality shopping.

Whatever the truth of this, the unusual combination of uses in both this project and the hypermarket Pavilions suggests one possible area of future development of shopping forms which as yet, and perhaps because of the specialisation of many developers, seems relatively unexplored.

3 Markets

In view of the more extreme predictions of economic collapse, it is perhaps fortunate that the simplest and most energy-conserving form of retailing—the trestle stall or barrow of the market—has survived the years of growth in such good shape. The great virtue of this trading form has traditionally been its flexibility, whereby it could move from place to place, offering customers a wide choice of goods and at the same time allowing traders to aggregate the

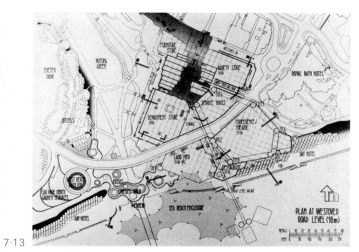

7·13

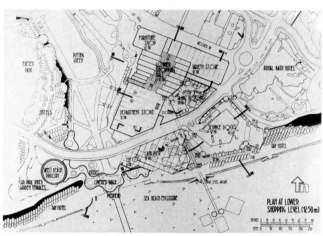

7·14

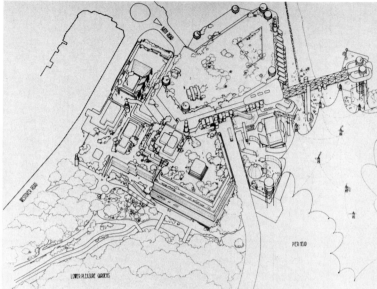

7·15

7·13 Bournemouth Steps Shopping Centre, England: plan at Westover Road level (18m)
Architect: Peter Cook; Archigram

7·14 Bournemouth Steps Shopping Centre, England: plan at lower shopping level (12·50m)

7·15 Bournemouth Steps Shopping Centre: axonometric

7·16 Bournemouth Steps Shopping Centre: interior view of arcade

7·16

day's demand for each commodity in each small town. Again the market was flexible in relation to the goods it sold, switching rapidly from one line of commodities to another in response to shortage and glut and performing a vital distributive function in swiftly disposing of perishable produce temporarily in surplus supply. Some of these characteristics often seem to be in conflict with the institutions which administer them and the regulations which govern trading seem to favour fixed establishments, dealing in fixed lines of goods on a permanent basis. This has tended to institutionalise many town markets and essentially change their character into that of collections of very small shops, and it is arguable whether this has been a beneficial metamorphosis. In addition, at any rate in the UK, the historical development of markets has produced an extremely uneven distribution across the country. It is therefore possible that an opportunity exists for a new extension of market operations to areas not presently covered, and perhaps predominantly at the district centre level. This could be achieved on a more informal, intermittent and inexpensive basis than that provided in the market hall provisions of the new integrated main centres, and could be a considerable benefit to the variety and attraction of, for example, circuits of new suburban district centres.

4 Corner Shops

In his article in *The Sunday Times* Andrew Lawson regrets the passing of the corner shop.[1] He points out that even in Victorian Times, Charles Dickens comments on the decline of the small linen drapers and chemists. The present day attempts to stabilise food prices and the rise of the large supermarket has meant the inevitable closure of the small grocer who cannot afford to cut his prices further. Many shops like Henry Dickens' off-licence grocery in Crookes, Sheffield are owned by the families that run them. Value Added Tax and National Insurance contributions for the self employed are further impositions.

Nevertheless, many corner shops still remain in the industrial towns of northern England. The off-licence still remains an important community shop supplying groceries and even occasionally retaining the old beer engines where beer could be bought on draught. Perhaps the specialised service these shops provide, like the corner delicatessen in the United States, is sufficient to justify their retention. They serve, as Andrew Lawson points out, as village shops and still survive in parts of south London, as a comprehensive group servicing the daily needs of the community. A modern version of the corner grocery can be seen in shops such as Down to Earth Community Supplies in Sheffield. This shop, run by a group of young people, caters mainly for the student population and sells all daily grocery needs in bulk, straight from sack, barrel or crate and eliminating wasteful package and containers.

7·17

7·17 The New Corner Shop: Down To Earth Community Supplies, Crookes, Sheffield: a corner grocery shop, catering mainly for a student population, which eliminates packaging and normal mass-marketing techniques

7·18 Down To Earth Community Supplies: interior

7·18

Key:
1 Rua Augusta
2 Linha 5 (underground rapid transport)
3 Rua Martinho Prado
4 Rua Olinda
5 Central ramp
6 Dove cot
7 Playground
8 Linha 4 (underground rapid transport)
9 Rua Consolacao
10 Void over motorway
11 Motorway
Scale: 1:4000

7·19 Praca Roosevelt, Sao Paulo, Brasil: site plan
Architects: Roberto Coelho Cardozo, A. Antunes Netto, M. De Souza Dias, J. C. Figueiredo Ferrai

7·20 Minitram at Sheffield: photomontage of minitram system over sunken pedestrian shopping precinct at road interchange
Architects: Robert Mathew, Johnson Marshall and Partners

5 Rehabilitation and Traffic

While the environmental benefits to shopping streets of pedestrianisation or reduced traffic penetration are generally recognised, there undoubtedly remain many instances in which miscellaneous urban spaces could be exploited for public and shopping uses. An example of this is the Praca Roosevelt in Sao Paulo,[2] where the architects A.A. Antusses Netto and M. de Souza Dias, with the landscape architect Roberto Coelho Cardoza, designed a layered structure to fill in the void left by the cutting of an urban motorway with a covered market, supermarket, shops, small theatre, play areas and cafés. This small development opportunistically adapts itself to spaces left by roads and high-rise buildings and successfully inserts a vital element into the middle of them.

A similar, if less ambitious, example occurs in Sheffield, England, in the creation of a pedestrian square at low level in the centre of a traffic island in Castle Square in the middle of the town. In effect no more than a confluence of underpasses across the traffic routes, the square and its approaches support a considerable amount of small stall shopping and function as positive pedestrian spaces. Another project proposed for that city suggest also the effects of future transportation systems upon existing city centres.

While cities such as Montreal have constructed new metro systems in recent years, the enormous costs of such projects, together with the widespread renewed interest in public transportation, have given rise to a number of alternative systems which aim to provide a similar segregation of traffic. One such system is Minitram, which was the subject of study contracts let in 1973 by the UK Transport and Road Research Laboratory to EASAMS Ltd. Hawker Siddeley Dynamics Ltd and planners Robert Matthew, Johnson-Marshall and Partners, involving its application to Sheffield.[3] The system comprised small, automatically controlled cab units running on a raised track which ran the length of the attenuated shopping core of the city, some 2400 m long, and connecting it to bus and rail stations. Cheaper than underground systems, and able to adapt to existing street patterns with little major disruption, the Minitram project gave an indication of the implications for shopping patterns should significant programmes of new public transportation systems be adopted for city centres. The implications of new public transportation forms could then be as significant in their impact upon the environment of existing city centres, and indeed upon the whole distribution and form of retail outlets, as has the automobile in the past 20 years.

6 Special Forms

In Chapter 5 it was possible to discuss only a few of the special forms of trading which have developed and which are responsible for much of the current variety in retailing methods. In addition to those mentioned, there has been rapid growth in a number of specialised fields, including Do-it-Yourself, Hi-Fi and electronics, Maternity and babywear, Frozen Food and Takeaway Food. Fashion and specialist shops for the young have continued to develop the field first opened up by the boutiques, and sometimes, as at Biba in London, with spectacular visual results.

These developments appear as a counterpart to the steady tendency of the large, highly-organised retail groups towards wider and more standard trading ranges; on the one hand there has been increasing standardisation in the marketing of the basic commodities, and on the other increasing fragmentation and specialisation in the sale of anything falling outside that net. The latter group is particularly associated with the growth in luxury or surplus spending power, and in a period of economic difficulty would seem most likely to be affected. Yet this area of trading has been a source of much invention, and whether the future lies with the bullion broker or the pawn shop, will continue to be a necessary leaven in the development of the industry.

These comments summarise a few of the strands which appear to offer new directions in shopping forms for the future. In the broad term many of the most successful shopping developments of the post-war period have been largely destructive in their results. In 1951, at the beginning of the period of development of the modern centres, Kenzo Tange, writing as a Japanese observing conditions in the west, noted that 'in modern capitalist societies of the west, urban cores have gradually been lost. The so-so-called business centres may be the new cores of capitalist societies, but can they be said to be cores of the lives of the citizens? . . . Amusements centres or shopping centres may be somewhat close to what I mean here by a core. However, if they are to be considered as cores in the sense of being places to cultivate the bodies and souls of the citizens, these by-products of Capitalism are too deeply related to consumption and pleasure and, being commercial undertakings, cannot be said to be healthy and desirable.'

In the period which has followed, the shopping element has been a key instrument of those opposing forces which have tended either to destroy and disperse the urban core, or, as in Tange's own Yerba Buena scheme, to reconstruct it in yet more complex form. It will perhaps be this function of the shopping structures of the next twenty years which will be their most important characteristic.

References

1 Lawson, Andrew 'Counter Revolution' *The Sunday Times* 30 March 1975
2 See *The Architectural Review* October 1971
3 *Minitram in Sheffield* report by Robert Matthew, Johnson-Marshall and Partners, London 1974

7·21 Praca Roosevelt, Sao Paulo: air view of shopping centre over road interchange

Appendix A
Glossary

CBD Central Business District: the main commercial centre, or 'downtown' area, of a larger town of regional status. In the UK the method of demarcation is described in full in the Census of Distribution

Department Store Large store, with at least 25 employees, selling a wide range of commodities, including clothing. The term 'Junior Department Store' is used for a smaller branch of a Department Store chain, usually in a suburban location and selling a more restricted range of goods than in the main stores

District Centre Middle tier of shopping centre hierarchy predominantly in range 10,000–25,000 m² GLA and serving catchment of 20,000–60,000 population; alternatively described as 'Community Centre'

GLA Gross Leasable Area: the most common measure of the size of a shopping building. The term refers to the total area let to traders, but excludes, in a shopping centre for example, the area of malls, service roads, landlord's plant rooms and other common areas. The GLA may be further reduced to the 'sales area' or 'net rental area', which comprises only that part devoted to selling, and excludes storage, food preparation, offices and similar support areas

Hypermarket Large self-service store trading in both convenience and durable goods. Generally at least 5,000 m² GLA, located in an out-of-town location and provided with extensive car parking

Local Centre Smallest classification of centres by functions, serving a local population of up to about 10,000 people with 2,500–7,500 m² GLA; also referred to as 'Neighbourhood Centre'

Multiple Retailing organisation having at least ten outlets, one with less being referred to as an 'Independent'

Regional Centre Centre with a major concentration of department stores and other durable goods outlets in a region, with a catchment of at least 100,000 population and GLA in excess of 40,000 m². Highest in the tripartite hierarchy of shopping centres

Superette Also 'bantamstore'; a small self-service store, generally in the range 100–350 m² GLA

Supermarket Medium size self-service store, of at least 400 m², and commonly of 2,000 m², GLA, selling a wide range of convenience goods and a basis of food sales

Superstore Similar in definition to 'Hypermarket', although a lower minimum area of 2,500 m² is accepted within the meaning of the term. An edge-of-town location is common in the UK

TBA Tyre, battery and car accessory sales; commonly an independent unit located in the parking areas of an out-of-town shopping facility

Appendix B
Cages: A Trend in Retail Distribution

by Jolyon Drury MA (Cantab) Dip Arch RIBA MIMH

Wire box pallets, cages as they are known in the UK, have been in use in Europe for a decade. Because of the slow development of hypermarkets and superstores in Britain, due to planning constraints, cages are only now beginning to be used in significant numbers. Cages offer considerable benefits to the retailer, and ultimately to the consumer, by:

1 Reducing the time spent in merchandising, the most time and labour intensive in-store activity. Cages reduce merchandising time to one twentieth of conventional packaging

2 Eliminating packaging nuisance at peak shopping periods

3 Giving maximum display for minimum area of selling space. Sales increase about 20% using cages

4 Reducing the size of stock rooms. By using cages, operators have liberated 1·5% of the sales area in addition

Cages are used mostly for dry goods, fast-moving lines, such as tinned stock, bottles and packeted commodities. But cages are beginning to be used for vegetables, and their potential for dairy goods is under discussion. It is predicted that 300 lines will be caged in superstores, and 100—150 in larger supermarkets. At present, 28 hypermarkets and superstores employ cages as the principal display method, but it is predicted that there will be over 200 outlets using cages by 1980. It is likely that there will be 250,000 cages in use by the end of 1976.

The introduction of cages on a large scale is bound to affect the design of the premises. Most of the large supermarket chains have cages on trial, and they are planning to introduce cages into superstores and their larger supermarkets in the near future. But the growth of cages as a unit load distribution medium is likely to penetrate further into the retail industry. Once the volume manufacturers have re-equipped packaging lines to load cages 'on-line', it is likely that they will be reluctant to continue packing fast-moving brands in parallel into conventional cardboard boxes, except for small quantities for the small shops. This implies that cages may be used as a general transport medium, with the possibility that the retail outlet will be too small to use the cage for display, but merchandise from it in the stock room. The cage will also be in demand from the cash-and-carry trade, which has space and merchandising problems too, and which accounts for 25% of all retail distribution.

The cage has its floor, sides and feet constructed from woven and welded bright zinc wire. The cage can be supplied with fold-down panels on two faces, and they all fold up for empty return transport. There are a number of cage sizes in use at present, because of the previous European development. Prospective operators are tending to choose cages to suit their existing conditions, and this has resulted in confusion, especially for the manufacturer of the goods. The Institute of Grocery Distribution has suggested two principal sizes:

B·1 Stacker truck handling cages, used here for hardware, in a 1560 mm aisle

B·2 Typical cage used for plastic bottles: note the double drop-front design for access

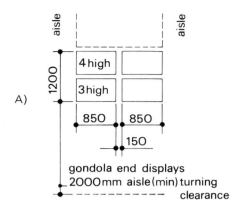

A)

gondola end displays
2000 mm aisle (min) turning
clearance

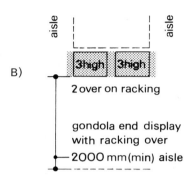

B)

2 over on racking

gondola end display
with racking over
2000 mm (min) aisle

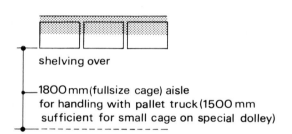

shelving over

1800 mm (fullsize cage) aisle
for handling with pallet truck (1500 mm
sufficient for small cage on special dolley)

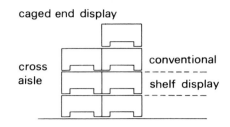

caged end display

cross aisle

conventional

shelf display

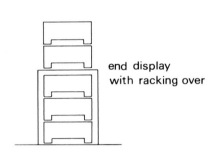

end display
with racking over

B·3 Cage displays: gondola end positions: A) shows a maximum impact position for a primary aisle B) is also for maximum impact, but the use of racking to hold back-up stock over the access display can save valuable area throughout the store

B·4 Cages in conventional aisles: placed under shelf displays. Such displays provide a high impact without prejudicing the shelf display overhead

1 1150 mm × 850 mm × 1000 mm high with 500 kg capacity
2 850 mm × 600 mm × 870 mm high with 300 kg capacity

These dimensions were chosen to be a compromise most suitable for current packaging, integration with delivery transport, and to suit 1000 mm and 1200 mm gondola display units. These sizes have yet to be endorsed by the British grocery trade. On the whole, the smaller size, known as the half-Euro cage, is preferred. As the planning authorities have kept British hypermarket floor-space low by European standards, the use of the larger cage would reduce the number of varieties that could be displayed.

The increase in cages will affect:
1 The design of the store's selling area
2 The area of back-up storage provided at the outlet
3 The unloading and handling facilities at the premises
4 The storage space at the manufacturer's premises

Apart from the disadvantages of having to re-equip to load cages, the manufacturer is faced with a warehousing problem. Compared with block-stacked palletised goods, cages demand twice the floor area, even though they can be stacked five high. The design of the cages' feet, about 25 cm² each, impose very high point loads on the floor.

Four adjacent stacks of the larger cage size could impose a load of 10 tonnes on an area of only 100 cm². The same provision also applies when considering the floor of the selling area, where five-high stacking has been suggested by some operators.

The introduction of cages also poses problems for distribution transport. Ideally, bulk haulage of cages demands side loading. This should not be a problem for hypermarkets and superstores, designed to receive maximum-sized vehicles, unless the building has been equipped with raised docks, for handling roll pallets from the ends of vehicles. But it does imply that smaller supermarkets may have to be equipped with a lift truck: these can be purchased cheaply, with a simple specification.[1]

Cages are best positioned in the selling area where their impact can be best utilised, typically at gondola end positions. Considerable stock-room space has been saved by placing back-up stock on racking above the display. This has increased visual impact and minimised the intrusion of handling equipment during shopping hours. Typical displays at aisle ends are:
1 Seven cages for fast-moving goods and promotions, arranged with a three-high picking stack and a four-high back-up

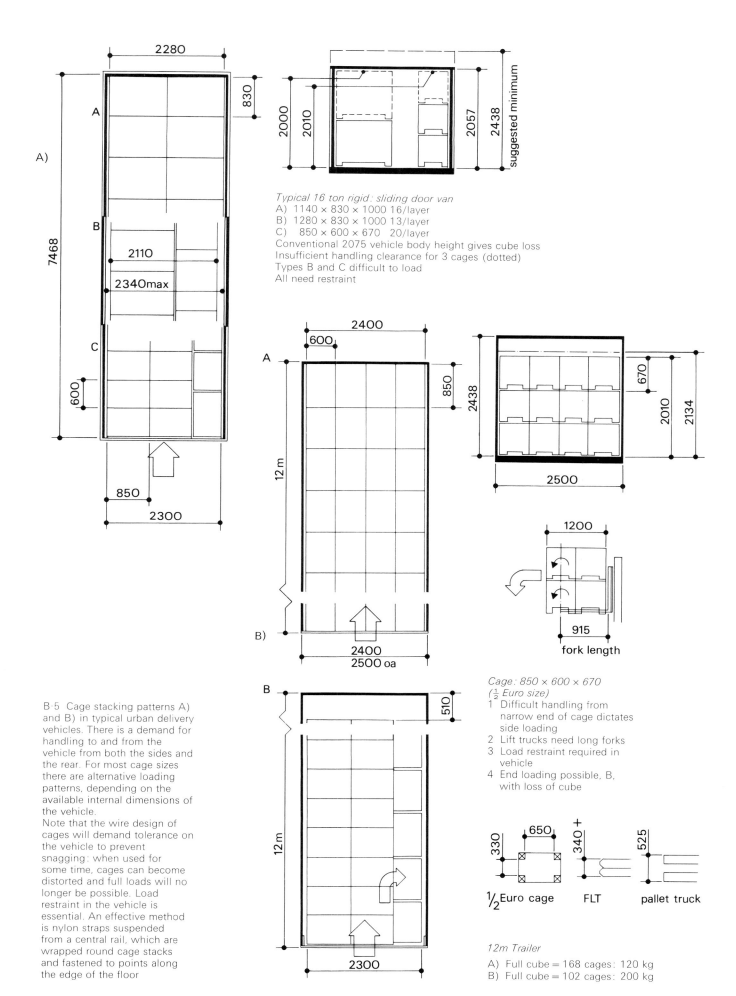

Typical 16 ton rigid: sliding door van
A) 1140 × 830 × 1000 16/layer
B) 1280 × 830 × 1000 13/layer
C) 850 × 600 × 670 20/layer
Conventional 2075 vehicle body height gives cube loss
Insufficient handling clearance for 3 cages (dotted)
Types B and C difficult to load
All need restraint

fork length

Cage: 850 × 600 × 670
($\frac{1}{2}$ *Euro size*)
1 Difficult handling from narrow end of cage dictates side loading
2 Lift trucks need long forks
3 Load restraint required in vehicle
4 End loading possible, B, with loss of cube

$\frac{1}{2}$ Euro cage   FLT   pallet truck

12m Trailer

A) Full cube = 168 cages: 120 kg
B) Full cube = 102 cages: 200 kg

B·5 Cage stacking patterns A) and B) in typical urban delivery vehicles. There is a demand for handling to and from the vehicle from both the sides and the rear. For most cage sizes there are alternative loading patterns, depending on the available internal dimensions of the vehicle.
Note that the wire design of cages will demand tolerance on the vehicle to prevent snagging: when used for some time, cages can become distorted and full loads will no longer be possible. Load restraint in the vehicle is essential. An effective method is nylon straps suspended from a central rail, which are wrapped round cage stacks and fastened to points along the edge of the floor

195

2 Three-cage display for slower-moving stock, with back-up stock overhead
3 Single cages placed in normal shopping aisles under gondola units for slow-moving goods

There should always be sufficient area for a day's stock to be contained without the intrusion of mechanical plant into the selling space during shopping hours. Handling plant should be pallet trucks (and standard types are too wide to accept the small cages end on), and for lifting, a reach or straddle truck. The latter is less expensive, and has the benefit of carrying the cages at low level over its wheelbase, useful for stability. To prevent speeding and stock damage in the selling area, a pedestrian controlled version is preferable.

Cages are beginning to make an impact on British retailing, and they should help to reduce distribution costs. Retail outlets employing cages indicate across the board savings of over 10% to the consumer, who has been paying 30% of retail prices to the cost of storage, handling and transport.

References

1 See Peter Falconer and Jolyon Drury *Building and Planning for Industrial Storage and Distribution* The Architectural Press Ltd: London 1975

Further Reading

Report on *Cage Distribution* conference: *Supermarketing* 31 October, 7 and 14 November 1975; *Materials Handling News* December 1975
'Learning to Love Cages' *Materials Handling News* September 1975, pp 127–31
'Hypermarkets in Europe' *Grocer* 1 November 1975, pp 70–72

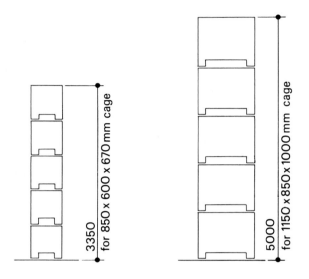

3350 for 850 x 600 x 670 mm cage

5000 for 1150 x 850 x 1000 mm cage

B·6 Stacking cages in the warehouse. Compared with block-stacked palletised goods, the same tonnage of goods in cages will demand approximately twice the area. This is due to the limited stacking height of cages and the lower-laden volume they imply

Bibliography

Books, Reports

1 SHOPPING CENTRES: GENERAL AND DESIGN

Capital and Counties Property Co Ltd *Design for Shopping* The Company: London 1970, 37 pp

Corporation of Glasgow *Recent Shopping Developments in Europe* The Corporation: Glasgow 1971, 76pp

Cullen Gordon *Townscape* The Architectural Press Ltd: London 1961; revised edition *The Concise Townscape* London: 1971 pp 151–154

Cumbernauld New Town *Report on Central Area* April 1960, 86 pp

Darlow, Clive (ed) *Enclosed Shopping Centres* The Architectural Press Ltd: London 1972, 221 pp

Evans, Hazel (ed) *New Towns: The British Experience* The Town and Country Planning Association: London 1972, pp 117–123

Gosling, David and Cullen, Gordon *Maryculter: A New Community Near Aberdeen* Kincardine County Council and Christian Salvensen Ltd: 1974, 89 pp

Gruen, Victor and Smith, Larry *Shopping Towns USA* Reinhold Publishing Corporation: London 1960, 228 pp

Hornbeck, J. S. (ed) *Stores and Shopping Centres* McGraw Hill Book Company: New York 1962, 181 pp

Irvine Development Corporation *Irvine New Town Plan* The Corporation. Irvine, Scotland 1971, pp 59–76, 109–116, 230–235, 288–293

Jones, Colin S. *Regional Shopping Centres: New York, London* International Publications Service 1970. 220 pp

Kaspar, K. *International Shop Design* Thames & Hudson and Andre Deutsch: London 1967

London County Council *The Planning of a New Town: Hook* The Council: London 1961, pp 53–65

Magnani (ed) *Negozi Moderni* Gorlich: Milan 1965

Marriott, Oliver *The Property Boom* Pan Books: London 1969

McKeever, J. Ross (ed) *The Community Builders Handbook* Urban Land Institute: Washington DC 1968, 526 pp

Multiple Shops Federation *Shopping Centres in North-West Europe* The Federation: London 1967, 28 pp
The Planning of Shopping Centres The Federation: London 1964

National Building Agency and New Towns Technical Liaison Committee *Shops: Part 2* The Committee: London 1968, 104 pp

National Economic Development Office *The Future Patterns of Shopping* HMSO: London 1971, 112 pp

Parly 2 (Chesnay, Paris) *Brochure* Christian Chassin: Paris 2, pp 34

Redstone, Louis G. *New Dimensions in Shopping Centres and Stores* McGraw Hill Book Company: New York 1973, 322 pp

Runcorn Development Corporation *Runcorn New Town* The Corporation: Runcorn, England 1967, pp 75–92

Seven Shopping Centres Institut for Center-Planlaegning: Copenhagen 1968, 16 pp

Shopping for Pleasure Capital and Counties Property Co Ltd: London 1969, 40 pp

2 STRATEGY, FEASIBILITY STUDIES, SHOPPING THEORY AND PREDICTIONS

Applebaum, William *Shopping Center Strategy: A Case Study of Planning Location and Development of the Del Monte Center, Monterey, California* International Council of Shopping Centers: New York 1970, 202 pp

Agergard E. and Olsen P. A. *The Interaction between Retailing and the Urban Centre Structure: A Theory of Spiral Movement* Institut for Center-Planlaegning: Copenhagen 1968, 42 pp

Daws, L. F. *On Shoppers' Requirements for the Location of Shops in Towns* Building Research Establishment Paper 23174: Watford, England 1974, 16 pp

Economic Development Council for the Distributive Trades *Distribution Efficiency and Government Policies* Nedo: London 1969

Economic Development Council for the Distributive Trades *Models Working Party: Urban Models in Shopping Studies* Nedo: London 1970

Eve, Gerald and Co. *Report on Aspects of Future Shopping Provision* Glasgow 1971, 34 pp

Journal of Property Management 'Probing Potential in New and Existing Shopping Centres' Institute of Real Estate Management: Chicago 1971, 64 pp

Journal of Property Management 'Feasibility Study Techniques: Apartment, Office, Shopping Centre Condominium' Institute of Real Estate Management: Chicago 1970, 32 pp

Scott, Peter *Geography and Retailing* Aldine Publishing Co: Chicago 1970, 129 pp

Stacey, N. A. H. and Wilson, A. *The Changing Patterns of Distribution* Pergamon Press: London 1965

3 FINANCING, VALUATION, MARKET RESEARCH

Graham, John & Co. *Financing Data: College Grove Shopping Center, San Diego* Seattle: 1960, 18 pp

Gunning, Francis P. *New Techniques in Financing* International Council of Shopping Centers: New York 1969, 6 pp

Hammer and Co. *Market Analysis: Springfield Mall* The Company: Virginia 1963, 41 pp

International Council of Shopping Centers *Depreciable Lives of Shopping Centers* Touche Ross & Co: New York 1973, pp 31

Lima Filho, A. de Oliveira *Uma analise de desenvolvimento de sistemas de varejo controlado na area metropolitana da Sao Paulo* PhD Thesis: Michigan State University 1972

Walker, Joan *Shopping Center Economics: Can Centers*

Work in Brazil? Property Consultants Inc: Northfield, Illinois 1973, 39 pp

Walker, Joan *Proforma Shopping Center Financial Analysis* Property Consultants Inc: Northfield, Illinois 1969, 17 pp

Walker, Joan *A economia dos centros comerciais* Banco Nacional Habitacao: Rio de Janeiro 1973, 35 pp

Walker, Joan *Market Research for Managers and Promotion Directors* International Council of Shopping Centers: New York 1974

4 *LEASING, TENANCIES, FRANCHISING*

American Institute of Real Estate Appraisers *Case Studies in Shopping Center Valuation* The Institute: Chicago 1964, 37 pp

Franchising Today Fransworth Publishing Co: Lynbrook, NY 1969, 1970, Vol I 376 pp; Vol II 424 pp

Information Bulletin: Insurance International Council of Shopping Centers: New York 1971, 8 pp

Lebhar, Ruth *Appraising Prospective Tenants* International Council of Shopping Centers: New York 1972, 12 pp

National Institute of Real Estate Brokers *Guide to Commercial Property Leasing* The Institute: Chicago 1970, 95 pp

Practicing Law Institute *Transcript Series No 10: Business and Legal Problems of Shopping Centers* 1970, 572 pp

5 *MANAGEMENT, PROMOTIONAL ACTIVITY*

Applebaum, William and Kaylin, S. O. *Case Studies in Shopping Center Development and Operation* International Council of Shopping Centers: New York 1974, 280 pp

Callahan, William *Shopping Center Promotions* International Council of Shopping Centers: 1972, 380 pp

Carpenter, Horace *Shopping Center Management* International Council of Shopping Centers: New York 1974, 196 pp

Information File: Public Use of Shopping Center Property International Council of Shopping Centers: New York 1972

Markin, R. *Retailing: Concepts, Institutions and Management* Macmillan and Co: New York 1971, 398 pp

Nyburg, Robert So. *Shopping-Center Merchants' Associations* International Council of Shopping Centers: New York 1970, 60 pp

Wingate, Schaller and Millar *Retail Merchandise Management* Prentice-Hall Inc: Englewood Cliffs NJ 1972, 386 pp

6 *MARKETING TECHNIQUES*

Department and Speciality Store Merchandising and Operating Results National Retail Merchants Association: New York, annual

Galt, James & Co. *Galt's Early Stages* The Company: Cheadle, England 1972, 220 pp

Galt, James & Co. *Manual for Galt Toyshops-in-Shops* The Company: Cheadle, England 1972, 11 pp

7 *TECHNICAL DATA, STATISTICS*

Annual Report of the Grocery Industry Progressive Grocer: USA, annual

British Market Research Bureau Ltd. *Shopping in the 'Seventies* IPC Women's Weeklies: London 1970

Consumer Buying Patterns in Self-Service General Merchandise Stores Mass Retailing Institute: New York 1971, 15 pp

Department of Trade and Industry, Business Statistics Office *Census of Distribution* London 1971

Directory of General Merchandise: Variety and Junior Department Store Chains Chain Store Guide: New York, annual

Directory of Shopping Centers National Research Bureau, Merchandising Division: Burlington, Iowa 1972

Directory of Supermarket, Grocery and Convenience Store Chains Chain Store Guide: New York, annual

Discount Store Census Discount Store News: New York, USA, annual

National Economic Development Office *The Future Patterns of Shopping* HMSO: London 1971, 112 pp

Sheldon's Retail Trade Phelon, Sheldon & Mansar: New York, annual

Shopping Centers 1970: Statistics (Catalogue No. 63-214) Ottowa, Canada 1972

Smith, Larry & Co. *Severance Center and Fringe Property Summary Data Report* Larry Smith & Co: Seattle 1960, 22 pp

Supermarkets: Sales Manual Issue Chainstore Age: USA, annual

8 *MECHANICAL SERVICES, HEATING, VENTILATING, AIR CONDITIONING*

Heating, Ventilating and Air Conditioning Guide for Commercial Buildings Stanats Publishing Co.: Cedar Rapids, Iowa 1971, 96 pp

9 *PEDESTRIANISATION, PARKING REQUIREMENTS, FREIGHT TRANSPORT REQUIREMENTS*

Freight Transport Association *Research Report No 1: Design Standards for Service and Off-Street Loading Areas* The Association: London 1972, 24 pp

Freight Transport Association *Research Report No 2: Study of Watford Service-Only Precinct* The Association: London 1972, 29 pp

Gray, John *Pedestrianised Shopping Streets in Europe* Edinburgh Pedestrians Association 61 pp

Matthew, Robert and Johnson-Marshall, Stirrat *Minitram in Sheffield* Road Research Laboratory 1974, 87 pp

Multiple Shops Federation *Standards for Service Areas in Shopping Centres* Multiple Shops Federation: London 1968, 8 pp

Urban Land Institute *Parking Requirements for Shopping Centres: Technical Bulletin No. 53* The Institute: Washington DC 1965, 24 pp

Wood A. A. *Norwich: London Street. The Creation of a Foot Street* Norwich Corporation 1969, 24 pp

10 BUILDING REGULATIONS, FIRE PRECAUTIONS, *STRUCTURAL REQUIREMENTS*

British Standard Code of Practice 3: Chapter IV: Part 2: 1968 *Shops and Department Stores*

Building Regulations 1972 *Town Centres and Shopping Precincts. Department of the Environment Circular 19/73* HMSO: London 1973

Fairweather L. and Sliwa J. A. *The Architects' Journal Metric Handbook* The Architectural Press Ltd: London pp 75–81

Fire Research Station *Report No 875: Control of Smoke in Enclosed Shopping Centres* 1971

Floor Loading in Retail Premises—Survey Building Research Station: CP 25/71 1971, 37 pp

Home Office, The *Fire Precautions in Town Centre Redevelopments* HMSO: London 1972

Heselden A. J. M., Wraight H. G. H. and Watts P. R. *Fire Problems of Pedestrian Precincts: Fire Research Station Report No 954* 1972

Phillips, A. M. *Smoke Travel in Shopping Malls: Fire Research Station Report No 864* 1971, 20 pp

11 SUPERMARKETS, HYPERMARKETS

Hoje Taastrup Storcenter Copenhagon: Kommand Itselskabet The Storcenter: 1968, 24 pp

Supermarkeder 1974 Per Press: Copenhagen 1974, 214 pp

12 DEPARTMENT STORES

Entwurf und Planung: Warenhaus und ein Kaufszentrum Georg Gallway: Munich 1972,

International Association of Department Stores *Commission of Chief Executives' Report* The Association: Paris May 1970, 33 pp

International Association of Department Stores *Commission on Department Stores in Shopping Centres: Report* The Association: Paris 1973 33 pp

13 MARKETS

Kirk J. H., Ellis P. G., and Medland, J. R. *Retail Stall Markets in Great Britain* Wye College, University of London: 1972, 110 pp

14 BIBLIOGRAPHIES

Artley, Alexandra (ed.) *The Golden Age of Shop Design: European Shop Interiors 1880–1939* The Architectural Press Ltd: London 1975. Contains bibliography on history of European shop décor

A selected Bibliography on Shopping Centers International Council of Shopping Centers: New York 1972

Kessler, Mary *Shopping Centers: Exchange Bibliography No 208* Council of Planning Librarians: Monticello, Illinois 1971

Myers, Robert H. *Suburban Shopping Centers* Small Business Administration: *Washington DC* 1970

Shopping Centres, Shops and Markets: Architectural Association Library Bibliography No 3 London 1973

Articles

15 SHOPPING CENTRES: GENERAL DESIGN

'Shops, Department Stores and Shopping Centres' *L'Architecture Francaise* (France) No 279–280 1965, Special Issue

'Regional Shopping Centres: Development in North America and Future in UK' *The Surveyor* (Great Britain) No 12 1966, pp 131–2

'Growth of Shopping Centres with Special Reference to USA' *Casa Bella* (Italy) No 311, 1966, pp 12–31

'Shopping Centres and Stores' *Architectural Record* (USA) April 1966, pp 160–163

'Retail Shops' *Neue Laden* (Germany) December 1967, Special Issue

'Shops, Stores and Shopping Centres' *Der Aufbau* (Germany) No 6 1968, Special Issue

'A New Approach to Shopping Centers' *Architectural Record* (USA) April 1968, pp 167–180

'Village Shopping Center' *House and Home* (USA) October 1968, pp 68–75

'Shopping Centres' *Architecture in Australia* (Australia) February 1969, Special Issue

'Shopping Centres' *Werk* (Switzerland) No 9, 1970, Special Issue

'Shopping' *Official Architecture and Planning* (Great Britain) January 1970, pp 29–55

'Planning Multi-Level Malls' *Chain Store Age* (USA) June 1970, pp 14–16

'Shopping Centres' *Werk* (Germany) September 1970, Special Issue

'Shops and Shopping Centres' *Deutsche Bauzeitschrift* (Germany) No 3, 1971, Special Issue

'Shopping Out Of Centres' *Official Architecture and Planning* (Great Britain) February 1971, pp 105–125

'Shopping Centres and Department Stores *L'Architecture Francaise* (France) May-June 1971 Special Issue

'Shopping' *Official Architecture and Planning* (Great Britain) July 1971, pp 539–543

Percival, R. N. 'Recent Shopping Developments in Europe' *Royal Town Planning Institute Journal* (Great Britain) September 1971, p 388

'Shops on the Move' *Design* (Great Britain) Part 1 April 1972 pp 25–29; Part II April 1972 pp 30–33

Schiller, R. K. 'Shopping Centres: The Measurement of the Attractiveness of Shopping Centres to Middle-Class Luxury Consumers' *Regional Studies* (USA) September 1972, pp 291–297

Wright, L. 'Edge of Town Shopping' *The Architects' Journal* (Great Britain) 25 October 1972, p. 932

Wright, L. 'Shopping The Environment' *The Architectural Review* (Great Britain) March 1973, pp 168–191

16 STRATEGY, FEASIBILITY STUDIES, SHOPPING THEORY AND PREDICTIONS, CONSUMER BEHAVIOUR

Davies, W. K. D. 'Centrality and the Central Place Hierarchy' *Urban Studies* (Great Britain) February 1967

Rhodes, T. and Whitaker, R. A. 'Forecasting Shopping Demand' *Town Planning Institute Journal* (Great Britain) May 1967

Lewis, J. Parry and Traill, A. L. 'Assessment of Shopping Potential and Demand for Shops' *(Town Planning Review* (Great Britain) January 1968, pp. 317–326

Hall, P. 'Planning Priorities for Shopping Centres' *Design* (Great Britain) April 1968, pp 45–47

Bacon, R. W. 'An Approach to the Theory of Consumer Shopping Behaviour' *Urban Studies* (USA) No 1 1971, pp 55–64

Murray, W. and Kennedy, M. B. 'A Shopping Model Primer' *Town Planning Institute Journal* (Great Britain) May 1971, pp 211–215

Halper, E. B. 'Giant Jigsaw: Putting Together a Shopping-Center Site *Real Estate Review* (USA) Summer 1971, pp 84–88

Blake, J. 'Future Pattern of London Shopping' *The Surveyor* (Great Britain) 13 August 1971, pp 16–19; 20 August 1971, pp 16–17; 27 August 1971, pp 32–34

Dacey, M. F. 'An Explanation for the Observed Dispersion of Retail Establishments in Urban Areas' *Environment and Planning* No 3 1972, pp 323–330

'Seeking Model Planning Procedures' *Shopping Centre World* (USA) March 1972, pp 37–38

Batty, M. and Saether, A. 'A Note on the Design of Shopping Models' *Royal Town Planning Institute Journal* (Great Britain) July/August 1972, pp 303–306

17 FINANCING, VALUATION, MARKET RESEARCH

Thomas, M. E. and Waide, W. L. 'Shopping Centres and Community Investment' *Official Architecture and Planning* (Great Britain) August 1967 pp 1094–1100

Lathrop, D. 'Revitalizing Downtown Shopping Centers' *Architectural Record* (USA) July 1969 pp 135–150

Appel, D. L. 'Market Segmentation: A Response to Retail Innovation' *Journal of Marketing* (USA) April 1970, pp 64–67

18 MANAGEMENT, PROMOTIONAL ACTIVITY

'Shopping Centers Become Centers For Social Political Activities' *New York Times* 7 March 1971, pF 1

'Shopping Centres Grow Into Shopping Cities' *Business Week* (USA) 4 September 1971, pp 34–38

19 *MECHANICAL SERVICES, HEATING, VENTILATING, AIR CONDITIONING*

'Lighting of Shops' *International Lighting Review* (Holland) No 2 1969, Special Issue

Throns, T. A. 'Shopping Centers' Central Systems' *Building Systems Design* (USA) February 1970, pp 38–41

Stinson, R. G. 'Shopping Centers—HVAC' *Building Systems Design* (USA) February 1970, pp 36–38

Steinman, W. R. 'Total Energy at Work in Pennsylvania: A Shopping Mall' *Ashrae Journal* (USA) September 1971, pp 60–63

Maxwell, A. and Bartlett, G. E. 'The Electric Environment In A Superstore' *Light and Lighting* August 1972, pp 270–272

20 *PEDESTRIANISATION, PARKING REQUIREMENTS, FREIGHT TRANSPORT*

Continini, E. 'Anatomy of the Pedestrian Mall' *American Institute of Architects Journal* February 1969, pp 42–50

Likierman A. and Wilcock A. 'Suburban Shopping Precincts—An Assessment' *Royal Town Planning Institute Journal* (Great Britain) April 1970, pp 138–141

'Sheffield—Castle Square, Roundabout and Pedestrian Shopping Precinct and Subway' *Concrete Quarterly* (Great Britain) July/September 1970, pp 24–5

Bell, R. A. 'Traffic Parking and the Regional Shopping Centre' *Traffic Engineering and Control* September 1971, pp 210–214

21 *BUILDING REGULATIONS, FIRE PRECAUTIONS, STRUCTURAL REQUIREMENTS*

Hinkley P. L., Butcher G. and Parnell A. 'Fires In Shopping Malls'
The Architects' Journal (Great Britain) 28 November 1973, pp 1319–1325

22 *HYPERMARKETS, SUPERMARKETS*

'Supermarkets—Financial Times Survey' *The Financial Times* (Great Britain) 2 May 1972, pp 19–30

Wolf, K. H. and Meissner, L. 'Fundamentals For Planning, Design and Rationalisation of Supermarkets' *Deutsche Architektur* (Germany) August 1972, pp 471–475

23 *DEPARTMENT STORES*

'Stores in Urban and Suburban Shopping Centers' *Architectural Record* (USA) July 1964, pp 135–150

24 *BOUTIQUES*

'Boutiques and Shopping Centres' *Deutsche Bauzeitung* (Germany) No 5, 1971, Special Issue

25 *MARKETS*

'Sheffield Castle Market' *The Architectural Review* (Great Britain) August 1962

'Padua—Covered Market' *Domus* (Italy) September 1970, pp 10–14

'San Francisco-Market' *Werk* (Switzerland) October 1971, pp 660–663

Shelton, B. 'Updating Market Halls' *Official Architecture and Planning* (Great Britain) January 1972, pp 43–46

'Paris: Les Halles: New Use for Old Shops' *Baum* February 1972, pp 154–155

'Leicester: Market Pyramids' *The Architects' Journal* (Great Britain) 19 April 1972, pp 822–23

Medland, J. R. 'In the Market Place' *New Society* (Great Britain) 28 September 1972, pp 609–613

Burgess, J. 'Street Markets: An Extentible Resource' *Built Environment* (Great Britain) August 1974, pp 403–425

Case Studies

26 *AUSTRALIA*

Shopping Centres *Architecture In Australia* February 1969, Special Issue

27 *AUSTRIA*

Candle Maker's Shop Vienna (Architect: H. Hollein) *Architectural Forum* (USA) June 1966, pp 33–37

28 *BELGIUM*

Shopping Centre: Woluwe Saint Lambert, Brussels (Architect: M. Blomme) *La Technique Des Travaux* (Belgium) May–June 1971, pp 161–65

29 *BRASIL*

Sao Paulo Praca (Architect: A. Antunes Netto and M. De Souza Dias) *The Architectural Review* October 1971, pp 253–254

30 *CANADA*

Downtown in 3-D: Montreal *Architectural Forum* September 1966, pp 31–49

Richards, J. M. Multi-Level City: Montreal *The Architectural Review* August 1967, pp 89–96

Urban Supertoy: York Square Toronto (Architect: Diamond and Myers) *Progressive Architecture* (USA) September 1969, pp 144–153; *Baumeister* October 1972, pp 1090–1101

Place Bonaventure: Montreal (Architects: Affleck, Desbarats, Dimakopoulos, Lebensold, Sise) *Architecture Canada* July 1967, pp 31–39; *Canadian Architect* September 1967, pp 42–66; *Architectural Record* December 1967, pp 139–148; *Moebel Interior Design* No 10 1968, pp 49–68; *Architectural Design* January 1968, pp 69–73; *Space Design* February 1968, pp 65–76; *Architectural Review* March 1968, pp 181–188; *Baumeister* March 1968, pp 261–269; *Concrete Quarterly* April 1968, pp 14–19; *Design* April 1968, pp 14–19; *Progressive Architecture* July 1968, pp 112–113; *Bauwelt* No 1 1969, pp 13–17

Sherway Gardens: Toronto (Architects: Murray & Fleiss) *Canadian Architect* April 1971, pp 39–44

Place Ville Marie: Montreal (Architects: I. M. Pei) *Werk* January 1972, pp 24–25

31 *DENMARK*

Rodovre Copenhagen Shopping Centre (Architects: Krohn

and Rasmussen) *Arkitektur* No 5 1967, pp 174–85; *Bouw* July 1971, pp 1102–8

Albertslund South New Town *Arkitektur* No 1 1969, pp 1–23

Scandinavian Shopping: Rodovre, Copenhagen; Hoje Tastrup Storcenter, Copenhagen; Skarholmen, Stockholm; (Pasila Zentrum, Helsinki) *Deutsche Bauzeitung* No 2, 1970, pp 114–120

32 *FINLAND*

Myllypuro Centre, Helsinki (Architect: E. Karvinen) *Arkkitehti* No 5 1968, pp 34–35

Shopping Centres, Finland; Leverkusen, Puotinharjn *Bauwelt* No 47 1966, pp 1361–79

33 *FRANCE*

Regional Shopping Centre: Parly 2 Paris (Architects: Douglass and Balick) *Glasforum* No 3 1970, pp 21–27; *Moebel Interior Design* No 5 1970, pp 43–41; *L'Architecture Francaise* May–June 1971; pp 7–9

Carrefour Hypermarket, Melun, France *Modener Market* September 1972, pp 10–22

Space Frames For 2 Shopping Centres In France. *Acier, Stahl, Steel* September 1972, pp 385–391

Regional Shopping Development in France *Chartered Surveyor—Urban Quarterly* September 1973, pp 36–40

34 *GERMANY*

Maintaunus Franfurt (Architects: Schwebes and Schoszberger) *Arkitektur Und Wohnform* 1965, pp 428–33

Europa Shopping Centre, Berlin (Architects: Hentrich and Detschnigg) *Bouw* 16 April 1966, pp 550–7; *Deutsche Bauzeitung* No 4 1966, pp 268–73; *Deutsche Bauzeitschrift* 1966, pp 357–64; *L'Architecture Francaise* 1968, pp 73–7

Centre: Mannheim-Vogelstang (Architect: Striffler) *Arkitektur Und Wohnform* July 1970, pp 218–23; *International Asbestos Cement Review* July 1971, pp 12–14

Northwest Centre, Frankfurt (Architects: Apel & Beckert) *Architectural Forum* October 1970, pp 30–37; *Werk* No 9 1970, pp 574–7

Supermarket Designs in East Germany *Deutsche Architektur* August 1972, pp 456–464

35 *GREAT BRITAIN*

Runcorn New Town Centre (Architects: Runcorn Development Corporation) *The Architects' Journal* 16 November 1966, p 1184; *Building* 18 November 1966, p. 136; *The Surveyor* 26 November 1966, pp 19–20; *The Architectural Review* January 1967, pp 11, 14–15; *Architectural Design* January 1967, p 25; *Neue Laden* February 1967, pp 13–15; *Bauen and Wohnen* December 1967, pp 469–472; *Zodiac* March 1969, pp 139–146; *The Architects' Journal* 21 June 1972, pp 1377–1392; *Architectural Design* June 1972, pp 373–374; *The Architectural Review* March 1973, pp 182–183; Runcorn Development Corporation *Town Centre Planning Report* December 1965, *Town Centre* October 1966, *Central Area Report* June 1967; Professor Arthur Ling & Runcorn Development Corporation *Master Plan* 1967, pp 75–92, p. 135; Grosvenor Estate Commercial Developments Ltd *Runcorn New Town Shopping Centre Guide* December 1969; Drivers, Jonas & Co & Runcorn Development Corporation *Runcorn New Town: Growth of Shops and Services in the Town Centre* February 1966, pp 27–151

Irvine New Town Centre (Architects: Irvine Development Corporation) *The Architects' Journal* 4 March 1970, pp 526–28; *The Surveyor* 3 April 1970, pp 26–27; *Architectural Design* November 1970; *The Architects' Journal* September 1971, pp 616–19; Ayrshire Land Need Study *Working Party Report* No. 1, 1968, No. 2 1969, No. 3, 1970; Irvine Development Corporation, *Information Mapping System by Computer* (A. Macdonald) 15 May 1973; Irvine Development Corporation, *Interim Revised Outline Plan* August 1969, pp 61–65; *Irvine New Town Centre: Report to Policy Group* September 1971, *Irvine Burgh Centre: CDA Proposals* June 1972, *Irvine New Town Central Area: Stage A Report* March 1971, *Irvine New Town Plan* January 1971, *Irvine New Town Centre: Car Parking Provision* October 1972

Harlow Shopping Centre (Architects: Harlow Development Corporation *Official Architecture & Planning* August 1967, pp 1108–11

Chelsea Drug Store, Kings Road, London (Architects: Garnett Cloughley & Blakemore) *The Architects' Journal* 17 July 1968, p 66; *Progressive Architecture* November 1968, pp 150–1; *The Architects' Journal* 18 June 1969, p 18–19; *Interior Design* June 1969, p 36

Blackburn Centre, Lancashire (Architects: BDP) *The Architectural Review* February 1970, pp 119–129; *Werk* No 9 1970, pp 589–91

London: Print & Map Shop, Bloomsbury (Architects: Colquohoun and Miller) *The Architectural Review* June 1970, pp 431–4

London: Miss Selfridge; Brompton Road (Architect: Howard Sant) *Interior Design* October 1970, pp 632–3

Arndale Centre, Poole, Dorset (Architect: Jones) *Building* 4 September 1970, pp 55–60

Doncaster: Opticians Shop (Architects: Aldington & Craig) *The Architectural Review* March 1971, pp 175–8

London: Print Shop, Baker Street (Conran Design Group) *Interior Design* October 1971, p 648

Runcorn, Cheshire: Local Centre Castlefields (Architects: Runcorn Development Corporation) *The Architects' Journal* 5 January 1972, pp 25–36

London: Boutique (Architects: Garnett Cloughley & Blakemore) *The Architectural Review* September 1972, pp 159–161

Just Looking Boutique, London (Architects: Garnett Cloughley & Blakemore) *The Architectural Review* September 1972, pp 159–161; *Design* September 1972, p 77

University Precinct Centre, Manchester (Architects: Wilson and Womersley) *The Architects' Journal* 6 December 1972, pp 1301–1316

Milton Keynes Centre (Architect: Derek Walker) *Architectural Design* June 1973, p 363

Habitat: Wallingford (Architects: Ahrends, Burton & Koralek) *The Architectural Review* August 1974, pp 74–79

36 *ITALY*

Cardin Boutique, Milano (Nino, Gabrio, Bini) *Domus* February 1970, pp 46–7

La Via Del Caterpillar (Cappai and Mainardis) *Casabella* July/August 1970

Shop In Plexiglass, Sorrento, Italy *Domus* September 1970, p 16

Project for a Mechanised Shopping Centre, Milano (Architect: Ramstein) *Bauen Und Wohnen* September 1970, pp 325–7

Furniture Showroom, Milano (Architect: Bellini) *The Architectural Review* March 1971, pp 168–170

La Rinascente Department Stores Turin (Architect: Gregotti) *Contra Spazio* March 1971, pp 2–19

Watchmaker's Shop, Milano (Architects: Achille and Castiglioni) *The Architectural Review* August 1971, pp 105–108

Supermarket SMA, (Architect: Corsica) San Vittore Olona *Domus* December 1971; *Werk* June 1972, pp 326–8

Torre Annunziata: Flower Shop *Domus* January 1972, p 24

Centro Domus (Architects: Studio Da, Milano) *Domus* April 1974

Ceramica Matteo D'Agostino, Milano (Architect: Castiglioni) and Boutique: Florence (Architects: Biocchi and Monsani) *Domus* September 1974

Boutique: Saluzzo (Architects: Prando and Roso) *Domus* October 1974

37 *JAPAN*

Tamagawa Takashimaya Shopping Centre Japan *Japan Architect* March 1970, pp 15–18

Omni-Rental Stores, Tokyo (Architect: Takeyama) *Japan Architect* August 1970, pp 63–9

Shopping Mall: Senri New Town *Japan Architect* October 1970, pp 40–44

Suburban Shopping Centre: Nakamozu Plaza, Osaka (Architect: Takenake Komuten) *Japan Architect* June 1971, pp 103–6

Lineage of Urban Design: Tokyo Bay Plan (Architect: Kenzo Tange) *Japan Architect* September–October 1971, pp 28–29, Special Edition

Street In A Building: Osaka *Japan Architect* July 1972, pp 70–71

38 *NETHERLANDS*

Shopping Centre: Beverwijk (Architects: Bleeker and Spruit) *Bouw* 26 February 1966, pp 310–3

Bijenkorf Department Store Eindhoven (Architect: Ponti) *Bouw* 24 January 1970, pp 142–7

Shopping Centre Versus Town Centre (Architect: J. Th. Gantvoort) *Town Planning Review* January 1971, pp 61–70

39 *POLAND*

Shop: Warsaw Poland *Architektura* (Poland) September 1970, pp 300–310

40 *SWEDEN*

Skarholmen Centre: Stockholm (Architects: Bowsen and Efvergren) *Interbuild* December 1967, pp 2709; *Arkitektur* No 11 1968, pp 32–9; *Baumeister* No 5 1969, pp 604–10; *Architect and Building News* 2 April 1970, pp 55–9

Frolunda: Goteburg (Architects: Klemming and Thelaus) *Deutsche Bauzeitschrift* No 7 1967, pp 1107–10; *Arkitektur* No 11 1968, pp 26–31

Taby Centre: Stockholm *Byggnadsindustrin* January 1968, pp 21–5; *Arkitektur* No 11 1968, pp 40–7; *Bauen Und Wohnen* No 9 1970, pp 328–32

41 *SWITZERLAND*

Schonbuhl Centre, Lucerne (Architect: Roth) *Progressive Architecture* November 1968, pp 130–7; *Bauen Und Wohnen* No 10 1968, pp 38–40; *Arkitekten* No 25 1968, pp 553–9; *Architettura* No 164 1969, pp 101–11

42 *TUNISIA*

SFAX: A Tunisian Medina (Architects: De Selm and Ricci) *The Architectural Review* December 1970, pp 364–366

43 *UNITED STATES OF AMERICA*

Market Street East: Philadelphia (Architects: Skidmore Owings and Merril) *Architectural Forum* November 1966, pp 34–43

Supergraphics *Progressive Architecture* November 1967, pp 132–151; October 1968, pp 148–208 (Special Issue); April 1969, pp 106–121

The Cannery: San Francisco (Architects: Esherick, Homsey, Dodge and Davis) *L'Architecture D'Aujourd Hui* August/September 1971 pp 42–3; *Architectural Forum* June 1968, pp 75–9; *Werk* No 10 1971, pp 660–3

Galleria, Houston Texas (Architects: Hellmuth, Obata, Kassabaum) *Architectural Record* July 1969, pp 143–50; *Architectural Forum* April 1972, pp 30–33

Shopping Centers (Forum 303 Arlington, Texas; Town East, Texas and Crossroads, Oklahoma City) *Architectural Record* March 1970, pp 119–132

Survey of Recent Shopping Centres in USA *Architectural Record* March 1970, pp 119–32

Design Research: Cambridge *Bauen Und Wohnen* August 1971, pp 347–50; *Contract* July 1970; *Architectural Record* May 1970, pp 105–112; *The Architectural Review* January 1972, pp 28–34; *Interiors* May 1970, pp 108–117

San Francisco: Ghiradelli Square (Architects: Wurster, Bernadi, Eammons) *Interiors* July 1970, pp 73–76

Childrens Toy Shops: New York City *Progressive Architecture* November 1970 pp 74–79

Midtown Plaza: Rochester NU (Architect: Gruen) *Deutsche Bauzeitschrift* No 8 1971, pp 1525–6

Heritage Village Bazaar: Soutbury, Connecticutt (Architects: Callister & Payne) *The Architectural Review* May 1971, pp 107–110; *Architectural Forum* April 1971, pp 59–60; *Architectural Record* May 1971, pp 107–110

Columbia, Maryland: Shopping Malls in Suburbia *Architectural Record* March 1972, pp 113–128

Communitas Residential and Commercial Centre Project Denver *Progressive Architecture* January 1975, pp 50–51

Faneuil Hall Market, Boston *Progressive Architecture* January 1975, p 61

Index

204